Building Cross-Platform Apps Using Titanium™, Alloy, and Appcelerator® Cloud Services

Aaron Saunders

WILEY

A catalogue record for this book is available from the British Library.

ISBN 978-1-118-67325-6 (paperback); ISBN 978-1-118-67324-9 (ePub); 978-1-118-67322-5 (ePDF)

Set in 10/12.5 ChaparralPro-Light by TCS/SPS

Printed in the United States by Bind-Rite

I dedicate this book to my father, Dennis Francis Saunders Sr., who supported me in my interest with computers way before computers where commonplace in society. He bought me my first computer—a Timex Sinclair—and I also remember the TRS-80 from Radio Shack. He passed away before the book could be finished, but he is the reason I became involved with computers.

Publisher's Acknowledgements

Some of the people who helped bring this book to market include the following:

Editorial and Production

**VP Consumer and Technology
Publishing Director:**
Michelle Leete

**Associate Director–Book Content
Management:**
Martin Tribe

Associate Publisher:
Chris Webb

Project Editor:
Kezia Endsley

Copy Editor:
Kezia Endsley

Technical Editor:
Chaim Krause

Editorial Manager:
Rev Mengle

Senior Project Editor:
Sara Shlaer

Editorial Assistant:
Claire Johnson

Marketing

Marketing Manager:
Lorna Mein

Assistant Marketing Manager:
Dave Allen

About the Author

AARON SAUNDERS is the CEO/Founder of Clearly Innovative Inc., a minority-owned digital solutions provider headquartered in Washington DC with offices in New York City. The firm shapes ideas into viable products and transforms clients' existing technologies into stunning solutions. Clearly Innovative is a leader in early adaption and implementation of cutting edge technologies, from mobile strategy and design to developing innovative web-based solutions. Clearly Innovative provides support and expertise through services focused on product strategy, user experience, design, and development.

Aaron is an experienced software developer with over 30 years of experience and has strong technical, communication, and collaboration abilities. He is highly adept at helping organizations add business value using mobile and web applications.

Aaron has a BA in Computer Science from Ohio Wesleyan University and an MBA with concentrations in Information Technology Strategy and Marketing from the NYU Stern School of Business.

Acknowledgments

This book would never have been started without the encouragement of Kwasi Frye to keep pressuring me to respond to requests to write a book.

This book would have never been completed without the patience and understanding of my wife Andrea Saunders who consistently gave me the time I needed to get this done, which was above and beyond the long hours of running a small digital agency, when I got home nights and sometime the whole weekend was spent writing code, reviewing chapters, and retesting the application for the book.

Thank you to Appcelerator for the platform you provided for me to start Clearly Innovative on, and thanks to all of the clients we worked with to develop mobile solutions and expand my knowledge of the Appcelerator platform and mobile application development.

Thanks to the team at Wiley who has been patient with me through the changes in the underlying Appcelerator platform that caused chapter rewrites, changes in the mobile user interface that required new screenshots, and delays in scheduling due to personal matters.

Thanks to Chaim Krause for being a great technical reviewer. I hope you learned something through the process.

Contents

Introduction

THIS BOOK IS a high-level overview of using Appcelerator Titanium Alloy and Appcelerator Cloud Services to build native, cross-platform solutions in JavaScript. There is and will probably for a long time be an argument about the benefits of cross-platform solutions like Appcelerator, yet competitors continue to enter the field.

First and foremost, Appcelerator Titanium Alloy is not Phonegap; Appcelerator renders native user interfaces and provides a robust and extensible framework of APIs to interact with the native device on iOS, Android, Blackberry, and Windows Phone. Phonegap uses the mobile device's web browser to render the user interface of the application and a collection of modules to interact with the device's native capabilities. It is an acceptable solution for some, but I choose to focus on Appcelerator in my business, Clearly Innovative, because I believed, from a business and cost perspective, that we could provide the client with the native performance at a much better price point.

This book walks you through the process of building a photo-sharing application for the iOS and Android platforms on the Appcelerator Platform using the powerful new Alloy framework. This application integrates Appcelerator Platform's MBaaS (mobile backend-as-a-service) and Appcelerator Cloud Services to create users, store photos, and implement push notifications in mobile applications.

The Appcelerator Community is very active through the Q&A forums, specific websites such as `http://www.tidev.io/`, and community-driven conferences like `http://ticonf.org/`. The Appcelerator company website documentation, training videos, and open sourced samples can provide you with additional supporting materials to help you get started in building your own great solution.

Building a great mobile solution is a fun yet sometimes challenging experience. It is my hope that this book makes the process a bit more enjoyable and manageable.

—Aaron K. Saunders

@aaronksaunders

https://github.com/aaronksaunders

Chapter 1

Installing and Configuring Appcelerator

THIS CHAPTER BRIEFLY outlines the installation process for the Appcelerator tools. More detailed step-by-step instructions can be found on the Appcelerator site at http://docs.appcelerator.com/titanium/3.0/#%21/guide/Setting_up_Studio-section-37540095_SettingupStudio-installingstudio.

Setting Up Titanium

To install Titanium Studio, download the installer from the Appcelerator website. You will need to log in using your Appcelerator credentials, so register for an account if you haven't done so already.

After launching Titanium Studio, you will need to configure native SDKs for each platform you want to support. Android works on both Mac and PC, but to develop for iOS you will need a Mac. See http://docs.appcelerator.com/titanium/3.0/#!/guide/Quick_Start for more information.

Installing Titanium on the Mac

To install Titanium Studio on the Mac, download Titanium Studio from Appcelerator and install it. Then install Xcode and the Android SDK. The following sections cover this process in detail.

Installing Titanium Studio IDE

1. Register for an account at www.appcelerator.com.

2. Download Titanium Studio at www.appcelerator.com/titanium/download, as shown in Figure 1-1. The download will begin automatically.

FIGURE 1-1: Downloading Titanium Studio from Appcelerator.

3. Open the disk image and drag the Titanium Studio folder into Applications, as shown in Figure 1-2.

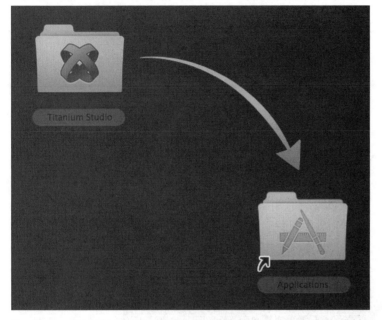

FIGURE 1-2: Dragging the Titanium Studio folder into the Applications folder.

4. Open Applications ⇨ Titanium Studio ⇨ TitaniumStudio, as shown in Figure 1-3.

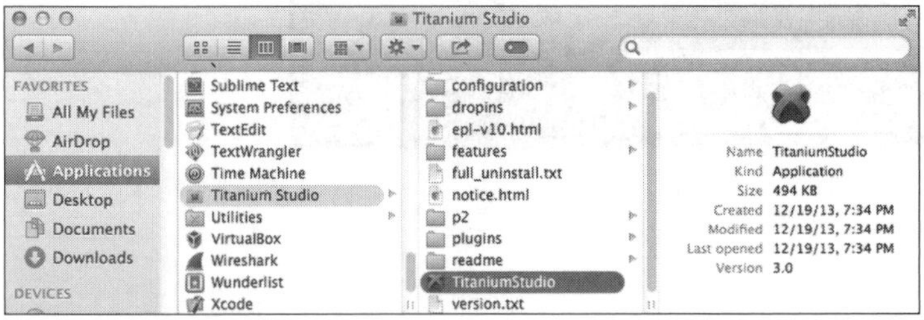

FIGURE 1-3: Launching Titanium Studio.

5. Check the box to use this folder as the default, and then click OK. See Figure 1-4.

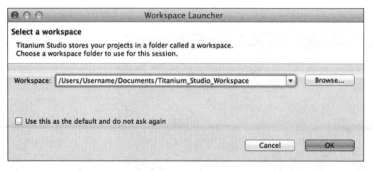

FIGURE 1-4: Selecting a workspace.

6. Log in using the account you created earlier. See Figure 1-5.

FIGURE 1-5: Logging in to use Titanium Studio.

Installing Xcode

Titanium Studio opens the Dashboard by default. You can reach the Dashboard again by clicking on the red home icon shown in Figure 1-6.

FIGURE 1-6: The Titanium Studio Dashboard is always accessible by clicking the red home icon.

1. Click the Get Started tab.

2. Scroll down to the Configure Native SDKs section and select iOS SDK. Click the Install or Update iOS SDK button on the left. See Figure 1-7.

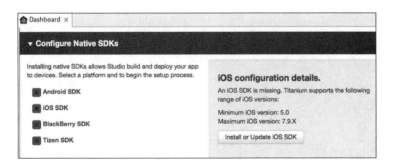

FIGURE 1-7: Selecting iOS SDK from the Configure Native SDKs section.

3. On the next window, click the Configure button. See Figure 1-8. This will launch the Mac App Store and take you to the Xcode download page, as shown in Figure 1-9.

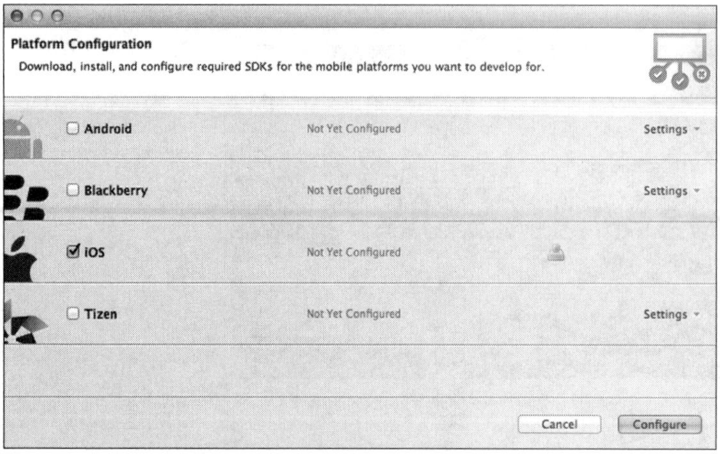

FIGURE 1-8: Platform Configuration window (iOS).

FIGURE 1-9: Installing Xcode from the Mac App store.

4. When it's finished, there should be a green checkmark next to iOS SDK, as shown in Figure 1-10.

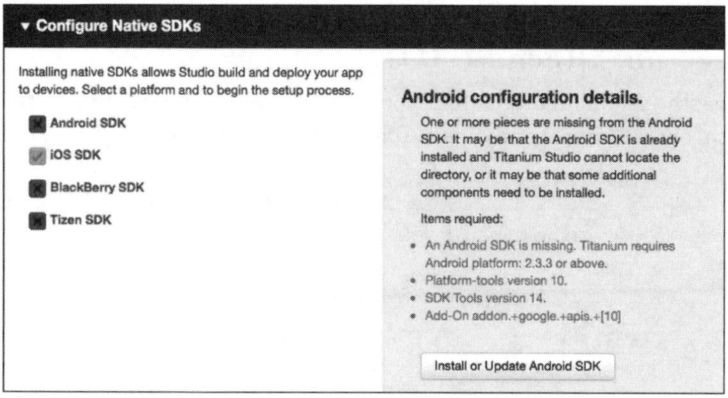

FIGURE 1-10: Configuring of the Native SDK section is complete.

5. Launch Xcode and accept the license agreement.

Installing the iOS Simulator

You will use the iOS Simulator regularly, so it's important to install it next. Open Xcode and navigate to Xcode ⇨ Preferences ⇨ Downloads. Select each available version of the iOS Simulator, as shown in Figure 1-11. Click the Check and Install Now button.

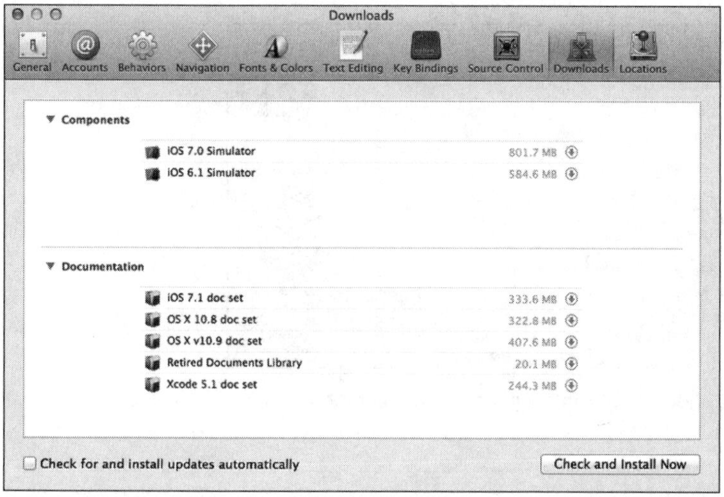

FIGURE 1-11: Downloading the iOS Simulator in the Xcode Preferences section.

Installing the Titanium Command-Line Interface to Use an Alternate IDE

If you choose not to use the Titanium Studio IDE, you will need to set up Titanium on the command line. To do so, open Terminal and run the following two commands.

| NOTE | Node comes with Titanium Studio, so npm should work. |

```
sudo npm install -g alloy
```

and

```
sudo npm install -g titanium
```

Installing the Android SDK

In the Titanium Studio Dashboard, select Android SDK and click Install or Update Android SDK. Then expand the Settings drop-down and select the Android API levels you want to support. Then click Configure. Note the Android SDK location: `/Users/<username>/Library/android-sdk-macosx/`. See Figure 1-12.

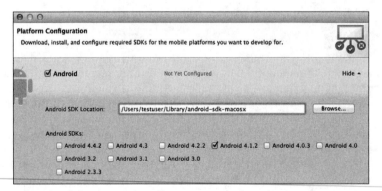

FIGURE 1-12: Installing Android SDKs in the platform configuration.

| TIP | `Library` is a hidden folder, but you can reach it using Finder ⇨ Go and then holding down the Option key to reveal its location. |

Installing Titanium Studio on Windows

To install Titanium Studio on Windows, download Titanium Studio from Appcelerator. Then install the Android SDK (Xcode requires a Mac, so you will not be able to deploy to iOS using Windows). The following sections cover this process in detail.

Installing Titanium Studio

Register for an account at www.appcelerator.com and then download Titanium Studio at www.appcelerator.com/titanium/download. See Figure 1-13.

FIGURE 1-13: Downloading Titanium Studio from Appcelerator.

1. Launch the downloaded executable and accept all the defaults in the install wizard. Titanium will install the Java Development Environment, Git, and Node. See Figure 1-14.

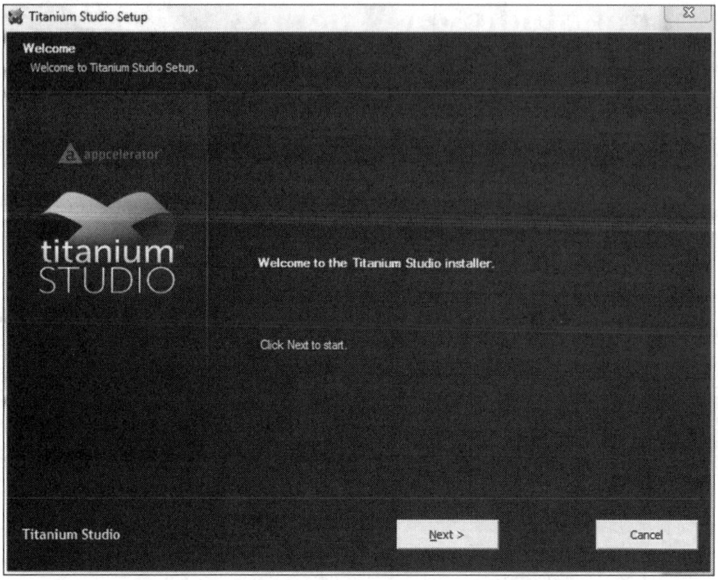

FIGURE 1-14: Titanium Studio Setup wizard.

2. After installation, launch Titanium by choosing Start ⇨ All Programs ⇨ Appcelerator ⇨ Titanium Studio. Check the box to accept the default folder location and click OK. See Figure 1-15.

> **NOTE** After completing Step 2, your projects will be saved in your `Documents\Titanium_Studio_Workspace\` folder by default.

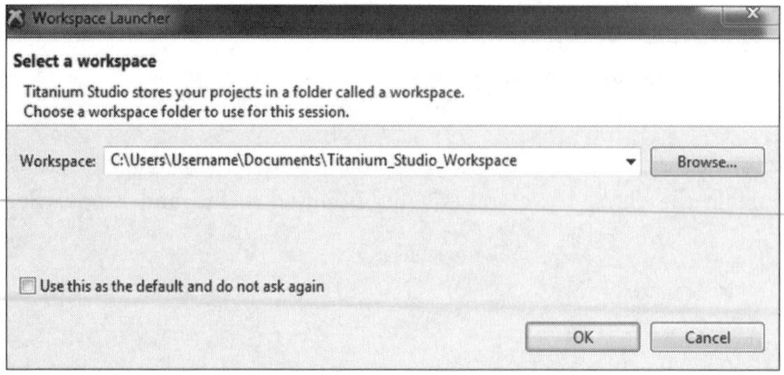

FIGURE 1-15: Selecting a workspace location.

3. Log in using the account you created earlier. See Figure 1-16.

FIGURE 1-16: Logging in to use Titanium Studio.

Installing Android SDK

Dashboard opens by default and you can come back to it later by clicking on the red home icon.

1. Scroll to the bottom of Dashboard to the Configure Native SDKs section.

2. Click Android SDK.

3. Click the Install or Update Android SDK button, as shown in Figure 1-17.

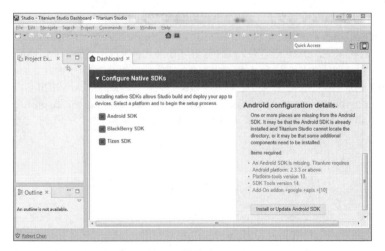

FIGURE 1-17: The Configure Native SDKs section.

4. Expand Settings and check the boxes for each Android API level you want to support.

5. Click the Configure button. See Figure 1-18.

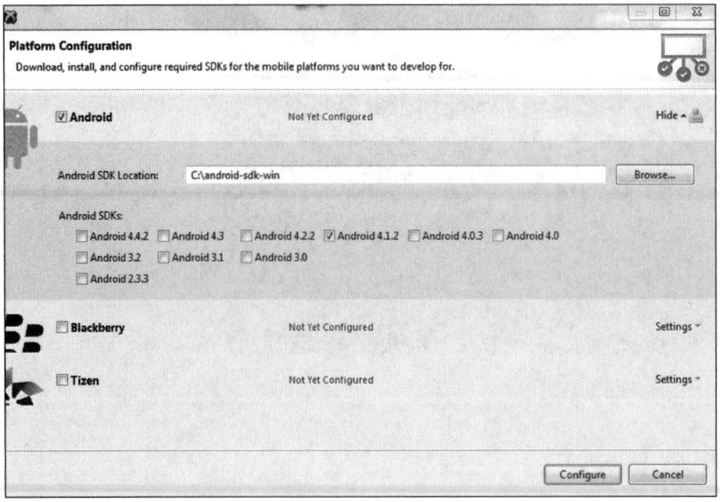

FIGURE 1-18: Installing Android SDKs in the platforms you want to support.

Note the Android SDK default location of `C:\android-sdk-win`. You may need to reopen Titanium Studio to refresh the Android SDK status. Look for the green checkmark.

Summary

To set up your environment, download and install Titanium Studio. On the Get Started tab in the Dashboard, you can configure native SDKs. The native SDKs enable you to deploy your app to platforms such as Android and iOS. The Android SDK link allows you to download and install different Android SDK versions. And on Mac, the iOS SDK link opens the Xcode download page on the Mac App Store. Use the Dashboard to verify whether each SDK was installed properly. When you're all set up properly, you're ready to move on to Chapter 2, where you learn about all that Appcelerator Cloud Services has to offer.

Chapter 2
Introducing Appcelerator Cloud Services

ONE OF THE bigger challenges in building a complex mobile application comes from an unexpected source, building the supporting backend systems for the application. The majority of applications out there interact with web services or databases to save or retrieve information for presentation in a mobile application. As a mobile developer, you need to find a solution since your goal is to develop mobile solutions, not build and maintain backend services and perform IT management and support.

The traditional approach is to build this backend system, find a place to host it, and then provide the appropriate resources to support it. Taking that approach in the mobile solutions world is cost-prohibitive, is an ongoing maintenance challenge, and is a financial burden on the mobile solution even before the application is launched.

Appcelerator Cloud Services provides a complete framework for integrating the backend services into your mobile application. These services are hosted and maintained by Appcelerator, the APIs are tested and supported by Appcelerator, and handling of the appropriate scaling as needed is also their responsibility. These Appcelerator-provided services enable you to create rich immersive mobile applications. You can extend the application's services with the `Node.ACS` product and most importantly leverage the infrastructure for the backend provided by Appcelerator.

Key features of the Appcelerator Cloud Services are available out of the box. For example, comments, ratings, and reviews are supported through the API with no additional coding on the mobile developer's side. Common location services such as check-ins and geo-querying are provided for all objects in the system. Photos and images are supported with built-in resizing, and blob storage comes ready to use. If the predefined objects do not meet your needs, you can save custom objects structured like JSON documents directly into the data store. Figure 2-1 shows all Appcelerator Cloud Services' pre-built objects.

FIGURE 2-1: All of the Appcelerator Cloud Services' pre-built objects.

An overview of Appcelerator Cloud Services can be found on the Appcelerator website at `http://www.appcelerator.com/cloud/`.

It is also important to know that even though you are using Appcelerator Cloud Services to integrate the Appcelerator Titanium mobile application, the framework provides a REST-based API, an iOS, and an Android native SDK that can be used for creating native applications.

Using the Appcelerator Cloud Services Console

To become more comfortable with Appcelerator Cloud Service, you are going to take a look at the Developer Console before you do any coding. You need to create an account at `https://my.appcelerator.com/auth/signup`. Figure 2-2 shows the sign-up page.

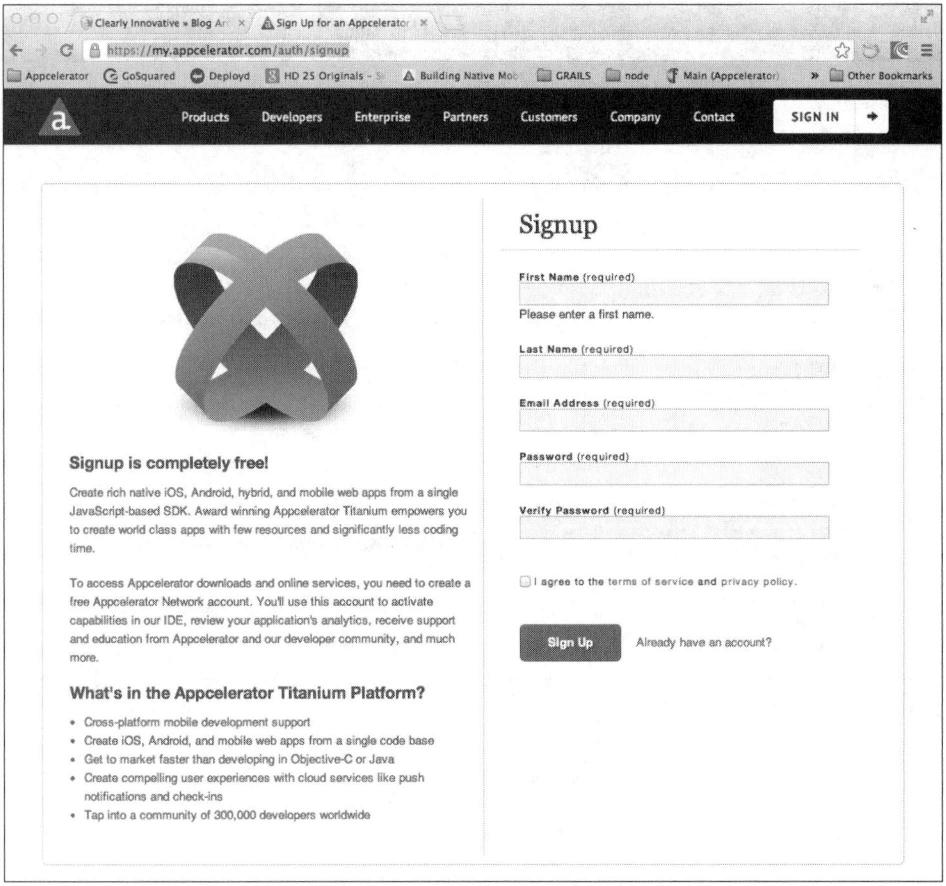

FIGURE 2-2: The Appcelerator developer's sign-up page.

Follow these steps to create an account:

1. Enter your information and click the Sign Up button. You should be forwarded to the developer's landing page. On the landing page is assorted information available to developers.

2. Click the link entitled Create an ACS App from the section called "Getting Started with ACS" on the developer's resources/landing page. Figure 2-3 shows this developer's landing page.

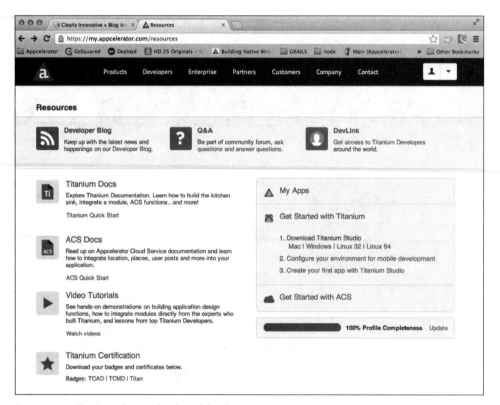

FIGURE 2-3: The Appcelerator developer's landing page.

3. On the Register A New App page, shown in Figure 2-4, enter a name and a brief description for your application. After the information is entered, click the Register App button.

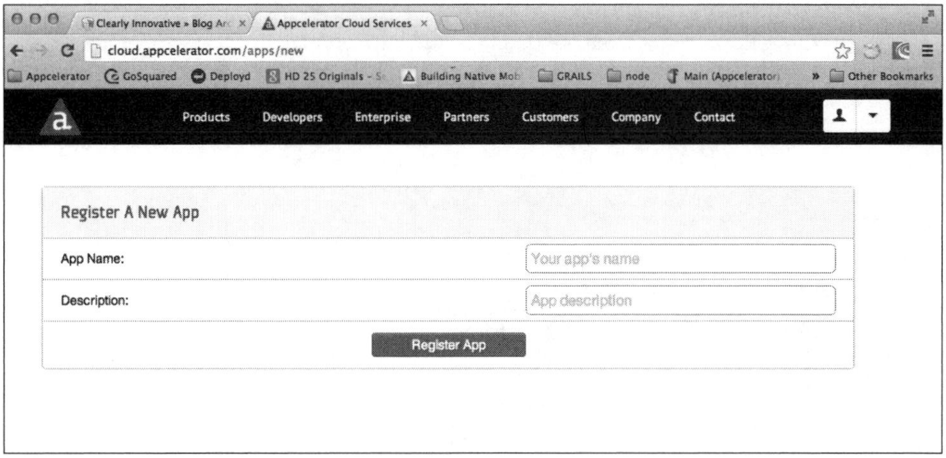

FIGURE 2-4: The Register A New App page.

If you created an app called `wileyone`, as the example here does, the resulting screen should look like Figure 2-5.

The left column provides basic overview information about your application and the right column shows the complete list of the predefined objects. You are going to create a user object first. Because most activities you will perform with Appcelerator Cloud Services require a user login, it's best to get that out of the way first.

4. Click on the link titled `Users(0)` at the bottom of the app page. The `(0)` represents the number of existing objects of that type.

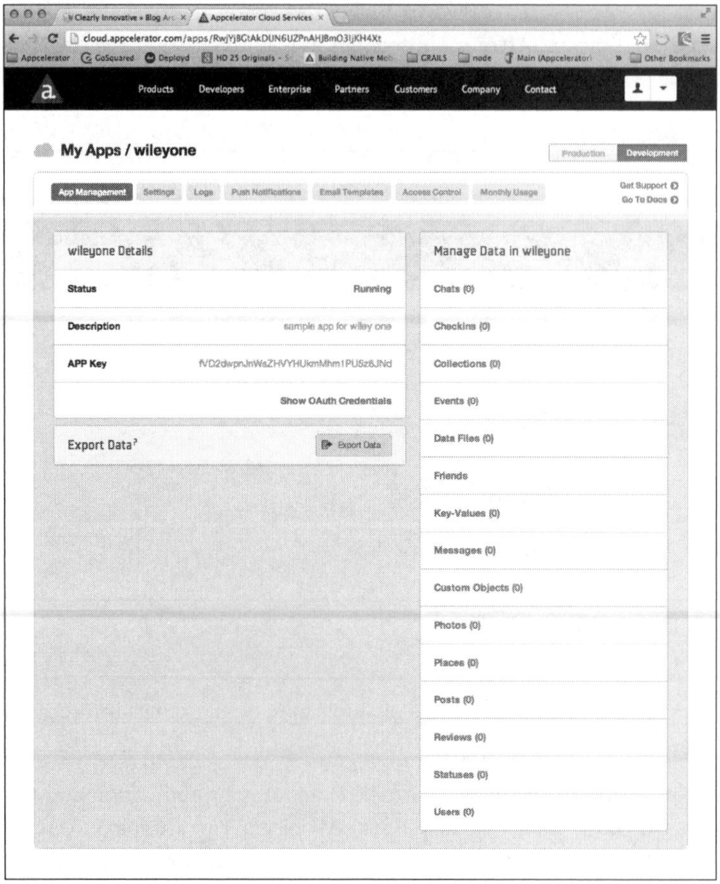

FIGURE 2-5: The Appcelerator Cloud Services app page.

Figure 2-6 shows the screen displaying the results of the query for all user objects. Since you have not created any yet, the screen is empty. On the top left, notice the All Users and Admin Users tabs. Don't worry about admin users, as they are covered later, when you create user accounts for testing the application.

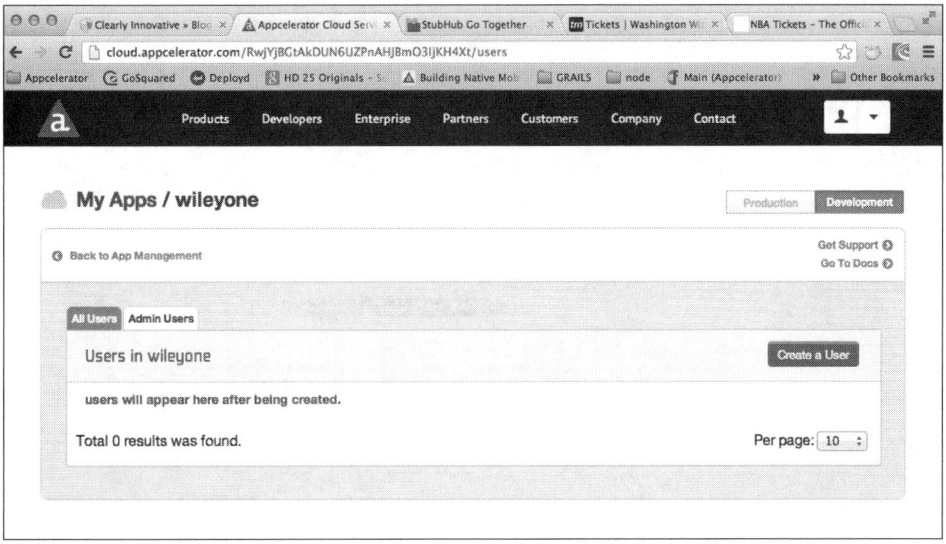

FIGURE 2-6: The Appcelerator Cloud Services new user page.

5. Next, click the Create a User button. Figure 2-7 shows the user input page you'll see next.

    Take a look at the input fields. You can see all the work and thought that went into defining the commonly used fields for users of the potential mobile application. If you need fields that are not included, you can extend the object using the `custom_fields` property, which is covered in more detail later, when you are extending objects in Appcelerator Cloud Services.

6. You can enter some basic data for the user in order to see how quickly the console gets going. Just enter an email address, username, and password. Figure 2-8 shows this page with some sample data.

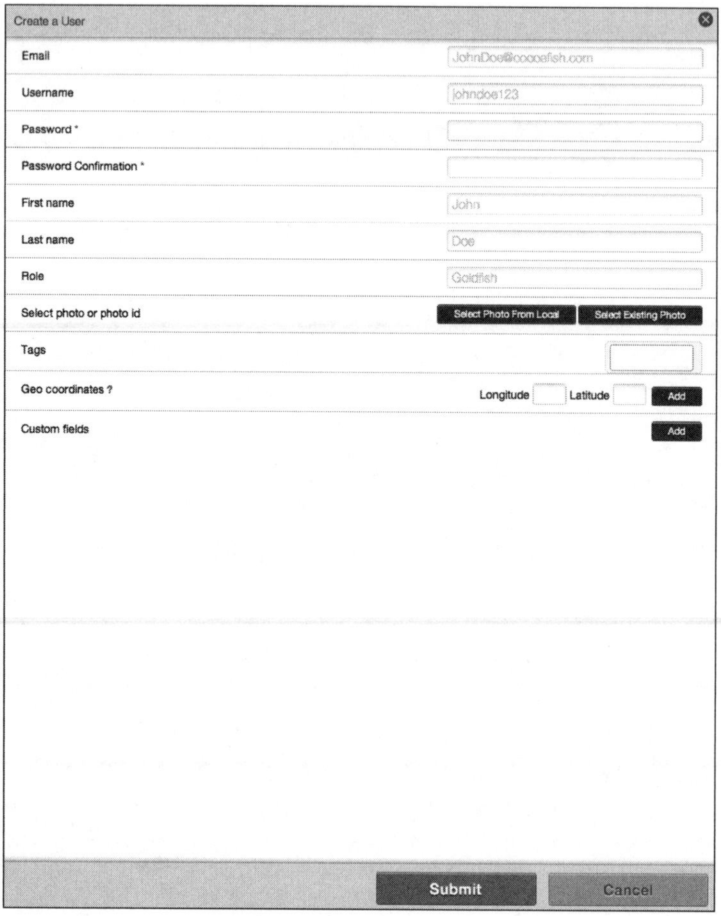

Create a User		⊗
Email		JohnDoe@icoodefish.com
Username		johndoe123
Password *		
Password Confirmation *		
First name		John
Last name		Doe
Role		Goldfish
Select photo or photo id		[Select Photo From Local] [Select Existing Photo]
Tags		[ ]
Geo coordinates ?		Longitude [ ] Latitude [ ] [Add]
Custom fields		[Add]

[Submit]   [Cancel]

FIGURE 2-7: Creating a new user.

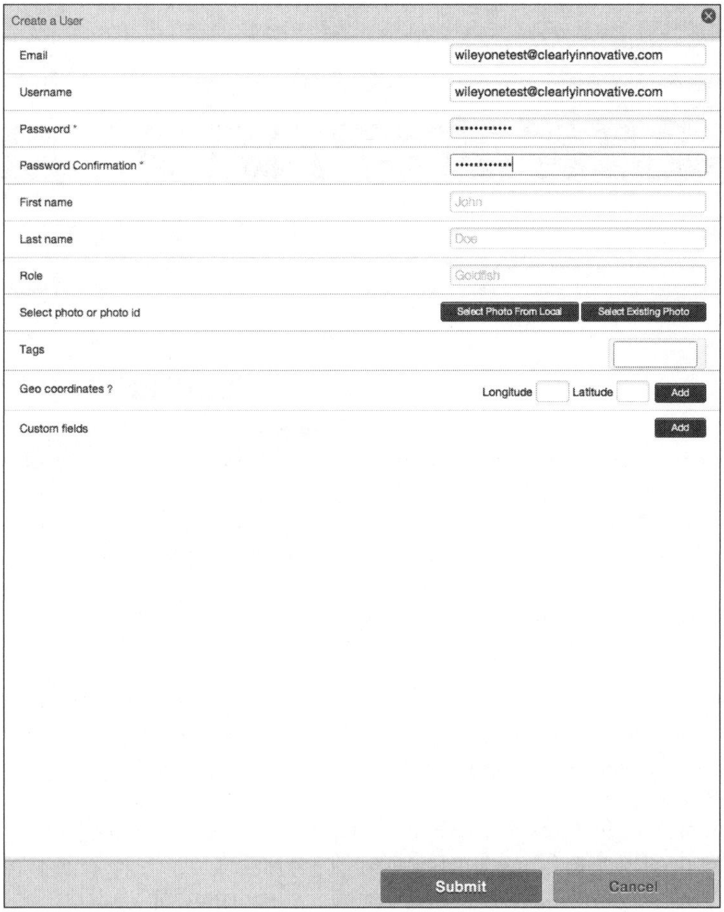

Create a User	⊗
Email	wileyonetest@clearlyinnovative.com
Username	wileyonetest@clearlyinnovative.com
Password *	•••••••••••
Password Confirmation *	•••••••••••
First name	John
Last name	Doe
Role	Goldfish
Select photo or photo id	Select Photo From Local Select Existing Photo
Tags	
Geo coordinates ?	Longitude □ Latitude □ Add
Custom fields	Add

Submit   Cancel

FIGURE 2-8: The New User Input page with sample data entered.

7. When you are done entering the data, click the Submit button to save the content to Appcelerator Cloud Services. Figure 2-9 shows the All Users tab after creating the new user.

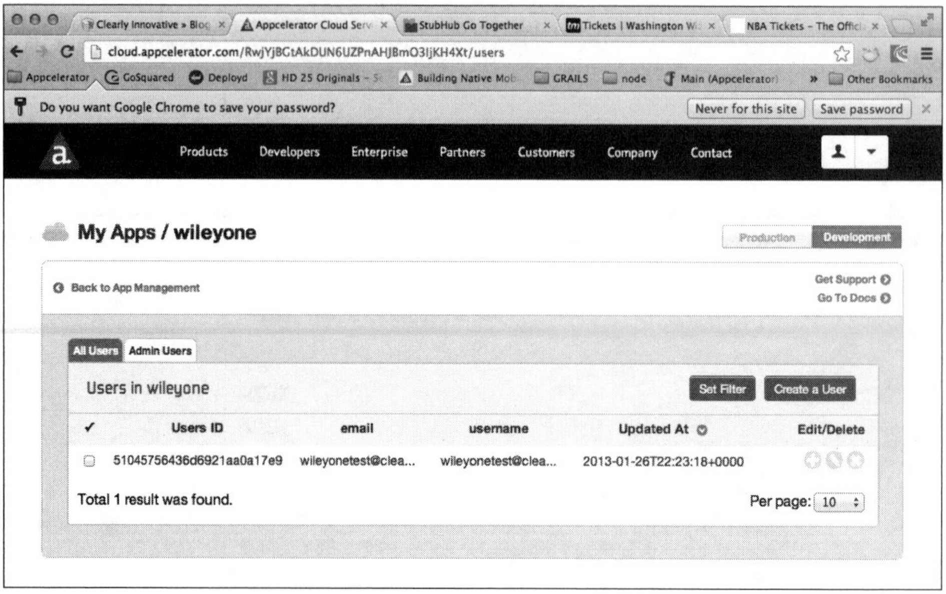

FIGURE 2-9: The All Users tab displaying the newly created user.

8. You can view the user's information by clicking the "expand icon," which looks like a plus sign, on the right side of the row of content. This will expand to show the fields associated with the user you just created. Figure 2-10 shows the expanded page.

The console supports additional features such as deleting objects, exporting objects, and setting filters on the object display page. These features are just a few of the many features provided by the console. It is a great place to verify information when your application is not doing what you expect or to pre-populate some content to get the development process started.

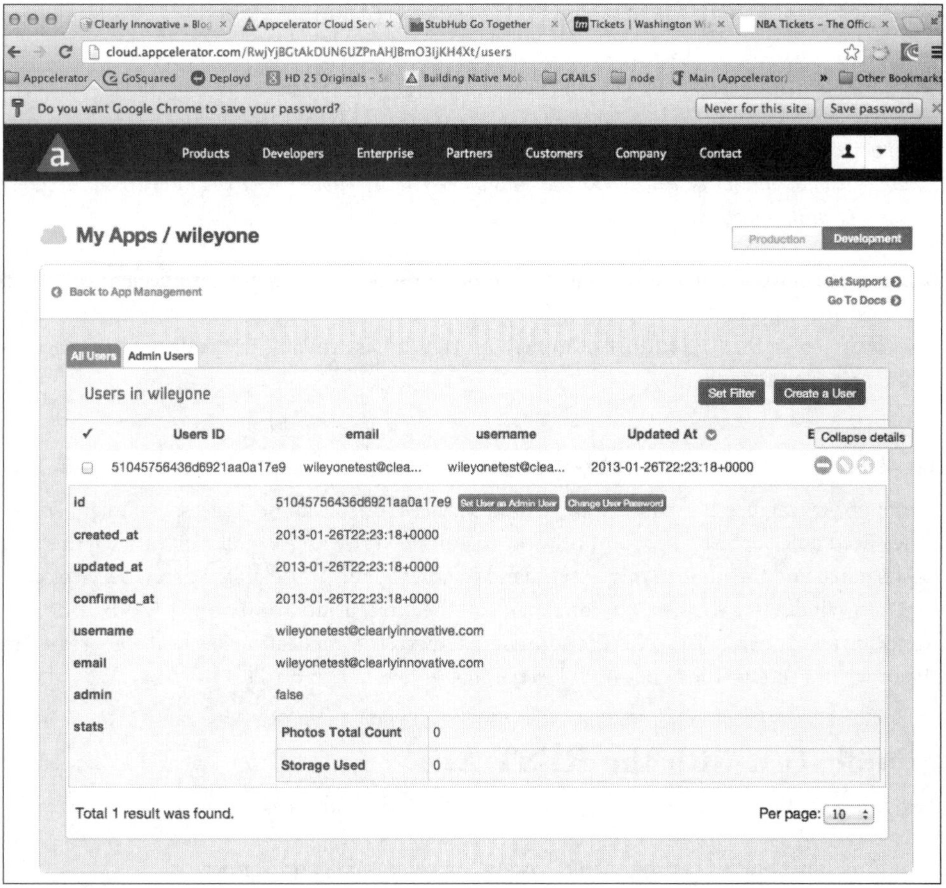

FIGURE 2-10: The All Users tab expanded to show the newly created user's field.

Using Appcelerator Cloud Services REST API

The Appcelerator Cloud Service has a REST API that allows you to create applications utilizing the framework as long as you have network capabilities. This means that Appcelerator Titanium apps and HTML5 applications utilizing AJAX clients both work.

Note the following from the Appcelerator Cloud Services documentation:

> *ACS is open to all app publishers, regardless of the development technology used to build the app-Titanium, Objective-C, Java, or HTML5 via frameworks like Sencha Touch or PhoneGap. Appcelerator Cloud Services provide a complete REST API along with iOS, Android, JavaScript, and ActionScript SDKs. Any device that can make HTTP requests over the Internet can securely use ACS as its server backend.*

Because the purpose of the book is to demonstrate how to integrate Appcelerator Cloud Services with Appcelerator Titanium Alloy through a mobile application, it contains only a brief overview of the REST API. Additional information is available in the developer's section of the Appcelerator website.

Installing curl on a Device

Although you can use the Appcelerator Cloud Services console in most cases, you might sometimes need quick access to content or want to quickly verify an API call. You can use the Mac OS terminal and the built-in `curl` command to access your Appcelerator Cloud Services content. On Windows machines, you can download the `curl` utility from `http://curl.haxx.se/download.html`. To access the content, you need the application key that was created in the previous section. The application key parameter is required on all REST API calls.

Simple Test with the REST API

Two important points to note when using the REST API and the console:

- You must always be logged in to access Appcelerator Cloud Services.
- You must save the `session_id` from the logged-in user to make Appcelerator Cloud Services REST API calls.

If you log in to the Appcelerator developer site and take a look at the documentation for the REST API, you can see examples of how to use the API. You can also see the appropriate parameters for making the REST API call. The information regarding the URL format and the parameters are specified in the documentation. Figure 2-11 shows an example API reference documentation.

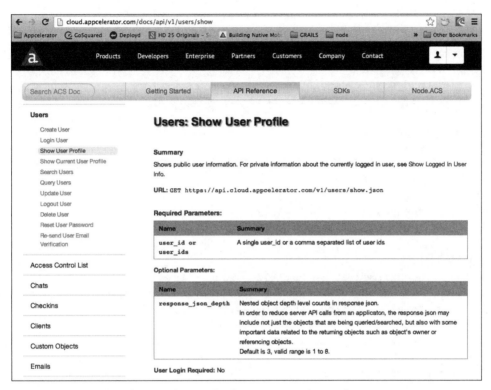

FIGURE 2-11: Sample of the Appcelerator Cloud Services API reference documentation.

You should now log in as the user you created in the previous section. The `cookies.txt` file will save the session information for use in other API calls. Type the information into the terminal, replacing the `key` parameter with your app ID.

```
$ curl -b cookies.txt -c cookies.txt -F
  "login=wileyonetest@clearlyinnovative.com" -F
  "password=wileyonetest"
  https://api.cloud.appcelerator.com/v1/users/login.json?key
  =[your-app-id]
```

The response should look something like the following code snippet, which indicates that you have successfully logged in to Appcelerator Cloud Services and the session information has been saved in the `cookies.txt` file. Please also note that all Appcelerator Cloud Services responses are in the JSON format. The `meta` section that follows always includes information about the specific query as well as a `response` section that lists the information on the objects that are returned from a successful request.

```json
{
  "meta": {
    "code": 200,
    "status": "ok",
    "method_name": "loginUser",
    "session_id": "Pn5a6z19prBWTiu2tI_MONtg7-M"
  },
  "response": {
    "users": [
      {
        "id": "51045756436d6921aa0a17e9",
        "created_at": "2013-01-26T22:23:18+0000",
        "updated_at": "2013-01-27T21:47:21+0000",
        "external_accounts": [

        ],
        "confirmed_at": "2013-01-26T22:23:18+0000",
        "username": "wileyonetest@clearlyinnovative.com",
        "email": "wileyonetest@clearlyinnovative.com",
        "admin": "false",
        "stats": {
          "photos": {
            "total_count": 0
          },
          "storage": {
            "used": 0
          }
        }
      }
    ]
  }
}
```

Now you'll use the Appcelerator Cloud Services REST API to update the user object you created. If you recall, the user object has a first_name and a last_name field, which you did not set when the object was created. You can set those object properties on the command line using curl:

```
$ curl --verbose -b cookies.txt -c cookies.txt -X PUT --data-
  urlencode "first_name=Aaron" --data-urlencode "last_name=Saunders"
  "https://api.cloud.appcelerator.com/v1/users/
          update.json? key=[your-app-id]"
```

You can get the value for `your-app-id` from the Appcelerator Cloud Services console on the Appcelerator website. After you log in to `my.appcelerator.com/apps`, select the appropriate application, and click Manage ACS. The new window will display a field titled "App Key," which is the value to use for `your-app-id`.

The result shows the updated user object:

```
{
  "meta": {
    "code": 200,
    "status": "ok",
    "method_name": "updateUser",
    "session_id": "Pn5a6z19prBWTiu2tI_MONtg7-M"
  },
  "response": {
    "users": [
      {
        "id": "51045756436d6921aa0a17e9",
        "first_name": "Aaron",
        "last_name": "Saunders",
        "created_at": "2013-01-26T22:23:18+0000",
        "updated_at": "2013-01-27T21:59:00+0000",
        "external_accounts": [

        ],
        "confirmed_at": "2013-01-26T22:23:18+0000",
        "username": "wileyonetest@clearlyinnovative.com",
        "email": "wileyonetest@clearlyinnovative.com",
        "admin": "false",
        "stats": {
          "photos": {
            "total_count": 0
          },
          "storage": {
            "used": 0
          }
        }
      }
    ]
  }
}
```

The same REST API used from the command line can be integrated into your Appcelerator Titanium mobile application, and in most cases the integration is done for you. For those who are interested, this section presents the same function performed previously using the REST API incorporated in a Titanium mobile application.

To connect to the service, you use the Appcelerator Titanium framework's `http` client class, as well as the same appkey and API URL that you used on the command line.

> **NOTE** This sample contains some advanced topics. Information about the `Ti.Network.HTTPClient` can be found in the Appcelerator Titanium documentation at `http://docs.appcelerator.com/titanium/latest/#!/api/Titanium.Network.HTTPClient`.

```javascript
var url = "https://api.cloud.appcelerator.com
        /v1/users/login.json?key=[your-app-id]";
var client = Ti.Network.createHTTPClient({
    //  called when the response data is available
    onload : function(e) {
        var results = JSON.parse(client.responseText);

        // display results on console
        Ti.API.info(JSON.stringify(results,null,2));
    },
    //  called when an error occurs, including a timeout
    onerror : function(e) {
        var results = JSON.parse(client.responseText);

        // display error results on the console
        Ti.API.err(JSON.stringify(results,null,2));
    },
});
// Prepare the connection
client.open("POST", url);

// Send the request with parameters
client.send({
    login :"wileyonetest@clearlyinnovative.com",
    password : "wileyonetest"
});
```

When you run this code, you will see the same results as when the REST API call was executed from the command line using `curl`. The function's parameters are provided as a parameter to the `httpClient`'s `send` method.

The previous section described how to use Appcelerator Cloud Services from the console, from the terminal using `curl` and using the HTTP client to make requests. The next section demonstrates the preferred integration method, which is to use the Cloud Services library and application properties provided by Appcelerator.

Integrating Appcelerator Cloud Services

Appcelerator Cloud Services are tightly integrated with the Appcelerator Framework. Integrating the functionality is as simple as setting an option when creating an application. This section shows you how to include Appcelerator Cloud Services in your application using the Appcelerator Titanium Studio project creation wizards.

Launch Appcelerator Titanium Studio and choose File ➪ New ➪ Titanium Project, as shown in Figure 2-12.

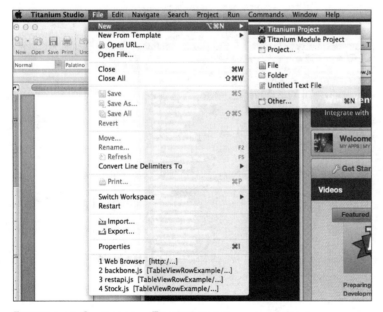

FIGURE 2-12: Creating a new Titanium project.

Enter the information for the project you are creating. This example names the project `wileyTwoSample` and the `app.id com.ci.wileytwosample`, as shown in Figure 2-13.

Note two important points here:

- The app ID must be unique; this is a requirement from iOS and Android SDKs.

- The app ID is usually structured in the reverse domain name format.

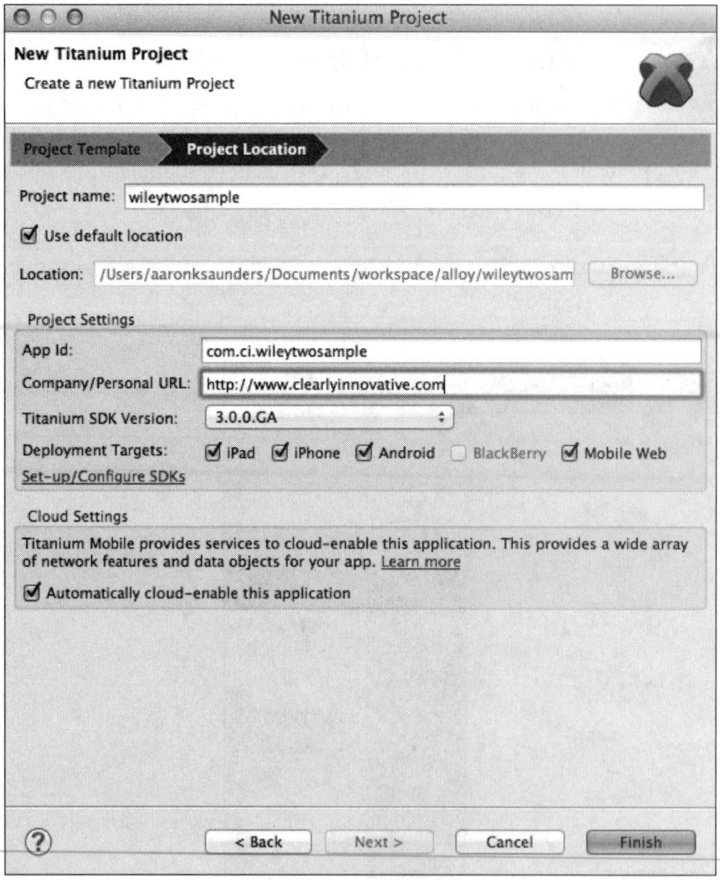

FIGURE 2-13: The new project with its completed fields.

Note the Cloud Settings section at the bottom of Figure 2-13. This is checked by default on all projects created in Titanium Studio. It cloud-enables your application by including the `ti.cloud.js` module in your application and setting the default authentication keys in the `tiapp.xml` file. These authentication properties are read by the `ti.cloud.js` module so as to provide access to your Appcelerator Cloud Service content. (When you *cloud-enable* your application it means that the connection to Appcelerator Cloud Services has been configured for you and the application has been set up in the Appcelerator Cloud Services console for you.)

After the project is created, you will be presented with the application configuration screen, which is a clean UI representing the XML inside of `tiapp.xml`. You can see the inclusion of the `ti.cloud` module and the Cloud Services API keys. Figure 2-14 shows the `tiapp.xml` user interface screen.

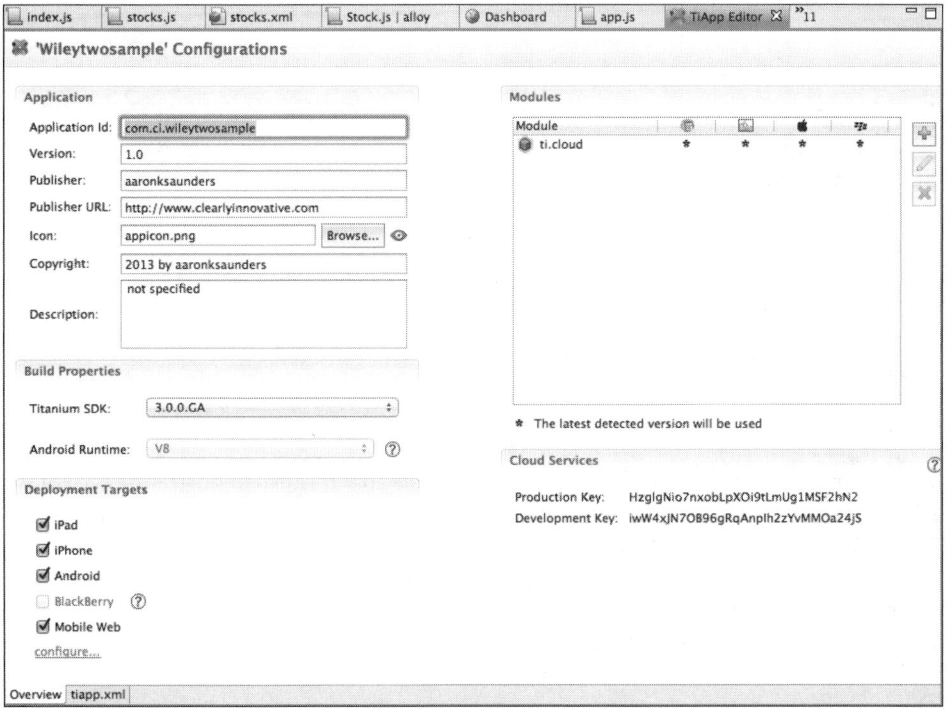

FIGURE 2-14: The tiapp.xml user interface screen.

If you view the raw XML in the `tiapp.xml` file, you can see the Appcelerator Cloud Services keys that were added to the application:

```
<property name="acs-oauth-secret-production"
  type="string">jm9LjW6cNiDOJLD5pCJW8RWgluxM5FYB</property>
    <property name="acs-oauth-key-production"
  type="string">80H9F4B0Dm7i04FEjmV1CNbjrGzUcLeQ</property>
    <property name="acs-api-key-production"
  type="string">HzglgNio7nxobLpXOi9tLmUg1MSF2hN2</property>
    <property name="acs-oauth-secret-development"
  type="string">nRAB8IJR5zWSgPq73HYLnYGTTFWCdXEf</property>
```

```
    <property name="acs-oauth-key-development"
 type="string">exjDF3XgNFvhHSV4rGLhkHqkdq1yDVc3</property>
    <property name="acs-api-key-development"
 type="string">iwW4xJN7OB96gRqAnpIh2zYvMMOa24jS</property>
```

At the bottom of the file you can see the inclusion of the `ti.cloud` JavaScript module:

```
<modules>
    <module platform="commonjs">ti.cloud</module>
</modules>
```

The `ti.cloud` JavaScript module supports most of the features of the Appcelerator Cloud Services API; please note that in some cases features will be available in the REST API before they are included in an updated `ti.cloud.js` JavaScript module.

> **NOTE** From the Appcelerator documentation regarding Appcelerator Cloud Services support in the JavaScript module: *Note that when new APIs are added to ACS, they may not be immediately available in the* `Titanium.Cloud` *module. The version listed after some APIs indicates the Titanium Mobile SDK release that included support for that API. (Note that the* `Titanium.Cloud` *module version is not always the same as the SDK version that it ships with.)*

The `Titanium.Cloud` module also includes a sample application demonstrating each of the ACS request types. You can find this in the modules folder under the Titanium SDK folder. For example:

```
/Library/Application Support/Titanium/modules/commonjs/
ti.cloud/<version>/example
```

Simple Example of Integrating Appcelerator Cloud Services

To help you get comfortable with Appcelerator Cloud Service, this section starts with a simple example that modifies the project you created previously. It doesn't go into too much detail about the Alloy application structure, because the purpose here is simply to demonstrate the Appcelerator Cloud Service integration.

Alloy applications have *models*, *views*, and *controllers*. In this application you are going to add some code to create a user object. Business logic will be included in the controllers, so you need to modify the default `index.js` controller with the Appcelerator Cloud Services code.

Model-view-controller (MVC) is a software pattern for implementing user interfaces. It's described in more detail in Chapter 3.   **TIP**

Open the project you created previously and select the `index.js` file. Figure 2-15 shows Titanium Studio with Alloy, opened to the `index.js` file.

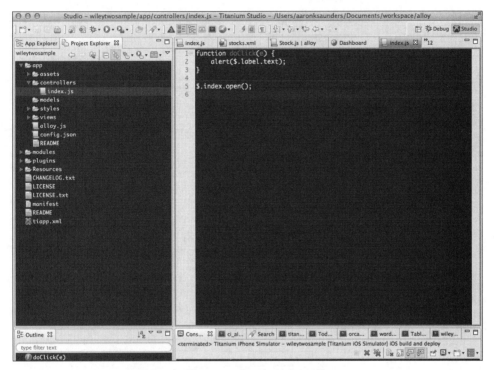

FIGURE 2-15: Titanium Studio with Alloy, opened to the index.js file.

The first step is to include the Appcelerator Cloud Services module in the application, as so:

```
var Cloud = require('ti.cloud');
```

Next you need to add some code to create a new user in Appcelerator Cloud Services. This will be the first user associated with this application since you are using the new Appcelerator Cloud Services application content created when you created the project.

Go to the Appcelerator Developer Center on the website to find the Appcelerator documentation. Because Appcelerator Cloud Services are integrated into the platform, you can access the documentation with the rest of the Appcelerator Titanium API calls at `http://docs.appcelerator.com/titanium/latest/#!/api/Titanium.Cloud`.

Figure 2-16 shows the Appcelerator developer documentation on Cloud Services.

FIGURE 2-16: Appcelerator developer documentation on Cloud Services.

Notice the complete list of Cloud Services objects listed in the left panel. Select the Users object for information about creating a new user with the Appcelerator Cloud Services API.

Click on the Users object and copy the sample code for creating a user. Paste the code into your `index.js` file and then save the file.

The `index.js` file is the first controller file executed in the Titanium Alloy application. By inserting the code here, you have a test harness so you can quickly demonstrate the interaction of the mobile application with the Appcelerator Cloud Services. Note that this is not the recommended approach for implementing Cloud Service integration since it does not follow the MVC pattern.

```
Cloud.Users.create({
    email: 'test@mycompany.com',
    username: 'test@mycompany.com',
    first_name: 'test_firstname',
    last_name: 'test_lastname',
    password: 'test_password',
    password_confirmation: 'test_password'
}, function (e) {
    if (e.success) {
        var user = e.users[0];
        alert('Success:\\n' +
            'id: ' + user.id + '\\n' +
            'first name: ' + user.first_name + '\\n' +
            'last name: ' + user.last_name);
    } else {
        alert('Error:\\n' +
            ((e.error && e.message) || JSON.stringify(e)));
    }
});
```

The `Cloud.Users.create` method takes a dictionary of parameters and a callback for when the function has completed. This example doesn't set all of the function's parameters. If you are interested in the complete set of parameters, you can review all of the optional and required parameters in the Appcelerator Cloud Services documentation at `http://cloud.appcelerator.com/docs`.

The function parameter information is not included in the Appcelerator Titanium Framework documentation; you must view the information at the Appcelerator Cloud Services documentation link (see `http://cloud.appcelerator.com/docs`).   **NOTE**

The parameters for the `Cloud.Users.create` method are shown in bold:

```
Cloud.Users.create({
    email: 'test@mycompany.com',
    first_name: 'test_firstname',
    last_name: 'test_lastname',
    password: 'test_password',
    password_confirmation: 'test_password'
```

```
}, function (e) {
    if (e.success) {
        // success
    } else {
        // error
    }
});
```

And the callback is shown in bold here:

```
Cloud.Users.create({
    email: 'test@mycompany.com',
    first_name: 'test_firstname',
    last_name: 'test_lastname',
    password: 'test_password',
    password_confirmation: 'test_password'
}, function (e) {
    if (e.success) {
        // success
    } else {
        // error!!
    }
});
```

In the previous example, you used an anonymous function as the callback and specified the parameters inline as a JavaScript object. You could have created a separate function and structured the code like this:

```
/**
 * callback function for Cloud.Users.create
 * @param {Object} e
 */
function createCallbackFunction(e) {
    if (e.success) {
        // success
    } else {
        // error
    }
}
```

```
// Trying to create a user
Cloud.Users.create({
    email : 'test@mycompany.com',
    username : 'test@mycompany.com',
    first_name : 'test_firstname',
    last_name : 'test_lastname',
    password : 'test_password',
    password_confirmation : 'test_password'
}, createCallbackFunction);
```

When the code is executed, it makes an asynchronous request to the server; the callback function is executed when the request completes. The results of the request are returned in a response object similar to the following output:

```
{
  "meta": {
    "code": 200,
    "status": "ok",
    "method_name": "createUser",
    "session_id": "Pn5a6z19prBWTiu2tI_MONtg7-M"
  },
  "response": {
    "users": [
      {
        "id": "51045756436d6921aa0a17e9",
        "email": 'test@mycompany.com',
        "first_name": 'test_firstname',
        "last_name": 'test_lastname',

        "created_at": "2013-01-26T22:23:18+0000",
        "updated_at": "2013-01-27T21:59:00+0000",
        "external_accounts": [

        ],
        "confirmed_at": "2013-01-26T22:23:18+0000",
        "username": 'test@mycompany.com',
        "email": 'test@mycompany.com',
        "admin": "false",
        "stats": {
          "photos": {
            "total_count": 0
          },
          "storage": {
            "used": 0
```

```
            }
          }
        }
      ]
    }
```

The object is specific to the Cloud Services object that the function is acting upon, which in this case is `Cloud.Users`. There is some commonality in the properties of the response object; where they vary is with the array of objects returned. So in the case of the `Cloud.Users`, user objects are returned. With `Cloud.Places`, a place object would be returned.

Now that you have seen the changes made to the application in the `index.js` file, try to launch the application and see what happens. Figure 2-17 shows the process of launching the application.

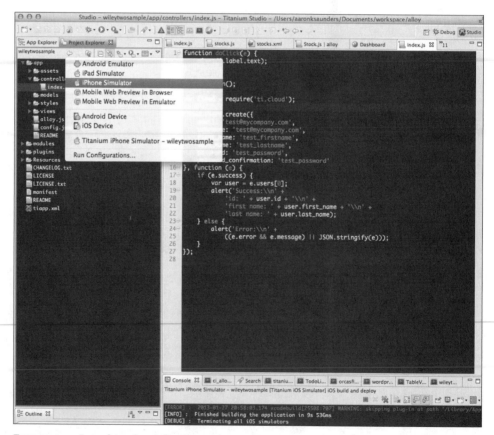

FIGURE 2-17: Launching the application.

Figure 2-18 shows the result of running the application.

FIGURE 2-18: The result of running the application.

Finally, Figure 2-19 shows the application results in the Appcelerator Cloud Services console.

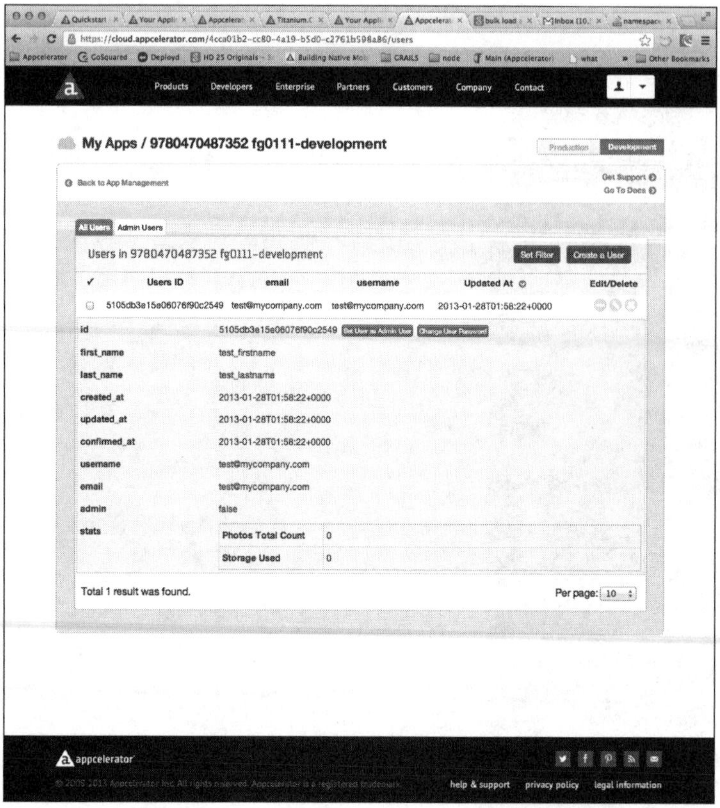

FIGURE 2-19: The application results in the Appcelerator Cloud Services console.

Summary

In this chapter you successfully created and cloud-enabled the mobile application with a scalable infrastructure supported by Appcelerator. You interacted with the cloud services using curl, using the Appcelerator Network HttpClient, and finally using the preferred method with the Cloud module library.

The next chapter starts to get into more detail of the Appcelerator Titanium Alloy framework; combining the structure of the framework with the full-featured cloud services provides you with a powerful technology stack for creating mobile solutions.

Chapter 3
Appcelerator Titanium Alloy Overview

ALLOY IS A new application framework by Appcelerator Titanium. It provides an MVC—Model-View-Controller—framework for developers to build cross-platform mobile applications. You are not required to use Alloy when building apps with Appcelerator Titanium, but after you understand the benefits of the framework, you will want to. Also note that even with Alloy, you can still fall back to the more traditional application structure in situations when you believe the Alloy approach doesn't fit.

Alloy provides a clean, well-defined MVC structure for building your applications. This structure follows the convention over configuration approach, which means if you structure and build your app following a specified set of conventions, the framework is self-configuring.

> The Model-View-Controller (MVC) triad of classes (first described by Krasner and Pope in 1988) is used to build user interfaces in Smalltalk-80. Looking at the design patterns inside MVC should help you see what the term "pattern" means. MVC consists of three kinds of objects. The *Model* is the application object, the *View* is its screen presentation, and the *Controller* defines the way the user interface reacts to user input. Before MVC, user interface designs tended to lump these objects together. MVC decouples them to increase flexibility and reuse. **NOTE**

From an Appcelerator Titanium perspective, MVC means you now have a well-defined structure for your applications based on a proven framework that is utilized in many programming languages today.

Understanding the Model-View-Controller (MVC) Framework

The *model* in MVC stores and maintains the data that your application works with. This can be local data stored in a SQLite database or a flat file but the same model maintains the data, whether it comes from a remote web service, a REST-based API, or a document store like MongoDB or Couchbase. The key here is that if the code/function has to do with managing or manipulating data—the CRUD—then it most likely belongs in the model.

CRUD refers to the major functions that are implemented in relational database applications. Each letter stands for a standard SQL statement and HTTP method:

- Create or add new entries
- Read, retrieve, search, or view existing entries
- Update or edit existing entries
- Delete/deactivate existing entries

The following code snippet represents the simplest form of a model that you would use in your mobile solution.

```
exports.definition = {
    config : {
        // table schema and adapter information
    },

    extendModel: function(Model) {
        _.extend(Model.prototype, {
            // Extend, override or implement Backbone.Model
        });

        return Model;
    },

    extendCollection: function(Collection) {
        _.extend(Collection.prototype, {
            // Extend, override or implement Backbone.Collection
        });

        return Collection;
    }
}
```

You'll learn about more of the advanced aspects of the model when you read about sync adapters and data binding later in the chapter.

The *view* is pretty straight forward, and usually the easiest to understand. It is the presentation layer of the application. All things that the user will interact with directly are considered the view. The `view.xml` files are XML-based representations of the user interface built using the Appcelerator objects defined in the various Titanium namespaces. The following code shows a sample view file of a window containing a label. The label has a click event associated with it. When the label is clicked, the function `doClick` from the associated controller is executed.

Notice the `id` property on the view elements. It allows you to access the object from inside the controller.

You'll read more about views later in this chapter when you start to integrate all of the pieces of the framework together and build a functional application.

The following code snippet represents the simplest form of a view that you could use in your mobile solution.

```
<!-- Create a window object and add a label to it -->
<Alloy>
    <Window id="main_window" class="container">
        <!-- on click event, call controller function doClick -->
        <Label id="hello_label" onClick="doClick">
            Hello, World
        </Label>
    </Window>
</Alloy>
```

Another important capability of Alloy when creating views is the use of the `Require` XML tag. It allows you to include other views or widgets in a view.

You can expand the previous example by adding a header to the window containing a title. Create the new view using the command line or by the menu item:

```
alloy generate controller header
```

Then add a simple label with a title inside the `header.xml` view file.

```
<Alloy>
  <View class="container">
    <Label>My Sample Title</Label>
  </View>
</Alloy>
```

You can set the style on the new header file to make sure the header is at the top of the page and the label font is larger and bold. Add the following code in to the `header.tss` file:

The following code snippet represents an example of a `.tss` file that would hold the style information for a view in your mobile solution. Alloy uses the concept of convention over configuration, which in this case means the components are matched by their names— `header.js` for controller, `header.tss` for styles, and `header.xml` for view.

```
".container": {
  backgroundColor: "white",
  top : 0,
  height : Ti.UI.SIZE,
  width : Ti.UI.FILL,
  backgroundColor : "brown"
},
"Label": {
  font : {
        fontSize : 18,
        fontWeight : 'bold'
   }
}
}
```

Finally, when you put it all together, the updated `index.xml` view file looks like this:

```
<!-- Create a window object, add header then add a label to it -->
<Alloy>
    <Window id="main_window" class="container">
        <!-- header for window, using Require -->
        <Require type="view" id="header" src="header" />

        <!-- on click event, call controller function doClick -->
        <Label id="hello_label" onClick="doClick">
           Hello, World
        </Label>
    </Window>
</Alloy>
```

The *controller* is the heart of the business logic for your application; it is the glue that holds it all together. Going in one direction, the controller gets data from the model for the view to render. Going in the other direction, the user interacts with the view, which then triggers the controller to take a specific action with the view or to pass CRUD changes on to the model.

In the following sample controller file, you can see the `doClick` function mentioned previously. Note how the controller has access to the controls from the view by using the $ variable to access context variables like the `hello_label` and the `main_window` being used in the open statement at the end of the file.

```
// local/private function
function doClick(e) {
    alert($.hello_label.text);
}

// public exported function than can be accessed by other
// controllers
exports.changeLabelText = function(_text) {
    $.hello_label.setText(_text);
}

// $ Represents current scope of controller, open the window
// main_window that was defined in the view.xml
$.main_window.open();
```

Most applications will have multiple models, controllers, and views but this structure will help in architecting and maintaining your application.

Using Appcelerator Alloy with the MVC Framework

Appcelerator Alloy maps the MVC framework directly to its project file structure. As you can see in Figure 3-1, there is a folder corresponding directly to the components described in the description of MVC.

Alloy also includes an additional file type to further complement the framework, `.tss` files, which contain style information that is applied to views. This further separates the concerns—how you apply styles to the view is controlled through `.tss` files, which are structured very similar to cascading style sheet (`.css`) files you would find in an HTML website. These `.tss` files are then applied to the view at pre-compile time to determine layout color and presentation-related properties.

Name	Date Modified
▼ 📁 app	Feb 19, 2013 3:09 PM
alloy.js	Feb 6, 2013 10:48 AM
▶ 📁 assets	Feb 6, 2013 10:49 AM
config.json	Feb 19, 2013 1:37 PM
▶ 📁 controllers	Feb 6, 2013 10:48 AM
▶ 📁 lib	Feb 6, 2013 10:49 AM
▶ 📁 models	Feb 6, 2013 10:54 AM
README	Feb 6, 2013 10:48 AM
▶ 📁 styles	Today 7:48 PM
▶ 📁 views	Today 7:48 PM
▼ 📁 widgets	Feb 19, 2013 3:09 PM
▼ 📁 buttonToggle	Feb 19, 2013 3:09 PM
▼ 📁 assets	Feb 19, 2013 1:37 PM
▼ 📁 controllers	Feb 19, 2013 1:37 PM
widget.js	Today 5:56 PM
▼ 📁 styles	Feb 19, 2013 1:37 PM
widget.tss	Feb 19, 2013 5:31 PM
▼ 📁 views	Feb 19, 2013 1:37 PM
widget.xml	Feb 19, 2013 1:59 PM
widget.json	Feb 19, 2013 1:37 PM
▶ 📁 build	Today 6:29 PM
CHANGELOG.txt	Feb 6, 2013 10:48 AM
LICENSE	Feb 6, 2013 10:48 AM
LICENSE.txt	Feb 6, 2013 10:48 AM
manifest	Feb 6, 2013 10:48 AM
▶ 📁 modules	Feb 6, 2013 10:52 AM
▶ 📁 plugins	Feb 6, 2013 10:48 AM
README	Feb 6, 2013 10:48 AM
▶ 📁 Resources	Feb 8, 2013 3:33 PM
tiapp.xml	Feb 19, 2013 1:48 PM

FIGURE 3-1: Appcelerator Alloy folder project structure.

Using the view file you created previously, add the following code to the file.

```xml
<!-- Create a window object and add a label to it -->
<Alloy>
    <Window id="main_window" class="container">
        <!-- on click event, call controller function doClick -->
        <Label id="hello_label" onClick="doClick">
            Hello, World
        </Label>
        <Label id="blue_label" >Blue Label</Label>
    </Window>
</Alloy>
```

You could style the index.tss file like this:

```
// This is applied to any element with the class attribute
// assigned to "container"
".container": {
    backgroundColor:"white",
    layout:"vertical",
},
// This is applied to all Labels in the view
"Label": {
    width: Ti.UI.SIZE,
    height: Ti.UI.SIZE,
    color: "#000" /* black */
},
// This is only applied to an element with the id attribute
// assigned to "label"
"#blue_label": {
    color: "blue"
}
```

In this example, the index.tss file is specific to the index.js controller, but you can create global-level styles by using an app.tss file.

Also since Appcelerator supports cross-platform development, you can have platform-specific styles using specific selectors in your .tss files:

```
// This is applied to all Labels in the view
"Label": {
    width: Ti.UI.SIZE,
    height: Ti.UI.SIZE,
    color: "#000" /* black */
},
// This is applied to all Labels in the view, when the device
// is an android device
"Label[platform=android]": {
    color: "green"
},
```

The relationship of the .tss files to the .xml view files is similar to the HTML files and the .css files in a web application.

Backbone.js

Alloy includes additional JavaScript libraries to assist in structuring the MVC pattern when developing applications; one such library is called Backbone.js.

NOTE Backbone.js gives structure to web applications by providing models with key-value binding and custom events, providing collections with a rich API of enumerable functions, and providing views with declarative event handling. Backbone.js connects it all to your existing API over a RESTful JSON interface. See `http://blog.iandavis.com/2008/12/09/what-are-the-benefits-of-mvc/`.

Alloy's implementation focuses specifically on integration of models, collections, and event binding. The view and routing implementation of Backbone.js is not leveraged in Alloy.

Backbone.js has a dependency on `underscore.js`, which provides a set of utility functions that are exposed by default on the model and collection objects. They can also be applied to your application object. See `http://underscorejs.org/` and `http://backbonejs.org/`.

Backbone.js in Alloy: Models and Collections

Models are a representation of the data in your mobile application. Backbone.js provides the basic functions for maintaining the data. The model objects can be extended to provide customized functionality to your model. Alloy models inherit the default `Backbone.Model` functionality.

A *collection* is a set of models of a specific type. The collection is comprised of the models and a set of functions to manage the collection/list of models. The collection objects can be extended to provide customized functionality to your models. Alloy models inherit the default `Backbone.Collection` functionality.

Models and collections are contained in one model file in Alloy; the basic file starts off like this:

```
exports.definition = {
  config : {
    "columns" : {
      name : 'TEXT',
    },
```

```
  // specify sync adapter information here
    "adapter" : {
      "type" : "sql_new",
      "collection_name" : "stuff",
      "idAttribute" : "stuff_id" // if not using id as the id
    }
  },

  extendModel : function(Model) {
    _.extend(Model.prototype, {
        // add code here to extend the model
    });
    // end extend model

    return Model;
  },
  extendCollection : function(Collection) {
    _.extend(Collection.prototype, {
      // add code here to extend the collection
    });
     // end extend collection

    return Collection;
  }
}
```

As stated, the models represent the data and the supporting methods in your mobile application. When your model needs to be read, saved, or modified, Backbone.js has a default persistence strategy that it applies which is based on the default HTTP verbs. This default strategy assumes convention over configuration in that the models are wired to function perfectly with a REST-based API in response to the HTTP verbs.

The following table outlines how your application's actions map to HTTP verbs and how that is then represented in Backbone.js sync adapters:

Action	HTTP Verb	Backbone Sync Method
Insert new book	POST	create
Get a specific book	GET	read
Get all books	GET	read
Update a book	PUT	update
Delete a book	DELETE	delete

These simple code snippets reflect the previous table's actions:

```
// create a new model, passing the name of model
var model = Alloy.createModel("stuff");
model.set({"name":"Aaron", "age":22});
model.save(); // POST: create


// get a model by model id
var model = new Stuff();
model.fetch(10); // GET: read


// get a collection of models
var collection = Alloy.createCollection("stuff");
collection.fetch(); // GET: read


// update a model
var model = new Stuff();
model.fetch(10); // GET: read
model.set({"age":45});
model.save(); // PUT: update


// delete a model by model id
var model = new Stuff();
model.destroy(10); // DELETE: delete
```

The model file defined here will support all of the actions described in the table without any additional changes. Sometimes you need your model or collection to support additional functionality, which is where extending the model object comes in.

Assume you have a model object that stores dates. You know that dates are usually stored in some format that is not easy for end users to read. You could extend the model to encapsulate rendering and produce prettyDate. This involves converting the timestamp into a formatted date string.

```
extendModel : function(Model) {
    _.extend(Model.prototype, {
```

```
    // @return a pretty version of the date using
    // moment.js date utilities
    // @see http://momentjs.com/
    //
    prettyDate : function() {
        var _model = this;
        var date_update = model.get("date_update");
        return moment.unix(date_update).calendar();
    }
});
    // end extend model
```

You can then just call the function on the model:

```
// create a new model
var model = Alloy.createModel("stuff");

// query a model with the id 10
stuffModel.fetch("10");

// now show normal date
stuffModel.get("date_update");

// show pretty date
stuffModel.prettyDate();
```

Collections can be extended in the same manner; see the following example where you're looking for items in the collection that match.

Models and collections can both be created as global singleton instances; they can be created by using the instance method available on both objects.

```
// create a new global model of type "stuff"
var globalStuffModel = Alloy.Model.instance("stuff");
// create a new global collection of type "stuff"
var globalStuffCollection = Alloy.Collection.instance("stuff");
```

Now to retrieve the object you can call the same method and it will return the object or create a new instance of one.

Using Sync Adapters

Sync adapters are commonJS libraries that you can include in your Alloy application to control how your models interact with the persistence mechanism of your application. In the default Backbone.js, there is an assumption that there is a library providing AJAX communication with the server—usually jQuery.

Alloy doesn't currently provide a default sync adapter to replace the default AJAX interaction provided by jQuery; you must specify a specific sync adapter to provide that functionality.

Alloy provides a few ready-made sync adapters. In the `adapter` object, set the `type` to use one of the following:

- `sql` for the SQLite database on the Android and iOS platforms.

- `localStorage` for HTML5 local storage on the Mobile web platform.

- `properties` for storing data locally in the Titanium SDK context.

- `sync` for mimicking the default Backbone.js AJAX functionality. This behavior supports REST-based APIs.

Basic Sync Adapter Construction

Because the sync adapter must follow the interface provided by Backbone.js, you can follow the previous table for understanding the methods you must support. `Backbone.Sync` was designed to support web/AJAX interaction, which is based on the HTTP verbs listed in the table.

```
// Alloy Sync Adapter Snippet to show key function sync,
// which handles the mapping of Backbone.Sync calls to
// specific REST actions or API calls
module.exports.sync = function (method, model, options) {

switch (method) {

        // GET: Model.fetch and Collection.fetch methods to
        // retrieve data.
        case 'read':
            break;

        // POST: Model.save and Collection.create methods to
        // an initialize model if the IDs are not set.
        case 'create':
            break;
```

```
        // DELETE: Model.destroy method to delete the model
        // from storage.
        case 'delete':
            break;

        // PUT: Model.save and Collection.create methods to
        // update a model if they have IDs set.
        case 'update':
            break;
        default :
            error = 'ERROR: Sync method not recognized!';
    }

    if (error) {
        options.error(model, error, options);
        model.trigger('error');
    } else {
        options.success(model, error, options);
        model.trigger('sync');
    }
};
```

Backbone Model Events

Backbone models trigger events based on certain actions. These actions can be subscribed to so that developers can take specific actions in the application. The default behavior for models is to fire a sync event when the sync adapter is called. If the call is not successful, the model should fire an error event.

```
// Listening for a sync event from model named
// currentCollection
$.currentCollection.on('sync', function() {
    Ti.API.info("the model is being modified");
});
```

When writing your own adapters, be sure to respect the convention of triggering the proper events. Follow the conventions of the standard Backbone.js adapter and return the new model, the network client object, and the original options that were passed into the sync adapter function.

```
// Inside of a custom sync adapter when starting
// sync adapter call
model.trigger('request', model, xhr, options);
```

```
// Inside of a custom sync adapter on successful
// sync adapter call
model.trigger('sync', model, resp, options);

// Inside of a custom sync adapter on error
// sync adapter call
model.trigger('error', model, resp, options);
```

Model-View Data Binding

A simple explanation of *model-view data binding* is the capability of changes in models and collections to be automatically reflected in the presentation layer of the application, or the views. Appcelerator Alloy currently only supports `TableViews` and the base `View` object; additional Appcelerator `View` objects will be supported in future Alloy releases.

Demo Project for Model View Binding

You can use the Titanium Studio menus to create the new demo project. Follow these steps to do so:

1. Choose File ➪ New ➪ Titanium Project, as shown in Figure 3-2.

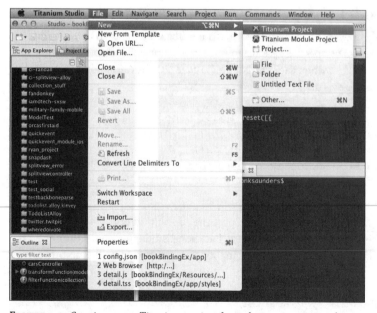

FIGURE 3-2: Creating a new Titanium project from the menu command area.

2. Select Default Alloy Project, as shown in Figure 3-3.

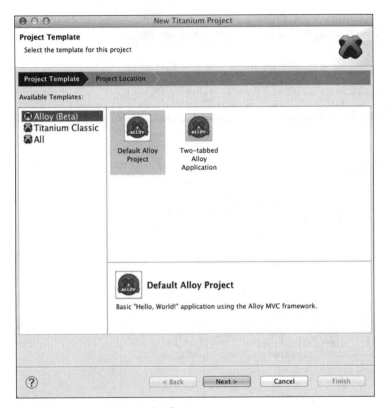

FIGURE 3-3: Select the Default Alloy Project option.

3. Figure 3-4 shows the New Titanium Project window, where you define the new project's name and settings. For the project name, enter demo_project. For the app ID, enter com.ci.demoproject. Finally, enter an URL for the Company/Personal URL.

Creating the Model File

First you need to create a model file. You will use the properties sync adapter to store the information since you don't want the complexity of creating a database and defining rows and columns in this introductory example.

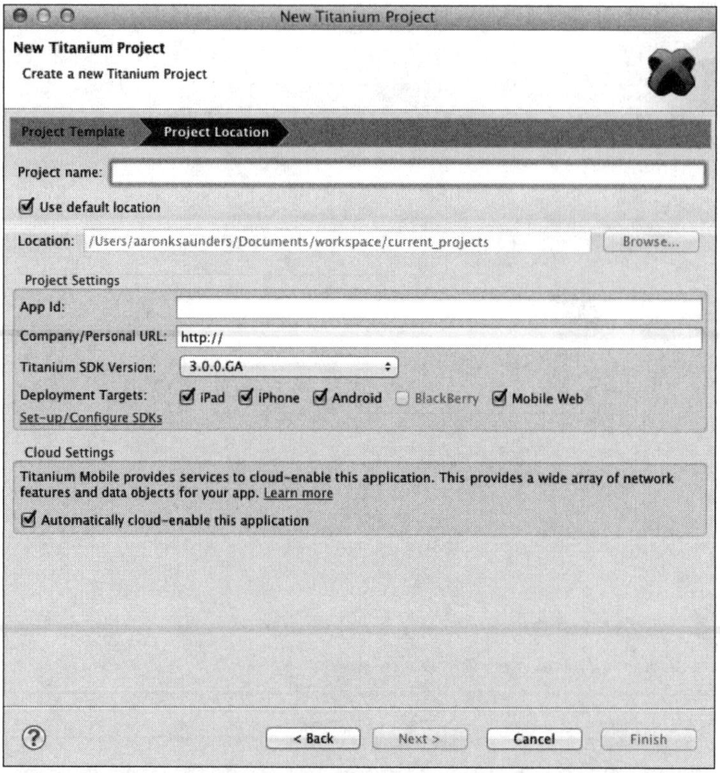

FIGURE 3-4: Enter the project information in this window.

The model you are creating will have two properties, called `make` and `model`. Since you are using the `properties` sync adapter, there are no predefined columns to represent these fields. The JSON representation of this model would look something like this:

```
{
    "make" : "Honda",
    "model" : "Accord"
}
```

You can use the Titanium Studio menu command to create the model JavaScript file, as shown in Figure 3-5. Simply choose New ➪ Alloy Model.

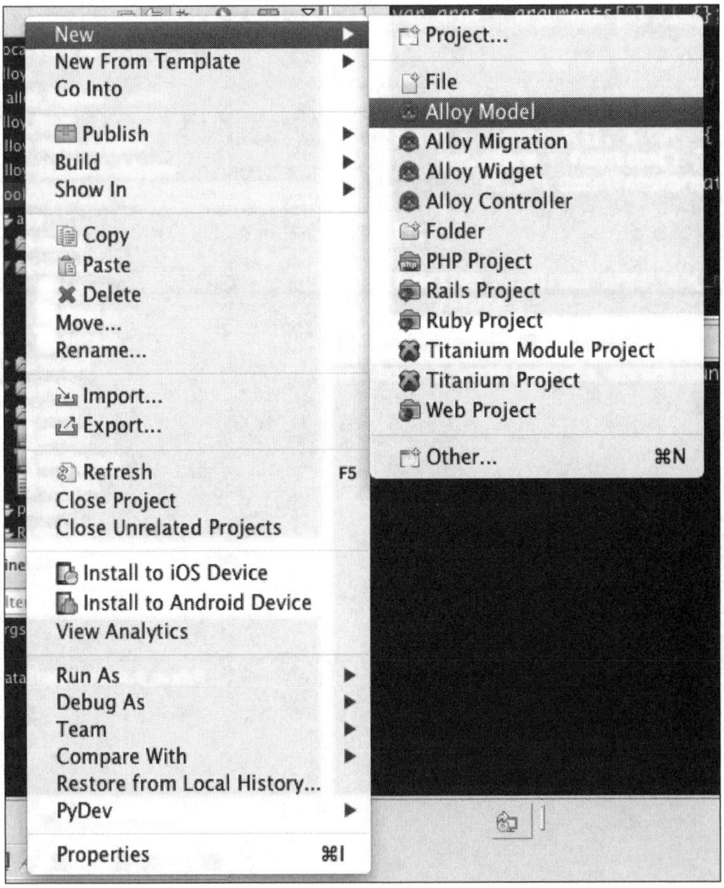

FIGURE 3-5: Creating a new model from the menu options.

You then enter the model name of cars in the field and select localStorage. You will be using the properties sync adapter, but it is not available in the menu. You will edit the value in the resulting model file, as shown in Figure 3-6.

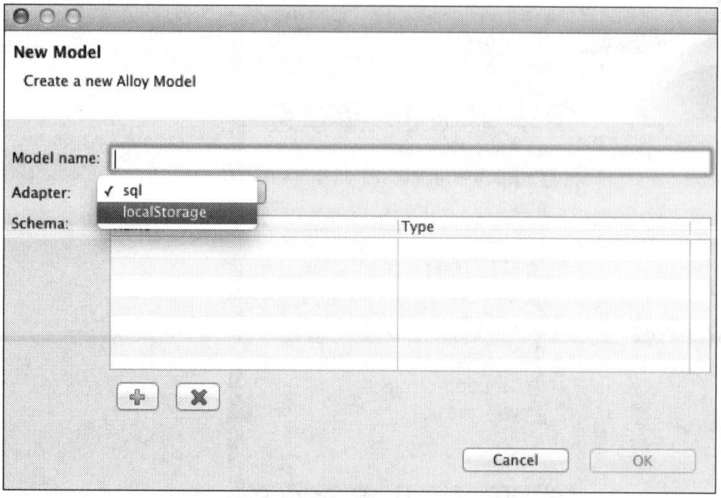

FIGURE 3-6: Entering a name for your new model.

Open the file and make the edits shown in the following code. The model file should look similar to this in the end:

```javascript
// models/cars.js
exports.definition = {
 config: {

    adapter: {
      type: "properties",
      collection_name: "cars"
    }
  },
  extendModel: function(Model) {
    _.extend(Model.prototype, {
      // extended functions and properties go here
    });

    return Model;
  },
  extendCollection: function(Collection) {
    _.extend(Collection.prototype, {
      // extended functions and properties go here
    });
```

```
    return Collection;
  }
}
```

Since you are going to use `index.xml` for the view, you need to replace the existing content with the code that follows. When you are finished, the contents of the `cars.xml` view file should look similar to this:

```
<Alloy>
    <Collection src="cars" />
    <Window id="mainWindow" class="container">
        <TableView dataCollection="cars" dataTransform="transform"
            dataFilter="filter">
            <TableViewRow title="{title}" modelId="{id}" />
        </TableView>
    </Window>
</Alloy>
```

First, you declared the collection of cars in the view file:

```
<Collection src="cars" />
```

This creates a global instance of a collection object based on the model `cars`. Since this is a global instance, you can access it in the code like this:

```
Alloy.Collections.cars
```

Next, you associate the collection to the table using the `dataCollection` property. You then set a few more properties on the collection for filtering and transforming the data that appears in the table. In this example, those functions are defined in the controller associated with the view but could also be global functions. You'll read more about this when you read about the controller JavaScript file.

```
<TableView dataCollection="cars" dataTransform="transform"
           dataFilter="filter">
```

Now replace the code in `index.js` with the following code. First you will see the `transform` function. This function is called for every model in the collection and allows the contents of the model to be modified for rendering in the `TableView`. Note that the properties returned from the `transform` function's model can be actual model properties or properties derived from the properties in the model.

In the following example, you concatenate the model and the `make` properties to create the title that you'll display in the table:

```
// Convert the model and make into a title property
function transform(model) {
    // Need to convert the model to a JSON object
    var carObject = model.toJSON();
    return {
        "title" : carObject.model + " by " + carObject.make,
        "id" : model.cid
    };
}
```

In the following example, you concatenate the model and the make to create the title that you'll display in the table:

```
// Show only cars made by Honda
function filter(collection) {
    return collection.where({
        make : 'Honda'
    });
}
```

This `close` event listener is required to ensure the bindings from the `TableView` are cleaned up correctly and there are no memory leaks.

```
// Free model-view data binding resources when this
// view-controller closes
$.mainWindow.addEventListener('close', function() {
    $.destroy();
});
```

Next, add an event listener on the window so that when the window is completely open, you'll set the contents of the collection. The `TableView` is bound to the collection so when it detects that the contents of the collection have changed, it will automatically refresh itself.

```
// add the data to the collection AFTER the window is opened. The
// generated data binding code is listening for specific events
// to force a redraw... reset is one of them.
$.mainWindow.addEventListener("open", function() {
    Alloy.Collections.cars.reset([{
        "make" : "Honda",
        "model" : "Civic"
    }, {
        "make" : "Honda",
        "model" : "Accord"
    }, {
        "make" : "Ford",
        "model" : "Escape"
    }, {
        "make" : "Ford",
        "model" : "Mustang"
    }, {
        "make" : "Nissan",
        "model" : "Altima"
    }]);
});
```

Finally you open the window.

```
$.mainWindow.open();
```

When you run the application, you should see the output shown in Figures 3-7 and 3-8.

When Alloy generates the code based on the view configuration, it sets the `TableView` so it can respond to changes in the collection. As mentioned, all the application needs to do is trigger one of these events against the collection and the table will refresh itself.

FIGURE 3-7: Application running in iOS.

Creating the Collection Object

A few points regarding creation of the collection object.

Even though you can create the collection object in the controller, as so:

```
Alloy.Collections.instance("cars");
```

In most cases it will not work if you attempt to create the collection in the same controller that is associated with the view you are attempting to render. The issue here has to do with the way Alloy generates code. All of the view code from the `view.xml` file is executed before any controller code. When this view code is executed, Alloy performs the event binding discussed previously. It will fail since the collection objects have not been created yet.

FIGURE 3-8: Application running in Android.

A solution I have used—when you must create the collection in the application code and not the view file—is to create the collection in a parent controller and then load a different child view to render the collection. So if you use the current example, the `index.js` file would create the collection and then create a new collection-view pair to actually render the table.

The `index.xml` file contents will need to be copied to the new child view. You need to create a new view-controller pair, naming the new set of files `cars` to render the information. You'll use `index.js` as an overall application initialization starting point:

```
<!-- index.xml -->
<Alloy>
    <!—Nothing needed here    -->
</Alloy>
```

The `index.js` file now just sets up collection by creating a global instance. This function will create the collection based on the model name provided or return the global instance of the collection if one exists.

```
// controllers/index.js
// Defining the Collection in the controller and not the view
Alloy.Collections.instance("cars");
```

You now create the new view-controller pair named `cars`. It will render the information and provide the supporting functions for interacting with the model and the view.

You can use the menu commands and interface to create the new controller, as shown in Figures 3-9 and 3-10.

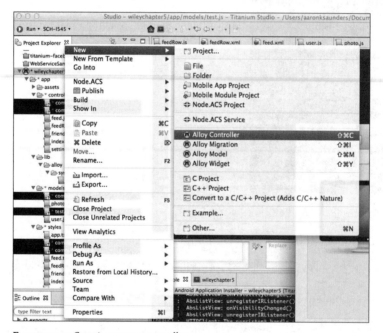

FIGURE 3-9: Creating a new controller.

A controller is created by using the `Alloy.createController` function and passing the name of the desired controller.

```
// controller/index.js
// create a new controller for view-controller pair
// that will eventually render the table
var carsController = Alloy.createController("cars");
```

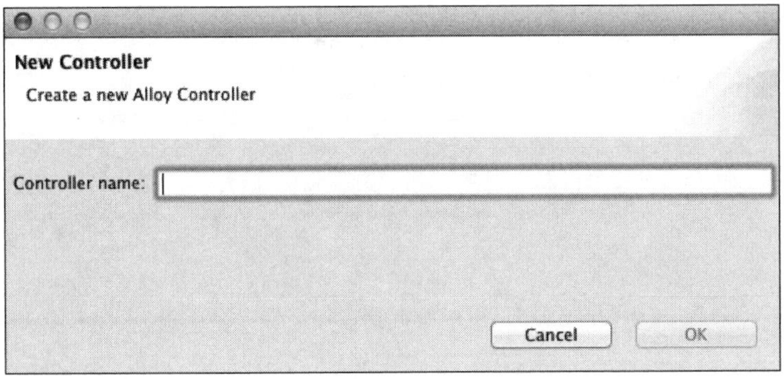

FIGURE 3-10: Name your new controller.

Then you initialize the collection with the sample data. Notice you use the `reset` method on the collection to trigger the controller to redraw the content.

```
// controllers/index.js
// add the data to collection after the
// view-controller pair is created
Alloy.Collections.cars.reset([{
    "make" : "Honda",
    "model" : "Civic"
}, {
    "make" : "Honda",
    "model" : "Accord"
}, {
    "make" : "Ford",
    "model" : "Escape"
},{
    "make" : "Nissan",
    "model" : "Altima"
}]);
```

Open the main window in the `cars` controller to show the content.

```
// open the view to show table
carsController.mainWindow.open();
```

Show the `cars` view; notice the collection is not defined in `cars.xml` as it was in the previous example.

```
<Alloy>
  <!-- notice there is no collection defined here -->
  <Window id="mainWindow" class="container">
    <TableView dataCollection="cars" dataTransform="transform"
        dataFilter="filter">
      <TableViewRow title="{title}" modelId="{id}"/>
    </TableView>
  </Window>
</Alloy>
```

In the cars.js file, you have moved over the transform and filter functions from the index.js file. You need to do this because the TableView processing is being done in the cars.js controller and not in the index.js controller any longer.

```
// controllers/cars.js
function transform(model) {
    // Need to convert the model to a JSON object
    var carObject = model.toJSON();
    return {
        "title" : carObject.model + " by " + carObject.make,
        "id" : model.cid
    };
}


// Show only cars made by Honda
function filter(collection) {
    return collection.where({
        make : 'Honda'
    });
}


// Free model-view data binding resources when view-controller
// closes
$.mainWindow.addEventListener('close', function() {
    $.destroy();
});
```

You can run the application at this point and see the original list of cars displayed when the application is first launched, as is shown in Figures 3-7 and 3-8.

Data Binding with Models in Appcelerator Titanium Alloy

This chapter has covered data binding with model collections, so now it's time to take a moment to see how data binding works with models in Appcelerator Titanium Alloy.

This section builds on the example created previously to show a detail screen of a specific car based on the user selecting a car in the `TableView`.

Updating the cars.js Controller File

First you make some changes to the existing application's `cars.js` controller file to listen for click events on the `TableView` and take action when the user clicks on a row in the view.

As you can see in the following code, you are creating the new controller instance with the `Alloy.createController` function and passing in the name of the controller to create.

```
$.table.addEventListener('click', function(_event) {
    var detailController = Alloy.createController('detail');
});
```

The `Alloy.createController` function allows for passing in arguments in a JavaScript hash; you pass in the model object of the item you want to render in the detail screen. In this case you want to show the car object that the user clicked on in the `TableView`.

You will find the `car` model object by the object's ID. Backbone.js allows for querying the collection for specific objects based on the ID. In this case, the `properties` sync adapter does not assign specific IDs so you can access the model object by using the _getByCid function from the Backbone collections.

Now put it all together and open the new car `detail.js` controller:

```
$.table.addEventListener('click', function(_event) {

    // get the correct model
    var model =
        Alloy.Collections.cars._getByCid(_event.rowData.modelId);

    // create the controller and pass in the model
    var detailController = Alloy.createController('detail', {
        data : model
    });
```

```
    // get view returns the root view when no view ID is provided
    detailController.getView().open({
        modal : true
    });
});
```

Creating the New Controller/View for the Detail Display

You need to create the new controller and view files for the detail display. You follow the same process as before of clicking on the project menu and selecting File ⇨ New Controller, but enter the name detail instead.

The model data binding in the detail.xml view file looks very similar to how the data binding was implemented for the collection in the cars.xml file. You specify a model object for the view to work with, but you add the instance property to indicate that this is not a global variable, but one that is local to the collection associated with this view.

```
<Model src="cars" instance="true" id="car">
```

Next you associate the model of the window object; notice the use of the $ variable when specifying the object. This is to indicate once again that the object is a local instance variable defined in the controller.

```
<Window id="detailWindow" model="$.car">
```

Access the model's properties once again using the $ variable to access the local object.

```
<Label id="make_lbl" text="{$.car.make}" ></Label>
<Label id="model_lbl" text="{$.car.model}" ></Label>
```

Putting it all together, notice the addition of the Button object, which has been added to the window. In the detail.js controller, you listen for the click event on the button to trigger the closing of this window.

```
<!-- detail.xml -->
<Alloy>
    <Model src="cars" instance="true" id="car">
    <Window id="detailWindow" model="$.car" >
        <Label id="make_lbl" text="{$.car.make}" ></Label>
```

```
        <Label id="model_lbl" text="{$.car.model}" ></Label>
        <Button id="closeBtn">Close Window</Button>
    </Window>
</Alloy>
```

Here's the associated .tss file for the car detail view:

```
".container": {
    backgroundColor: "white"
},
"#detailWindow" : {
        title:"Car Detail Window",
        layout:'vertical',
        backgroundColor: 'white'
},
"Label" : {
        top:10,
        textAlign:'center',
        font: {
            fontWeight:'bold',
            fontSize:18
        },
        color: '#000',
        height:Ti.UI.SIZE
},
"#closeBtn" : {
    top : "20dp"
}
```

Completing the Controller for the Detail View

The controller for handling events and showing the detail view has a few interesting changes.

As noted, you can pass parameters into the controller when creating it; the following pattern is one way to get the first argument if provided or set it to an empty object:

```
var args = arguments[0] || {};
```

The last new pattern specific to data binding and models relates to how you set the data on the model you want to display in the view. Recall that you extracted the arguments from the controller and assigned them to the local variable called `args`. You now set the local `car` model object using the data in `args.data`.

```
$.car.set(args.data.attributes);
```

This can also be done using the `Model.toJSON()` function, as follows:

```
$.car.set(args.data.toJSON());
```

You use `set` since data binding is listening for specific events to trigger the redrawing of the view; `set` will trigger that event.

The final code for the `detail.js` controller file is shown here:

```
var args = arguments[0] || {};
// close the window when button is clicked
$.closeBtn.addEventListener('click', function() {
    $.detailWindow.close();
});

// instance variable used in data binding.
// we do this set here to trigger the events
// that will cause the data to be rendered
$.car.set(args.data.attributes);

// Free model-view data binding resources when this
// view-controller closes
$.detailWindow.addEventListener('close', function() {
    $.destroy();
});
```

You can run the application at this point and see the original list of cars displayed when the application is first launched, as is shown in Figures 3-7 and 3-8.

When you click on one of the cars listed in the view, you will be taken to the detail view. It shows the information of the specific car you selected, as shown in Figures 3-11 and 3-12.

FIGURE 3-11: The detail view when you click on Honda Accord from the main iOS list.

FIGURE 3-12: The detail view when you click on Honda Accord in main Android list.

Creating Widgets

Widgets are small MVC-based components that exist inside your application. The objective of a widget is to promote reusability across multiple projects. There are also multiple components provided by Appcelerator and third-party providers that can assist in quickly constructing basic functionality in your application.

Widgets are made up of the same components as full-blown applications, views, controllers, and styles. They can be used to encapsulate repeated functionality in your application or on multiple projects. This chapter uses a simple toggle button widget to explain how a widget is structured.

You need to create a new test project for the widgets section of this chapter. Follow the instructions for creating a new project as described in the beginning of the chapter and then create a widget. You can also create the widget using the command line from the terminal, like so:

```
alloy generate widget buttonToggle
```

Or you can create one from the Titanium Studio File menu. Be sure to name your widget, as shown in Figure 3-13.

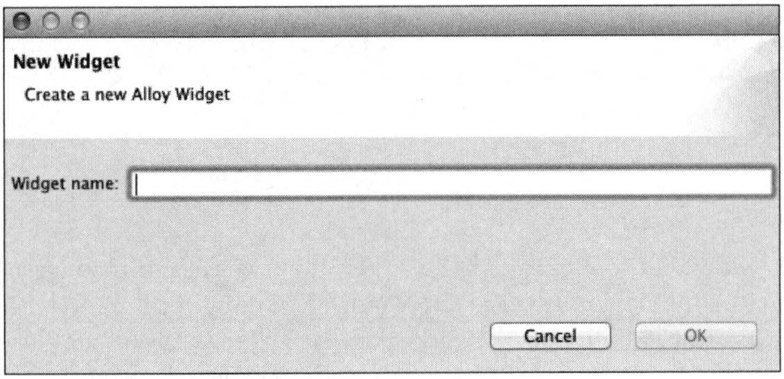

FIGURE 3-13: Naming the widget.

When the widget is created, Titanium will add the base files to your projects inside the directory titled `widgets`, as shown in Figure 3-14.

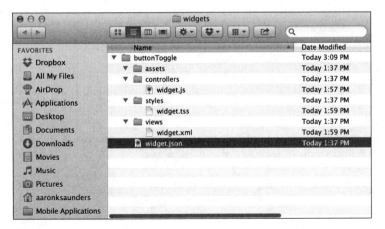

FIGURE 3-14: Widgets directory structure.

As you can see, the file structure in the `widgets` directory matches the overall structure of the project with the views and controllers directories.

This example creates a simple button that toggles between on and off. There are many ways to create such a button, but this approach was used to demonstrate the capabilities of widgets.

First you need a `widget.xml` file that contains the view that will be rendered when the widget is added to a view or window in the project. Add the following code to the `widget.xml` file:

```
<Alloy>
  <View id="container" >
    <Button id="on">Button is On</Button>
    <Button id="off">Button is Off</Button>
  </View>
</Alloy>
```

You have created a view with the ID `container` to hold the buttons you're going to toggle. This code also created two buttons and specified an ID for each one. One button is on and the other is off. Finally, text was added to the buttons. Since there is no specific layout information provided, the buttons will be drawn on top of each other, which is what you want.

Next up is the `.tss` file, which will contain style information for the view. Add the following code to the file:

```
"#container": {
    height: Ti.UI.SIZE,
    width: Ti.UI.SIZE
}
```

What you are doing here is wrapping the buttons in a view container. You set the width and height to `Ti.UI.Size` to make sure that the view is only as big as the items you have placed inside.

The controller will draw the widget on the screen and handle the user interaction with the buttons. Modify the `widget.js` file by including the following code:

```
// event handler for when the user clicks button
$.container.addEventListener('click', function(_event) {

  // hide the clicked item, show the unclicked one
```

```
    toggleButtonByIdClicked(_event.source.id);
})
// _buttonId name of the id clicked
function toggleButtonByIdClicked(_buttonId) {
  if (_buttonId === "on") {
    $.on.hide();
    $.off.show();
  } else if (_buttonId === "off") {
    $.on.show();
    $.off.hide();
  }
}
```

The container or button wrapper is accessed through `$.container`. You need to listen for any clicks inside the container. When you set the listener at this level, you'll get an event when the buttons are clicked.

Each of the buttons is assigned an ID in the `widget.xml` file. When the buttons are clicked, the ID is passed in the `event.source` object.

The rest of the code is pretty straightforward. You toggle the visibility of the objects using `hide` or `show`, depending on which item received the click event.

You can now add the widget to the view. You can do this either through the parent project or by using the view file, as follows: ʹ

```
<Alloy>
  <Window id="mainWindow" class="container">
    <Require type="widget" src="buttonToggle" id="buttonWidget"/>
  </Window>
</Alloy>
```

This means the controller that was using the widget has no change.

```
// open the window
$.mainWindow.open();
```

Or, you can programmatically add the widget to the view from inside the controller, as follows:

```
// create the widget
var toggleBtnWidget = Alloy.createWidget("buttonToggle");
```

```
// get the main view from the widget
$.mainWindow.add(toggleBtnWidget.getView());

// open the window
$.mainWindow.open();
```

The final step in using the buttonToggle widget is adding information about the widget to the config.json file, which can be found in the project's app directory.

```
{
    "global": {},
    "env:development": {},
    "env:test": {},
    "env:production": {},
    "os:ios": {},
    "os:android": {},
    "dependencies": {
        "buttonToggle": "1.0"
    }
}
```

Creating a More Complex Widget

Sometimes you need to initialize the widget before it is displayed in the view. Remember the idea behind widgets is that they can be reusable components across multiple projects. So it is very likely that you might need to configure or set up the widget differently based on the context of the project it is used in.

Since you can pass parameters into the widget, you can configure the widget at startup. Start with the buttonToggle widget you created and enhance it by processing arguments. Follow the same pattern used when processing controller parameters:

```
var args = arguments[0] || {};

// pass in default setting or set to 'on'
args.defaultState = args.defaultState || 'on';
```

You use the toggleButtonByIDClicked function at startup to simulate clicking on the button and to set the proper button as visible.

```
// set the initial state of the button
if (args.defaultState === "on") {
  toggleButtonByIdClicked("off");
} else if (args.defaultState === "off") {
  toggleButtonByIdClicked("on");
}
```

Here's the completed widget.js file:

```
var args = arguments[0] || {};
args.defaultState = args.defaultState || 'on';

// set the initial state of the button
if (args.defaultState === "on") {
  toggleButtonByIdClicked("off");
} else if (args.defaultState === "off") {
  toggleButtonByIdClicked("on");
}

// event handler for when the user clicks button
$.container.addEventListener('click', function(_event) {

  // hide the clicked item, show the unclicked one
  toggleButtonByIdClicked(_event.source.id);
})

/**
 * _buttonId name of the id clicked
 */
function toggleButtonByIdClicked(_buttonId) {
  if (_buttonId === "on") {
    $.on.hide();
    $.off.show();
  } else if (_buttonId === "off") {
    $.on.show();
    $.off.hide();
  }
}
```

You now can modify the widget declaration to set the default button parameter. You have the view.xml markup file for passing in the parameter.

```
<Alloy>
  <Window id="mainWindow" class="container">
    <Require type="widget" src="buttonToggle" id="buttonWidget"
          defaultState="off"/>
  </Window>
</Alloy>
```

And you have the programmatic approach when instantiating the widget from the controller:

```
// create the widget
var toggleBtnWidget = Alloy.createWidget("buttonToggle", null, {
  "defaultState": "on",
  "id" : "toggleBtnWidget"
});

// get the main view from the widget
$.mainWindow.add(toggleBtnWidget.getView());

// open the window
$.mainWindow.open();
```

Summary

This chapter covered the three key components of the Model-View-Controller pattern. You saw real examples of how they are implemented in Appcelerator Titanium Alloy. You also worked with the Widget framework, which can be used to develop reusable components that are completely self-contained. Chapter 4 moves on to creating a cross-platform photo-sharing application.

Chapter

Building a Cross-Platform Social Photo-Sharing Application

BECAUSE THE FOCUS of the book is on mobile development and not mobile design, this chapter uses a simple design to illustrate the concepts it's going to teach. Of course, mobile design is critical to the success of your app in the market. Mobile applications don't have user's manuals; if users can't make sense of the app after a few clicks, they will probably never use it again.

When building designs for clients, we usually try to create wireframes or simple mockups of the application screens. This process provides a baseline for what we believe we are trying to build and the images stimulate questions in a way that sometimes words on a page cannot.

Using Balsamiq to Design Mockups

I like to use simple tools for laying out the information since this is really more of a requirements/features/functions phase and not a user interface design phase. A simple tool I have used with success (and the one that's used for the images in this chapter) is Balsamiq.

The website sums up to two keys reasons I like Balsamiq:

- Mockups reproduce the experience of sketching on a whiteboard, but this allows them to be distributed, reviewed, and updated.
- These wireframes remove the distraction of the user interface design and put the focus on the features and the functions. The design team can then use these wireframes in a later phase of the project.

Let's walk through the sample mockup screens. To start with, Figure 4-1 shows a typical User Login screen.

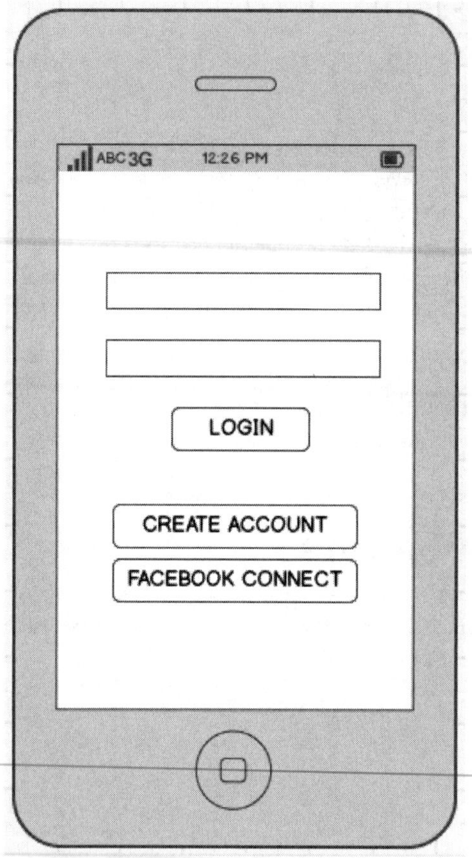

FIGURE 4-1: A typical User Login screen.

The point of the User Login screen is three-fold:

- Allows the users to log in to the system.
- Allows the users to create an account with an email and password.
- Allows the users to create an account with their Facebook credentials.

Figure 4-2 shows the screen that allows the users to create an account using their Facebook credentials. It allows the users to enter or edit account information, including a first name, last name, and a profile photo.

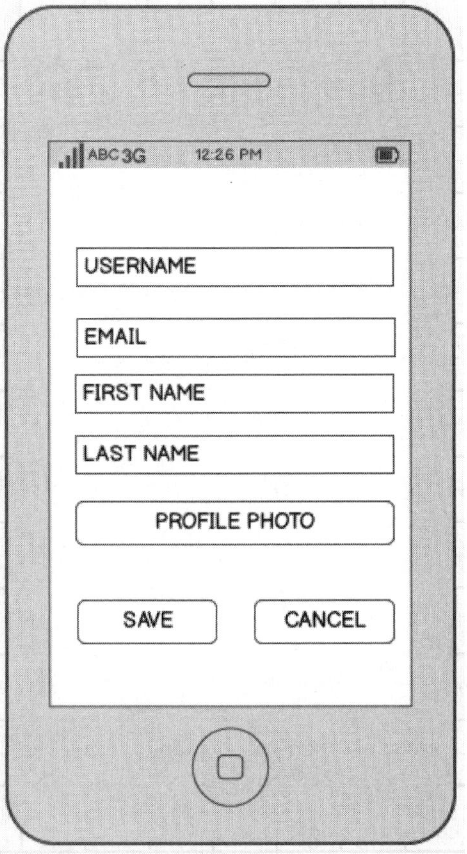

FIGURE 4-2: A standard Account Creation screen.

Figure 4-3 shows the Main Application screen, showing the Feed tab.

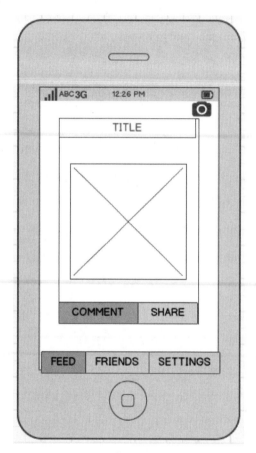

FIGURE 4-3: Main application screen with tabs.

The Main Application screen's job is the following:

- Allows users to toggle between the three tabbed sections of the application—Feed, Friends, and Settings.
- Allows the users to take a new photo by clicking the photo button.

The Feed tab of the Main Application screen is the default screen. It has the following characteristics:

- It's a scrolling view of the images associated with the user and any people the current user has identified as friends.

- Each photo has a title, tags, and captions associated with it.

- The photo container contains an action area that allows users to view or add comments and to share the image.

- Has an action area where there is a button for adding and viewing comments and for sharing the current image on Facebook.

Figure 4-4 shows the Photo Comments screen.

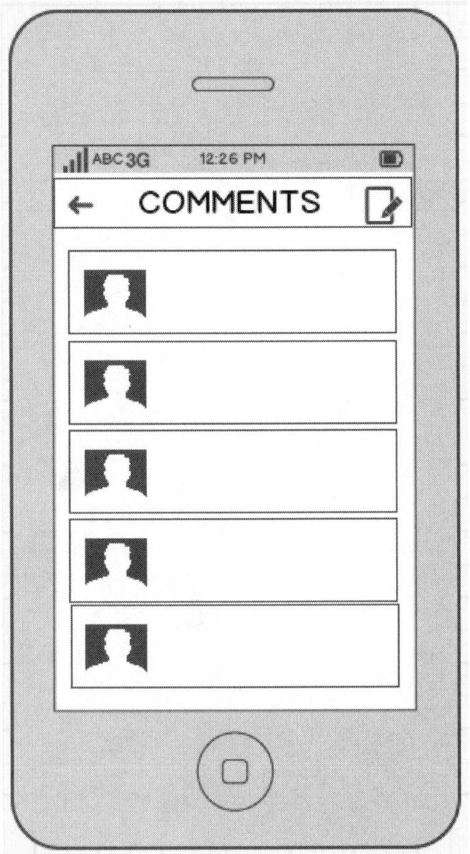

FIGURE 4-4: List view of a Photo Comments screen.

The purpose of the Photo Comments screen is as follows:

- Shows a list of comments associated to the current photo.

- The comment element contains the photo of the user who entered the comment, the time and location of the comment, and the comment text.

- Photo comments can be deleted by the user who entered the comment by swiping the comment row.

- New comments can be created by clicking the New Comment button, which is shown in the upper-right corner of the image.

- Users click the back button to return to the Main Application screen.

Figure 4-5 shows the New Photo Comment screen.

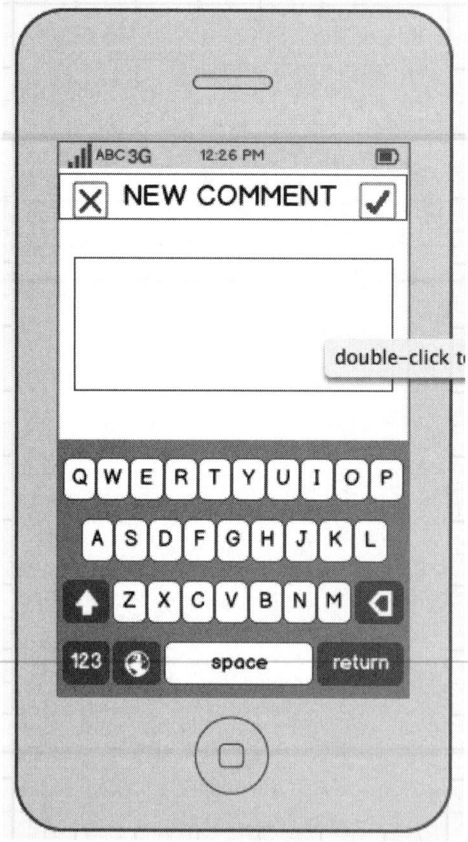

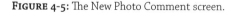

FIGURE 4-5: The New Photo Comment screen.

The New Photo Comment screen has the following capabilities:

- Users can enter the text of the new comment for the specified photo.

- Users can share the comment and the photo on Facebook from this screen.

- The user's location is captured with the comment entry.

- Users can cancel the creation of the comment and return to the Photo Comments screen.

Figure 4-6 shows the Friends/All Users list screen.

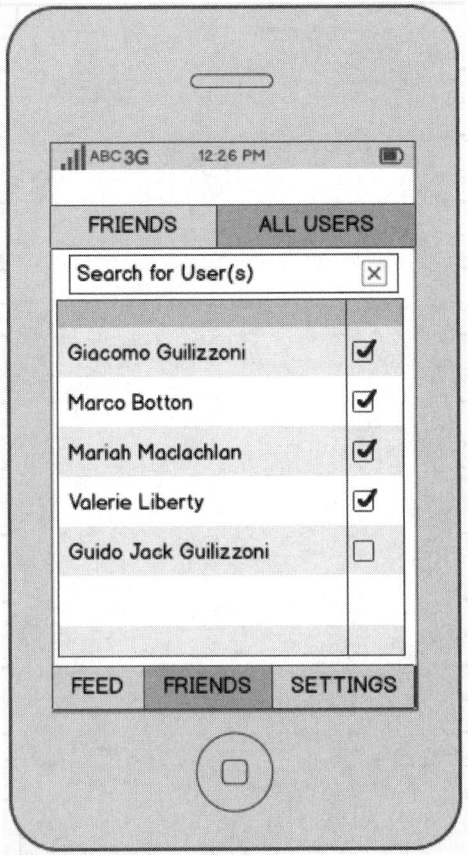

FIGURE 4-6: A list view of friends and all users.

Note the following functions of this screen:

- Includes a toggle button at the top to filter the list to display the user's current list of friends or to allow users to search for friends.

- The user list contains a search filter to narrow down the list of users when adding friends.

- The friend display row contains the profile photo, the username, and the first and last names.

- When the user is viewing the Friends list, they can remove selected elements from it.

- When the user is viewing the list of all users, they can add the selected elements to the Friends list.

Figure 4-7 shows the Settings screen, which has the following characteristics:

- Shows the username, the first and last names, and the profile photo.

- All elements can be changed except the username.

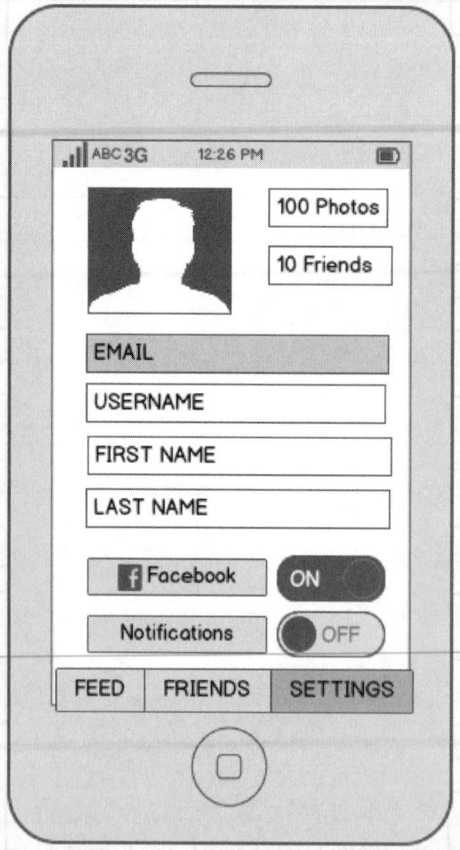

FIGURE 4-7: The Settings screen.

- Shows a Facebook on/off switch, which toggles Facebook functionality.

- Shows a notification on/off switch, which toggles notification alerts from the application.

Figure 4-8 shows the Photo Capture screen, which is a native camera interface for taking photos or using photos from the image gallery. It enables users to associate photos with their accounts.

FIGURE 4-8: Platform-specific photo capture screen.

Walking Through the Phone-Sharing App

This section walks through the process of building a mobile application for sharing photos through Facebook. The application will also allow you to comment on photos and choose other member's photos to include in your feed. Basically, this is a very simple version of all of the photo-sharing applications that exist today.

Along with showing you how to build this application, this section exposes you to the powerful benefits of Appcelerator Cloud Services and the Appcelerator framework. You don't need a Ruby or PHP developer for the backend services since they are provided for you; you don't need a hosting provider or a database administrator or a database designer; and most importantly, you don't need to be experienced in Objective-C or Java. This is where the huge benefits and efficiencies of the Appcelerator platform start to shine.

The following sections walk through the features and map them to the specific technologies.

User Accounts

This feature leverages the core functionality of the Appcelerator Cloud Services User objects. It also allows the users to create accounts utilizing an existing account in Facebook. Appcelerator Cloud Services allows you to integrate/create accounts using a Facebook ID.

The User Settings screen provides some basic information about the users, allows the users to log out of the application, and allows them to configure the Facebook integration.

Camera

Appcelerator Framework native device integration provides access to the Camera and the photo gallery. Users have complete access to the flash, as well as the front-facing and rear-facing cameras, which will provide users with the perfect shot to share on their mobile applications.

Photo Uploading

The Appcelerator Cloud Services Photo object provides the ability to upload photos and resize them into various dimensions for full-screen viewing, viewing as a thumbnail preview, and for sending to a friend at the original size. You need all of those different sizes so that the app efficiently utilizes the mobile device's bandwidth and user interface experience. It's important to avoid creating poor experiences by attempting to render large images unnecessarily.

You'll also get photo storage in the cloud that can scale to your needs. Don't underestimate the value of cloud storage when dealing with images; this is a powerful feature that simplifies the process.

The app will also determine the location of the user when the photo was taken so you can show the images on the map. This enables use of Appcelerator Cloud Services to perform geo-queries in order to find images based on distance from a certain location. A title, tags, and a simple caption are also saved with each photo; all of those pieces of data can be queried on, just like the location.

Social Integration with Facebook

As mentioned previously, the powerful integration of the Facebook API Appcelerator allows you to create accounts based on existing Facebook credentials. However, the integration does not stop there. You can use the API to share the photos from the application. Even if you choose not to associate your user account with Facebook, you can still connect to Facebook to share the images with your friends.

When uploading the images, the app will leverage not only the Appcelerator Facebook integration, but also the image-processing feature of Appcelerator Cloud Services. This way, the larger image is uploaded to Facebook automatically. Therefore, when users view the image on a PC or want to print a photo, they will have the better quality original.

Finding Friends

What good is a social mobile application if you cannot find friends to share your photos with or if it is too difficult to follow your friends' photo updates? Not very good. Appcelerator Cloud Services has the ability to find friends, create friends lists, and block access to content based on the list of friends.

The app will give users the ability to find friends and create a feed of just their friends' photos for a more personalized experience. If a user's friend's photos get too racy or annoying, they can use the Friends List feature to remove them from their feed.

Commenting and Rating of Media

Appcelerator Cloud Services provides a way to allow users to comment and rate objects. You can associate the object with other comments, posts, and photos, which is what you'll do in the example application in this book. Users will be able to comment on photos, like photos, and see how others commented on photos in the application. They'll also be able to query the comments based on the users or on the photo. Users can also delete their comments if they decide to make a change.

Just as with photos, the app will associate a location with the commenter so users can see how far their images have been shared across the globe, based on the location of the comments.

Push Notifications

Appcelerator Cloud Services provides objects for sending push notifications to users. You can send these notifications to specific users, user groups, or to "channels" that can be created for users to subscribe to. In this example application, users receive notification when they get a new friend, when a friend posts a photo to the system, or when they receive a comment about one of their photos. This is one way to keep users engaged and returning to the application.

Application Flow

Figure 4-9 shows the high-level flow of how the application fits together.

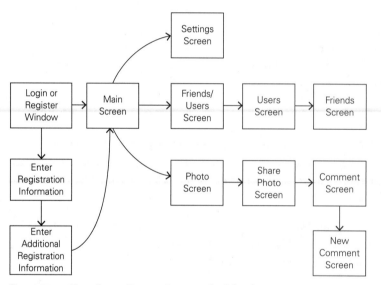

FIGURE 4-9: How the application flows at a high level.

Summary

Now that you have a basic understanding of the user interface and have seen sample diagrams of the layout, you have a foundation for what you will build throughout the rest of the book. The diagrams are representative of what you will build, but since you will be building a cross-platform solution, there will be some differences in the user interface elements on iOS and Android. Chapter 5 explains the development process you'll go through when building cross-platform apps.

Chapter 5

Development Process for Cross-Platform Apps

IN CHAPTER 4 you walked through the application's entire user interface and reviewed the wireframes/mockups for it. You reviewed the high-level features of the overall application. The next step is to write some code!

Because the most important piece of functionality for the cross-platform social photo-sharing application that you're building in this book is integration with the camera, this chapter jumps right into the camera functionality so you can see some immediate value in the product you're building.

When adding new functionality into Alloy applications, the usual pattern is to introduce new files for all of the components of the Model-View-Controller framework you read about in Chapter 3.

Creating the Project for This Chapter

To create the project you'll use in this chapter, you need to open Titanium Studio and create a new project. If you are unfamiliar with this approach, review Chapter 2, where new project creation is covered.

Select File ⇨ New ⇨ Titanium Project, as shown in Figure 5-1.

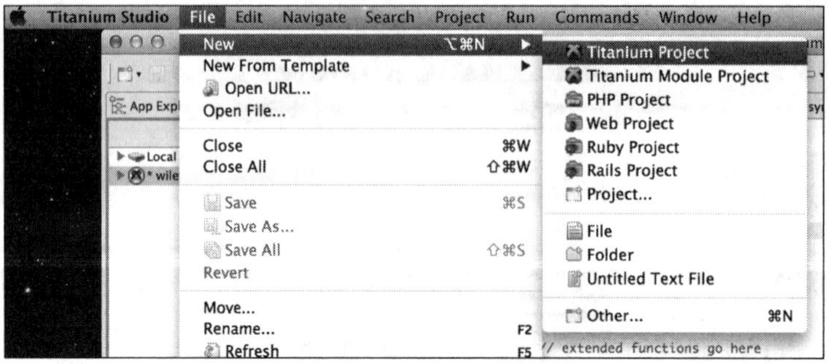

FIGURE 5-1: Creating a new Alloy project in Titanium Studio.

Figure 5-2 shows the window where you need to enter a project name and application ID. Be sure to check the Automatically Cloud-Enable this Application option. Then click Next.

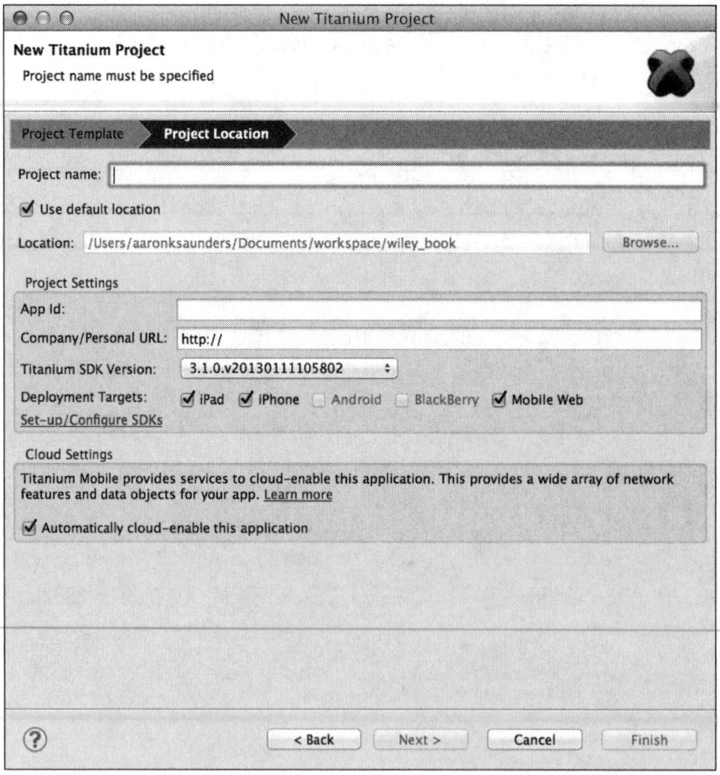

FIGURE 5-2: Setting project-specific properties when creating a new project.

Be sure to use the Alloy Project Template provided. When selecting the project template, choose Two-Tabbed Alloy Application (shown in Figure 5-3) and then click Next.

FIGURE 5-3: Select the Two-Tabbed Alloy Application template.

When you're done entering information, click the Finish button. After the project is created and the application is registered with ACS, you will be presented with the project configuration screen shown in Figure 5-4.

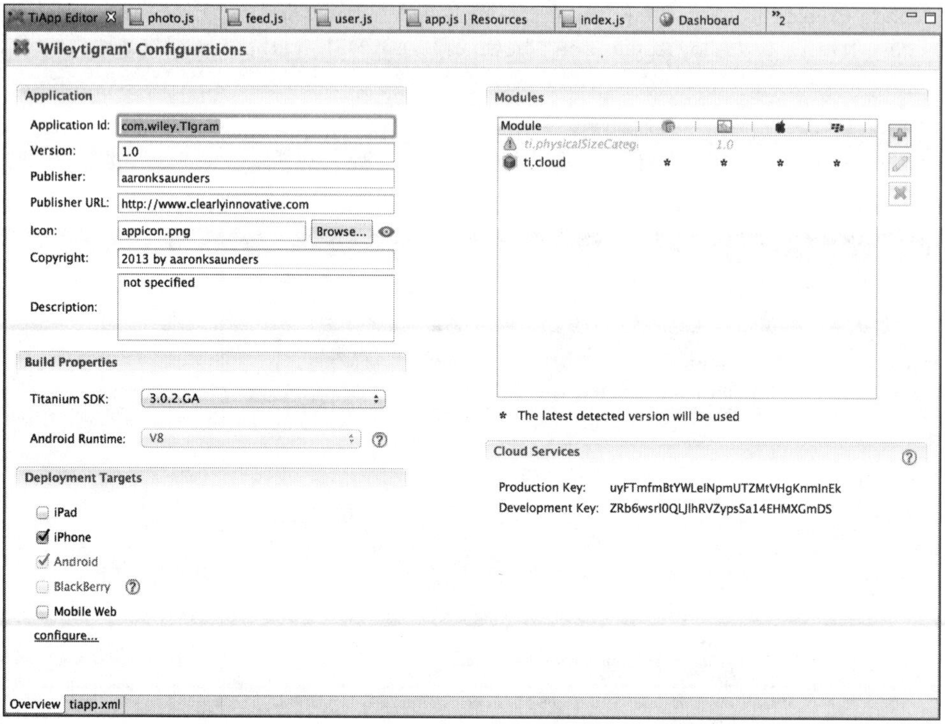

FIGURE 5-4: Enter the information in the required fields to set up your project.

Preconfiguring Appcelerator Cloud Services

In this application, you'll be integrating Appcelerator Cloud Services as the datastore for the information required by the application. To integrate with ACS, you need to have a user account with authorized credentials. Because you'll be working with the user account in later chapters, you'll create an Administrative User Account for now directly in ACS. This account is used throughout the application until the user accounts are introduced in a later chapter.

Enter the following URL into your browser: `https://my.appcelerator.com/apps`. Then find your application by the project name you specified and click on Manage ACS. If you are asked to log in again, you'll need to enter your credentials and continue. Figure 5-5 shows a list of all of the applications you have created, those with Cloud Services enabled and those without.

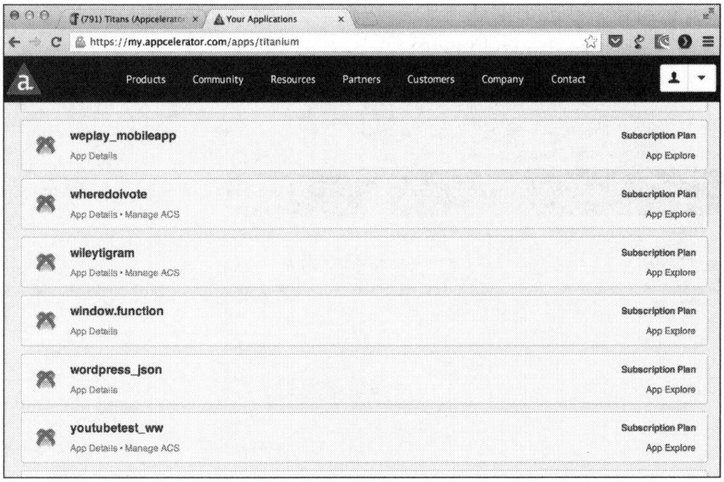

FIGURE 5-5: The Appcelerator Cloud Services console list shows your ACS-enabled apps.

Now you're going to create an admin user that will have access to all objects in the application.

First switch to the development instance of ACS by clicking the Development button in the ACS console. See Figure 5-6.

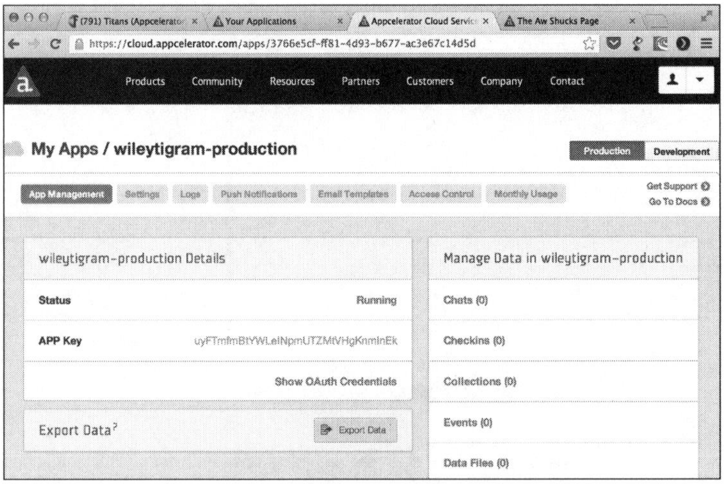

FIGURE 5-6: Select the proper button to switch between development and production services.

Scroll to bottom of the screen and click the User link, then click the tab Admin Users, then the button Create an Admin User, as shown in Figure 5-7.

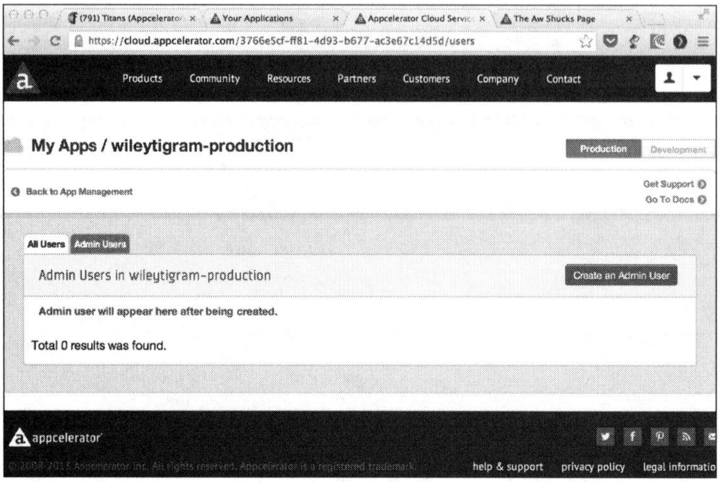

FIGURE 5-7: Click the Create an Admin User button.

Now you need to enter the required information for creating the admin user (see Figure 5-8). For this example, enter `wileytigram_admin` for the username and `wileytigram_admin` for the password to keep things simple. When you're finished, click Submit to create the admin user.

FIGURE 5-8: Enter the minimum information to create the administrative user.

After the admin user is created, the console should be updated to look like Figure 5-9.

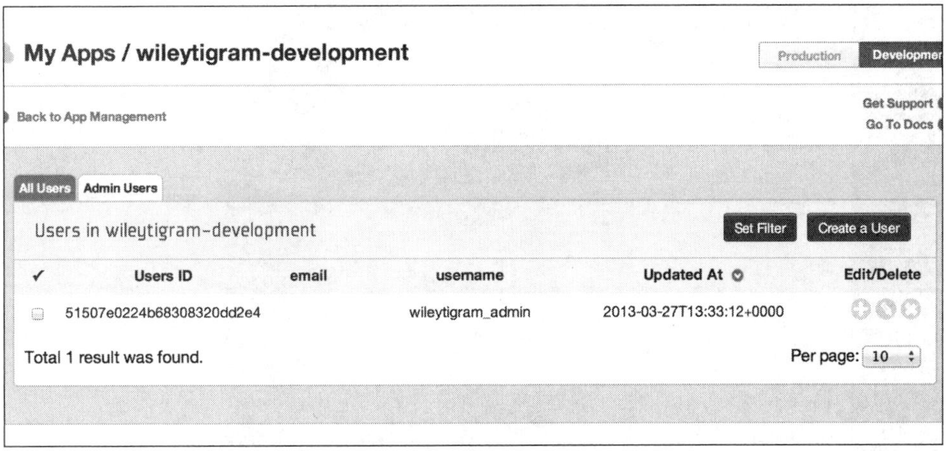

FIGURE 5-9: Updated view of the console after the administrative user has been created.

Now that you have set up the user account, you can exit the ACS console and get back to the application that needs to be created.

Creating the User Interface

The Alloy template you used when constructing the project created the basis for the application you're going to build, but you need to make some changes to the files for better application structure.

First you'll create the controllers and views for the three tabs specified in the wireframes that you created in the previous chapter. You can do this by using the menu item in Titanium Studio for creating Alloy objects.

Creating the Tab Group Files

Right-click on the project icon in the Project Explorer and select New ➪ Alloy Controller, as shown in Figure 5-10. You need to do this once for each of the tabs you're creating (Feed, Friends, and Settings). Figure 5-11 shows the window where you enter the new Alloy controller's name.

FIGURE 5-10: Creating a controller in Titanium Studio.

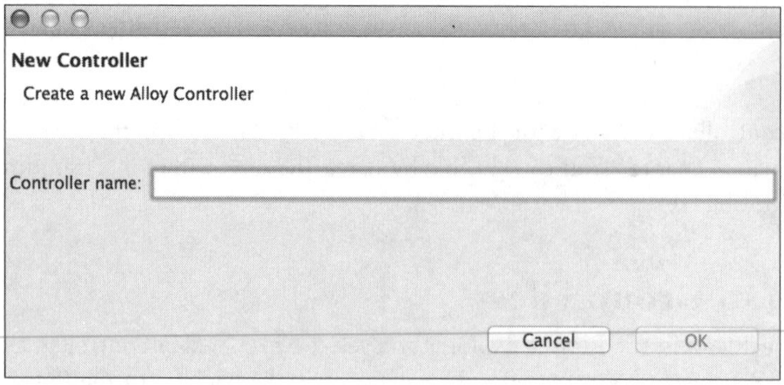

New Controller

Create a new Alloy Controller

Controller name: [   ]

Cancel   OK

FIGURE 5-11: Entering the name of the controller.

After you create an Alloy controller for all three of the tabs, you should have a project directory that looks similar to Figure 5-12.

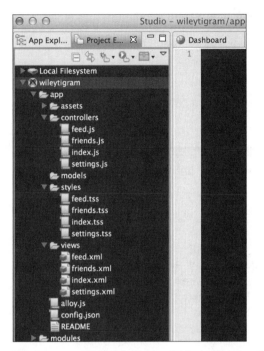

FIGURE 5-12: View of the Project folder in Titanium Studio.

Modifying index.xml and index.js for a Better Application Structure

The initial `index.xml` file created by the project template assumes that all of the windows are created in the index controller. Because you know your application will become more complex than that, you're going to use the individual controllers created previously to separate and better organize the application. To do this, you'll use the Alloy `require` capability in the `index.xml` view file.

In the original `index.xml`, shown here, you created the tabs and windows associated with the tabs directly in the one controller and view set.

```
<Alloy>
    <TabGroup>
        <Tab title="Tab 1" icon="KS_nav_ui.png">
            <Window title="Tab 1">
                <Label>I am Window 1</Label>
            </Window>
        </Tab>
```

```
    <Tab title="Tab 2" icon="KS_nav_views.png">
        <Window title="Tab 2">
            <Label>I am Window 2</Label>
        </Window>
    </Tab>
  </TabGroup>
</Alloy>
```

This could very quickly become overly complex and difficult to maintain. Let's make some changes. Here's the updated `index.xml`, which provides for a better-structured application:

```
<!-- index.xml -->
<Alloy>
    <TabGroup>
        <!-- Tabs included via <Require> tag -->
        <Require id="feedController" src="feed"/>
        <Require id="friendsController" src="friends"/>
        <Require id="settingsController" src="settings"/>
    </TabGroup>
</Alloy>
```

Notice use of `require` for separation of functionality into the individual controllers. You specify the name of the resource file containing the controllers; notice you don't include the `.js` extension on the filename when using `require`. Also notice how you specify the ID for each of the controllers created in `index.xml`. This will provide access to the controller associated with the required file.

One last change before you move on. You need to clean up the `index.js` controller file for now to just call `$.index.open()`. That call will initiate the action of creating the `tabGroup` and all of the associated views and controllers you will see in the next section.

Reviewing the Basic Window and Tab File Structure

Now take a look at what is in each of the three views. The window and the tab creation are now in the specific view files. Each of the files looks similar to the following listing. The only difference is that the name for the file, window, and tab correspond to the specific functions mentioned—feed, friends, or settings.

```
<!-- feed.xml -->
<Alloy>
   <Tab title="Feed">
      <Window title="Feed">
         <Label>This is a Feed tab</Label>
      </Window>
   </Tab>
</Alloy>
```

Setting the Default Styles for the Window and Tab Through the app.tss File

The tab and window title are both defined. Note that the code also removes the tab icon; you'll replace it later with a more appropriate icon. The code sets a label string in the window so that there is a visible indicator when you switch tabs.

The final change moves all of the style settings from index.tss to app.tss so the defaults can be utilized by all views in the application. To do this, you need to create a new file called app.tss and then copy the contents of index.tss to the newly created file:

```
"Window": {
   backgroundColor: "#fff"
},
"Label": {
   width: Ti.UI.SIZE,
   height: Ti.UI.SIZE,
   color: "#000",
   font: {
      fontSize: "18sp",
   },
   textAlign: 'center'
}
```

There are some default settings for application-wide resources that you can define once here in the application. This will help with minimizing some potential cross-platform issues when building your app. They are shown here and should be added to the app.tss file:

```
'Label[platform=android]': {
    color: '#000' // Android default to black
},
'Window[platform=android]': {
    modal: false // android windows all heavyweight
},
'TextField': {
    borderStyle: Ti.UI.INPUT_BORDERSTYLE_ROUNDED, // default style
    borderColor : 'black'
},
'TextField[platform=android]': {
    borderRadius: 6, // common default style
    borderColor : 'black',
    borderWidth : 1
},
'ImageView[platform=ios]': {
    preventDefaultImage: true // never image while loading remote
}
```

You can see the use of the platform attributes, [platform=ios], on the styles; it is a very powerful feature that you will use often as an alternative to platform-specific folders.

Once you've copied the file contents, rebuild the application to view the new three-tabbed application. Figure 5-13 shows the result.

Enabling the Camera Functionality on the Feed Tab

To demonstrate the functionality early, you're going to see what happens when you integrate the camera API now. The application should take a photo every time the user clicks the camera button on the Feed page. You want the application to take the image from the camera along with some miscellaneous information and display it in the feed. This Feed view will be displayed in a table view (using the TableView control) inside the window you've already created.

You will incrementally build out the functionality of the application through the chapters and then apply more professional styling in the end. The book's focus is on demonstrating value from the application early and often.

Updating the Feed View

Open the feed.xml file and add the code to display the camera button. You need to provide an ID for the button so you can access it from the feed controller file. You also need to add the TableView control to the window.

FIGURE 5-13: Basic application with the three tabs.

This approach will work for the IOS application since the navigation buttons are a standard pattern. Later in the chapter you will add Android support by introducing the ActionBar into the application. Notice in the view code that follows how the `RightNavButton` element is only used in the iOS application.

Notice in the following code how all of the objects have IDs. It's a good idea to get into the habit of adding IDs to objects when you add them to the view. These IDs will be required when you access the objects in the controller and also when you want to apply styles in the `.tss` files.

```
<Alloy>
   <Tab id="feedTab" title="Feed">
      <Window id="feedWindow" title="Feed">
         <RightNavButton platform="ios">
            <Button id="cameraButton">Camera</Button>
```

```
            </RightNavButton>
            <TableView id="feedTable"></TableView>
        </Window>
    </Tab>
</Alloy>
```

Adding Code to Listen for a Click on the Camera Button

It's time to start adding some controller code to respond to events in the views. You will start with the camera button that you added to `feed.xml`. Open `controllers/feed.js` to add the following code, which will listen for the click on the button you created. Remember to use the $ variable to access objects in the `view.xml` file; it makes it easy to access the `cameraButton` object to associate events or to change the object's properties.

```
OS_IOS && $.cameraButton.addEventListener("click", function(_event){
    $.cameraButtonClicked(_event);
});

// handlers
$.cameraButtonClicked = function(_event) {
  alert("user clicked camera button");
}
```

Adding a Custom Table Row to TableView

Every table needs rows, and since you're going to create a complex row, it is best to separate functionality into a separate view and controller. You use the same process when creating the controllers for tabs to create the controller and view for the rows. Name the rows `feedRow`.

Take a minute to look at the wireframe you're using for the design so you can see how the design maps to the XML structure used in the `feedRow.xml` file. Figure 5-14 shows the three tabs and Figure 5-15 shows the wireframe mockup.

Adding the FeedRow View

Here is the code for `feedRow.xml` view file:

```
<Alloy>
   <TableViewRow class="row">
      <View class="container">
         <Label id="titleLabel"></Label>
```

```
        <View id="imageContainer">
            <ImageView id="image"></ImageView>
        </View>
        <View id="buttonContainer">
            <Button id="commentButton">Comment</Button>
            <Button id="shareButton">Share</Button>
        </View>
      </View>
    </TableViewRow>
</Alloy>
```

FIGURE 5-14: The application with its three (empty) tabs.

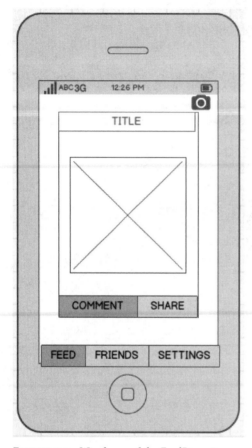

FIGURE 5-15: Wireframe of the FeedRow view.

The view `container` holds the whole row. The `Label` with the ID `titleLabel` will be inside of the `container` as will all of the other objects nested inside the XML element container. Next you create another view container with the ID `imageContainer`. Then you create an `ImageView` control with the ID `image` that will hold the photos. You place it inside of the `imageContainer` so it will be easier to place and style in the view.

Then you create another view container `buttonContainer`, this is also used for placement of the buttons. It's a good idea to add these containers for logical placement of objects. Finally, you create the two buttons—`commentButton` and `shareButton`—that will respond to click events and perform the appropriate actions.

> You might be wondering where the code for the FeedRow controller is. Usually the view and the controllers are created in pairs when structuring the application. The FeedRow you created will populate the table with objects from data retrieved using Appcelerator Cloud Services. Since you have not incorporated Appcelerator Cloud Services yet, the code for the feedRow controller is covered later in the chapter.
>
> **NOTE**

Integrating the Camera Functionality into the Application

Now that you have the interaction between the view and the button and you are capturing the click in the controller, you can start to integrate the core Appcelerator functionality.

Accessing the Device Camera in Appcelerator

Looking at the Appcelerator documentation, you find the `Titanium.Media` object, which contains the `showCamera` function you'll use to access the camera functionality. The documentation at `http://docs.appcelerator.com/titanium/latest/#!/guide/Camera_and_Photo_Gallery_APIs` provides an excellent overview of the functionality. We recommend you reference this Appcelerator documentation for specific details about the method and options.

Side-Stepping the Camera for Now

Since the camera works only when testing and you've not learned about the camera in full at this point, you need a way to get images into the application without using the camera. The following code solves the problem by determining whether the application is running in the simulator.

If the application is running on the simulator, you use the method `Titanium.Media.openPhotoGallery` and allow users to select from the photo gallery. Otherwise, you need to call `Titanium.Media.showCamera` to open the camera so the users can take a photo.

```
var photoSource = Titanium.Media.getIsCameraSupported()?

  Titanium.Media.showCamera : Titanium.Media.openPhotoGallery;
```

When the users click the camera button, the application will open the camera object using `Titanium.Media.showCamera()`. The API will display the camera and the default options for taking a picture. If the users take a new picture, a media object is returned that contains the information needed for displaying the photo in the Feed tab.

You'll create a function for processing the image for uploading to ACS, but will stub it out for now and just return the image with a temporary title, including the timestamp. This is sufficient at this point for getting an image to display in the `TableView` row.

Adding Camera API Calls to Feed Controller

Take a moment to look at the code added to the `feed.js` controller to respond to the click event and take the picture or load an image from the device's photo gallery:

```
$.cameraButtonClicked = function(_event) {
   alert("user clicked camera button");

   var photoSource = Titanium.Media.getIsCameraSupported() ?
      Titanium.Media.showCamera : Titanium.Media.openPhotoGallery;

photoSource ({
      success : function(event) {
         processImage(event.media, function(_photoResp){
            photoObject = _photoResp;
         });
      },
      cancel : function() {
       // called when user cancels taking a picture
      },
      error : function(error) {
       // display alert on error
         if (error.code == Titanium.Media.NO_CAMERA) {
            alert('Please run this test on device');
         } else {
            alert('Unexpected error: ' + error.code);
         }
      },
      saveToPhotoGallery : false,
      allowEditing : true,
      // only allow for photos, no video
      mediaTypes : [Ti.Media.MEDIA_TYPE_PHOTO]
   });
}
```

```
function processImage(_mediaObject, _callback) {
  // since there is no ACS integration yet, we will fake it
  var photoObject = {
    image : _mediaObject,
    title : "Sample Photo " + new Date()
  }

  // return the object to the caller
  _callback(photoObject);
}
```

This code retrieves the picture and the event.media object holding the picture that the user has taken. Following the wireframes provided, you need to place the image in the table view. You can accomplish that by creating the TableViewRow control, adding the items to the row, and then inserting the row into the table view. See http://docs.appcelerator.com/titanium/latest/#!/guide/TableViews for a detailed explanation about how to do this.

You will accomplish the creation of the customized tableRow that matches the wireframes by creating a TableViewRow control from the feedRow.js controller, which you created earlier in the application.

The file feedRow.js is straightforward assignment of the image object to the ImageView control and the text to the titleLabel property.

Revisiting the FeedRow Controller

Recall that earlier in the chapter you created the feedRow.xml view but did not complete the feedRow.js controller. Now that you have some data to add to the row you can complete that process.

Note that you can pass variables into the controllers when you create them. In this case, you're passing in the photoObject returned, which is a JavaScript object containing the image and its title. The controller can take only one additional parameter, so you pass in this object as a JavaScript hash and then retrieve each property and assign it to the appropriate object.

In this case, the arguments passed into the controller are the image and title, which is exactly what you need to set the properties in the feedRow.xml view.

Add this code to feedRow.js:

```
var args = arguments[0] || {};
```

```
// this is setting the view elements of the row view
// based on the arguments passed into the controller
$.image.image = args.image;
$.titleLabel.text = args.title || '';
```

Revisiting the Feed Controller to Add the Rows to the Table

Inside of feed.js you update the code to insert the row into feedTable every time a photo is taken. You utilize the returned value of the function processImage() to pass to the controller feedRow. Once the controller is created, calling the method getView() on the controller will return the TableViewRow object, which is then inserted into feedTable:

```
// code snippet from success handler in Titanium.Media.showCamera
success : function(event) {

    processImage(event.media, function(photoResp) {

        // create the row
        var row = Alloy.createController("feedRow", photoResp);

        // add the controller view, which is a row to the table
        if ($.feedTable.getData().length === 0) {
          $.feedTable.setData([]);
          $.feedTable.appendRow(row.getView(), true);
        } else {
            $.feedTable.insertRowBefore(0,row.getView(), true);
        }
    });

},
```

Adding Some Style to the Feed Table

To get the layout of the rows to look similar to the wireframes, you need to include some styling in the feedRow.tss file.

If you want the row to leave some room around the edges of the screen for example, you set the width of the row container to 90 percent of the screen width, as so:

```
".container": {
  layout: "vertical",
  width : '90%'
},
```

Since this application is being built for iOS and its screen width is 320dp, you have to set the size of the imageContainer for the photo to 300dp. Set the size of the actual photo to 280dp to leave room for a 10dp border. To center the image in the imageContainer, you set the top and the left properties of the image to 10dp:

```
"#imageContainer" : {
  width : '300dp',
  height :'300dp',
},
"#image" : {
  top : '10dp',
  left : '10dp',
  width : '280dp',
  height : '280dp',
},
```

For the button area, create buttonContainer and set the height to 42dp. This should be a sufficient size for the buttons. The width is set to Ti.UI.FILL, which instructs the button to use the entire width of the parent container. Set each of the buttons to be 50 percent of the width of the buttonContainer and set a default height of 32dp for the buttons.

```
"#buttonContainer" : {
  layout : 'horizontal',
  width : Ti.UI.FILL,
  height : '42dp'
},
"#commentButton" : {
  width : '50%',
  height : '32dp'
},
"#shareButton" : {
  width : '50%',
  height : '32dp'
}
```

Figure 5-16 shows the app with a sample photo shown on the screen.

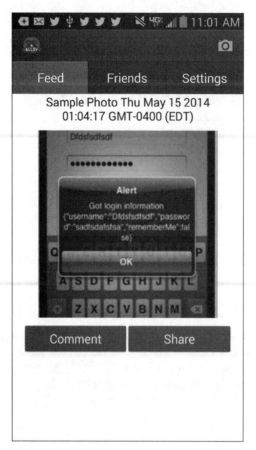

FIGURE 5-16: Application running with a sample photo.

Using the Android ActionBar for the Camera Button

If you are following along using Android as your development platform, you will have realized that there currently is no way to access the camera or the photo gallery to load images into the application. Normally in an Android application this would be accomplished through the inclusion of menus and menu items. In this application, you will use Appcelerator's implementation of the ActionBar.

Setting Up the index.xml View to Support the ActionBar

For the ActionBar to work properly, you need to set up the Android menus and associate them with the activity associated with `tabGroup` you created. You need to specify a function, called `doOpen`, to call when the window is opened to set up the menus in the ActionBar. You'll also set the ID on the `tabGroup` object so it can be accessed inside the `index.js` controller.

```
<!-- index.xml -->
<Alloy>
   <TabGroup id="tabGroup" onOpen="doOpen">
      <!-- Tabs included via <Require> tag -->
      <Require id="feedController" src="feed"/>
      <Require id="friendsController" src="friends"/>
      <Require id="settingsController" src="settings"/>
   </TabGroup>
</Alloy>
```

Modifying the index.xml View to Support the ActionBar

What the following code does is get the activity and add the menus to the activity. The `Ti.Android.SHOW_AS_ACTION_ALWAYS` parameter will keep the menu item in the ActionBar so it appears as a button. You also need to set the menu item's click event to call the same function to display the camera. You will notice this is the same function that was used in the iOS version of the application.

```
function doOpen() {

   if (OS_ANDROID) {
      var activity = $.getView().activity;
      var menuItem = null;

      activity.onCreateOptionsMenu = function(e) {

      if ($.tabGroup.activeTab.title === "Feed") {

         menuItem = e.menu.add({
           //itemId : "PHOTO",
            title : "Take Photo",
            showAsAction : Ti.Android.SHOW_AS_ACTION_ALWAYS,
            icon : Ti.Android.R.drawable.ic_menu_camera
         });
```

```
        menuItem.addEventListener("click", function(e) {
            $.feedController.cameraButtonClicked();
        });
    }
    };

    activity.invalidateOptionsMenu();

    // this forces the menu to update when the tab changes
    $.tabGroup.addEventListener('blur', function(_event) {
        $.getView().activity.invalidateOptionsMenu();
    });
    }
}
```

After the doOpen function is added, you remove the `$.index.open()` call and add `$.tab-Group.open()` to the end of the `index.js` controller.

Adding the Alloy Sync Adapter and Appcelerator Cloud Services

The current implementation of the application follows the MVC pattern discussed earlier in the book except for the persistence layer and the model. First you will learn how to replace the plain JavaScript object with the Alloy model object and then you'll integrate Appcelerator Cloud Services to save the model object to the cloud.

To integrate Appcelerator Cloud Services, you need to create the sync adapter to communicate with the cloud services.

Creating the User Model

To create a new model object, right-click on the project icon and then select New ⇨ Alloy Model, as shown in Figure 5-17. Enter **user** as the model name. You'll create the user model first since you need to log in before doing any interactions with ACS.

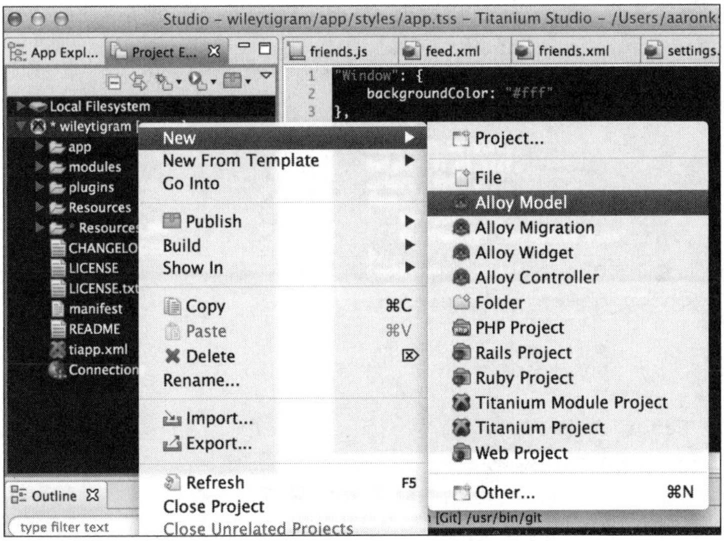

FIGURE 5-17: Creating a model in Titanium Studio.

Extending Alloy Models

The user model will be extended multiple times because there are specific functions required that do not follow the basic CRUD format that the sync adapter pattern closely follows. Extending the model is just a way you add functionality, such as login and logout.

This section focuses only on logging the users in; account creation and setup are discussed later in the book. When you learn how to implement those features, you'll also enhance the user model and the ACS sync adapter to support that functionality. Since extending the user model handles the login functionality, you won't be creating the sync adapter quite yet.

Logging the User In

Logging users in to ACS is pretty straightforward; when they provide a username and password, the app makes the `Cloud.Users.login` API call.

The models and adapter utilize the `ti.cloud.js` module, which is provided by Appcelerator. The process maps the appropriate REST verbs to the correct methods on the `ti.cloud` object for performing the reads, writes, updates, searches, and queries. This section starts with the user object, so it might be wise for you to review the ACS documentation on `ti.cloud` in preparation for additional details. You can find it at `http://docs.appcelerator.com/titanium/latest/#!/api/Titanium.Cloud.Users`.

Open the `user.js` model you just created and extend the model to support the user login function. The following code has been added and you can see—if you reference the documentation—that the login process is exactly as specified in the documentation. You provide a username and password and a function to call when the request is completed.

```
exports.definition = {

    config : {

        "adapter" : {
            "type" : "acs",
            "collection_name" : "users"
        }
    },

    extendModel : function(Model) {
        _.extend(Model.prototype, {

            /**
             * log user in with username and password
             *
             * @param {Object} _login
             * @param {Object} _password
             * @param {Object} _callback
             */
            login : function(_login, _password, _callback) {
                var self = this;
                this.config.Cloud.Users.login({
                    login : _login,
                    password : _password
                }, function(e) {
                    if (e.success) {
                        var user = e.users[0];

                        // save session id
                        Ti.App.Properties.setString
                          ('sessionId', e.meta.session_id);
                        Ti.App.Properties.setString
                          ('user', JSON.stringify(user));
                        _callback && _callback({
                            success : true,
                            model : new model(user)
                        });
                    } else {
                        Ti.API.error(e);
```

```
                    _callback && _callback({
                        success : false,
                        model : null,
                        error : e
                    });
                }
            });
        }
    // end extend

    return Model;
},

extendCollection : function(Collection) {
    _.extend(Collection.prototype, {

        // extended functions go here

    });
    // end extend

    return Collection;
},
}
```

Two important things to notice about the model configuration:

- The setting of the `adapter` type tells Alloy which sync adapter file to load for this model.

- The `collection_name` associates the model to the correct ACS object. This enables the model to access methods such as create and update on objects.

> You won't call a login method on the user model just yet. All models in Alloy must have a sync adapter associated with them. You create the model and specified the adapter as acs so now you need to create the sync adapter. You can use some of the code provided from the other adapters to get you started.   **NOTE**

Creating Appcelerator Cloud Service Sync Adapter

Since there is no sync adapter for Appcelerator Cloud Services, you'll see how to construct a simple one for supporting the objects included in this application. This adapter will provide the basic functionality for interacting with the object and illustrates the minimal requirements for constructing your own sync adapters in the future.

It's time to create the framework for the simple ACS sync adapter. Create a file called `acs.js` and add it to a newly created file path of `app/alloy/sync/acs.js`. Inside this file, add the following code as the basis for the adapter. (This code is copied from the `localStorage.js` adapter and is the common setup code utilized in the Alloy implementation of sync adapters.)

```
function S4() {
    return ((1 + Math.random()) * 65536 |
  0).toString(16).substring(1);
}

function guid() {
    return S4() + S4() + "-" + S4() + "-"
        + S4() + "-" + S4() + "-" + S4() + S4() + S4();
}

function InitAdapter(config) {
    Cloud = require("ti.cloud");
    Cloud.debug = !0;
    config.Cloud = Cloud;
}

function Sync(model, method, opts) {
    // Will be filled in later!!
}

var _ = require("alloy/underscore")._;

module.exports.sync = Sync;

module.exports.beforeModelCreate = function(config) {
    config = config || {};
    config.data = {};
    InitAdapter(config);
    return config;
};
```

```
module.exports.afterModelCreate = function(Model) {
    Model = Model || {};
    Model.prototype.config.Model = Model;
    return Model;
};
```

There are two important changes to note about this new code:

- All of the code from the `sync` function has been removed. It will be added later has you consider the specific concerns of each of the models you're going to support with the adapter.

- The code in `InitAdapter` has changed to instantiate the `ti.cloud` object. This is done so you can access it within the sync adapter and so you can access the object through the model configuration. Using the `ti.cloud` object is how you will access the methods created by Appcelerator to interface with the Cloud Service's objects.

Creating the Photo Model

You can use the Titanium Studio menu to create a new model object for the applications. Recall that you simply right-click on the project icon and select New ➪ Alloy Model. Then enter `user` as the model name. You'll create a `photo` model to store the information from the photo using ACS.

You need to make only two adjustments to the file to set the `adapter` to `acs` and the `collection_name` to `photos`; the bulk of the work is done in the sync adapter that you'll be updating. See the modified `models/photo.js` file for changes to the photo model:

```
exports.definition = {

  config : {

  "adapter" : {
      "type" : "acs",
      "collection_name" : "photos"
   }
  },

  extendModel : function(Model) {
    _.extend(Model.prototype, {

      // extended functions go here
    });
    // end extend
```

```
    return Model;
},

extendCollection : function(Collection) {
  _.extend(Collection.prototype, {

    // extended functions go here

  });
  // end extend

  return Collection;
},
}
```

Modifying the ACS Sync Adapter to Support the Photo Model

Throughout the application, you'll be referencing the Appcelerator Cloud Services `ti.cloud` library to access the methods you need to interact with the services. To implement the save functionality of the photo model, you make a call to `Cloud.Photos.create()`. See `http://docs.appcelerator.com/titanium/latest/#!/api/Titanium.Cloud.Photos` for more information about working with Photo Objects and Appcelerator Cloud Services.

You can modify the sync adapter you created at `assets/alloy/sync/acs.js` to handle photo models and user models. At this point, you're going to add the `processACSPhotos` function with code, but `processACSUsers` will be added as a functional placeholder with no additional code.

You branch on the specific object type by using the `collection_name` specified in the model file for each of the specific models. You branch on the if-condition based on the specific object type you are processing in the sync adapter.

```
function Sync(method, model, options) {
    var object_name = model.config.adapter.collection_name;

    if (object_name === "photos") {
        processACSPhotos(model, method, options);
    } else if (object_name === "users") {
        processACSUsers(model, method, options);
    }
}
```

Inside of processACSPhotos you'll create a switch statement to support all of the REST verbs that the ACS adapter must support. For now, though, you'll add only the functionality for creating a new model and saving it to Appcelerator Cloud Services.

```
/**
 * this is a separate handler for when the object being processed
 * is an ACS Photo
 */
function processACSPhotos(model, method, options) {
    switch (method) {
        case "create":
            // include attributes into the params for ACS
            Cloud.Photos.create(model.toJSON(), function(e) {
                if (e.success) {

                    // save the meta data with object
                    model.meta = e.meta;

                    // return the individual photo object found
                    options.success(e.photos[0]);

                    // trigger fetch for UI updates
                    model.trigger("fetch");
                } else {
                    Ti.API.error("Photos.create " + e.message);
                    options.error(e.error && e.message || e);
                }
            });
            break;
        case "read":
        case "update":
        case "delete":
            // Not currently implemented, let the user know
            alert("Not Implemented Yet");
            break;
    }
}
```

To save the photo, you'll make use of the functionality provided by the ACS library. All you need to do is ensure that you have the proper parameters set and the library does the rest. When passing the JavaScript object back into the success handler, the Backbone.js framework will update the model object and return a properly structured and functional model.

If you review the `user.js` file and look at the `login` function, you can see how the `ti.cloud` object is used to call the `login` method on the `user` object. This is consistent with the pattern you'll use through the `user` and `photo` models.

Model and Sync Adapter Working Together

Now that you have the sync adapter in place and have created the user and photo models, it's time to access the Appcelerator Cloud Services features; but you must log in to Appcelerator Cloud Services before doing anything else. At this point in the development process, you simply log the user into ACS whenever the application starts up. This is not the final solution, but as stated earlier, this approach resolves the requirement of being logged in to access ACS objects and methods.

User Login with User Model

You're going to use the administrative user created earlier through the console and log in to ACS. Because you do not want the application to continue until the user is successfully logged in, the idea is to open the main view only after a successful login.

Replace the code in `index.js` with the following code, which creates a user object from the model file and calls the `login` method that you added to the `model` object.

```
// when we start up, create a user and log in
var user = Alloy.createModel('User');

// we are using the default administration account for now
user.login("wileytigram_admin", "wileytigram_admin",
  function(_response) {
    if (_response.success) {
      // open the main screen
      $.index.open();
    } else {
      alert("Error Starting Application " + _response.error);
      Ti.API.error('error logging in ' + _response.error);
    }
});
```

This will log you in to Appcelerator Cloud Services and return the user object associated with the account. You'll use this information later in the display and account management, but there is no use for the information at this time.

Here's a sample JSON response from logging in a user or querying a user object:

```
{
    "users": [
        {
            "id": "51507e0224b68308320dd2e4",
            "created_at": "2013-03-25T16:40:34+0000",
            "updated_at": "2013-03-27T02:50:54+0000",
            "external_accounts": [],
            "confirmed_at": "2013-03-25T16:40:34+0000",
            "username": "wileytigram_admin",
            "admin": "true",
            "stats": {
                "photos": {
                    "total_count": 8
                },
                "storage": {
                    "used": 13069205
                }
            }
        }
    ],
    "success": true,
    "error": false,
    "meta": {
        "code": 200,
        "status": "ok",
        "method_name": "loginUser",
        "session_id": "wQGKymtbiazRLsRSDSGq-tJp6n4"
    }
}
```

Using the Photo Model in the Feed View

In the earlier implementation, the app did not save the photos anywhere; it simply took the photo from the camera and added it to the row. You're learning to incrementally add functionality to the application, so now you'll see how to change the code to save the photo to Appcelerator Cloud Services. After receiving a successful response from the server, the app will add the photo to the feed.

Modifying processImage to Create a Photo Model and Save It to ACS

Calls to the Appcelerator Cloud Services are asynchronous so you need to change processImage to support the asynchronous nature of the Appcelerator Cloud Services library. You have to make the API call to save the photo to Appcelerator Cloud Services. Then, when the app receives a response from the server, you have to tell it to take the appropriate next steps.

In processImage, you need to provide Appcelerator Cloud Services method Cloud.Photos.save() the correct parameters. You can use the image from the camera or gallery for the one required parameter, photo. Note that this code shows a temporary title; the final settings help define the sizes of the images you want the service to create.

Additional information on the parameters for this library call can be found at http://cloud.appcelerator.com/docs/api/v1/photos/create.

```
var parameters = {
  "photo" : _mediaObject,
  "title" : "Sample Photo " + new Date(),
  "photo_sizes[preview]" : "200x200#",
  "photo_sizes[iphone]" : "320x320#",
  // We need this since we are showing the image immediately
  "photo_sync_sizes[]" : "preview"
}
```

This code creates two photos from the original image of various sizes. One size is for displaying the photo in the feed table, which is appropriate for displaying on mobile devices, and the other size is for a PC display, which would be a larger photo.

The ACS sync adapter is simple enough that, after setting the parameters, you just need to create the model and call the save method.

```
var photo = Alloy.createModel('Photo', parameters);

photo.save({}, {
  success : function(_model, _response) { debugger;
    Ti.API.info('success: ' + _model.toJSON());
    _callback({
        model : _model,
        message : null,
        success : true
        });
    },
```

```
error : function(e) { debugger;
   Ti.API.error('error: ' + e.message);
   _callback({
         model : parameters,
         message : e.message,
         success : false
   });
 }
});
```

After you make these changes to the `processImage` method, you have integrated the ACS and Alloy models. The Alloy model `save` method takes an options parameter, which contains the success and error callbacks. The method returns from the ACS sync adapter the newly created model and the server's response on success. When an error occurs, the `save` method returns the original parameters and the error message that Appcelerator Cloud Services returned. The `save` method then calls the `callback` method, called `_callback`, that was passed into `processImage` and attempts to add the image to the feed table.

Here's a sample JSON object response when saving or querying a photo object:

```
{
    "photos": [
        {
            "id": "51525f8ee0b1ba6667001160",
            "filename": "b2b87f0.png",
            "size": 897507,
            "md5": "1f6555c2a04a89415c4fb412ed20f224",
            "created_at": "2013-03-27T02:55:11+0000",
            "updated_at": "2013-03-27T02:55:11+0000",
            "processed": false,
            "user": {
                "id": "51507e0224b68308320dd2e4",
                "created_at": "2013-03-25T16:40:34+0000",
                "updated_at": "2013-03-27T02:50:54+0000",
                "external_accounts": [],
                "confirmed_at": "2013-03-25T16:40:34+0000",
                "username": "wileytigram_admin",
                "admin": "true"
            },
```

```
            "title": "Sample Photo Tue Mar 26 2013 22:55:...",
            "urls": {
                "preview": "http://storage.cloud..._preview.png",
                "original": "http://storage.cloud... _original.png"
            },
            "content_type": "image/png"
        }
    ],
    "success": true,
    "error": false,
    "meta": {
        "code": 200,
        "status": "ok",
        "method_name": "createPhoto"
    }
}
```

Modifying the Feed Controller to Display a Photo After It Is Processed by the Cloud

This section returns to the cameraButtonClicked function in controllers/feed.js and shows you how to update the behavior of the success handler on the method call to work with the new asynchronous processImage method. The major changes are that the program now handles an error condition from processing the image and the object processResponse contains the model associated with the saved photo, as well as additional error information if needed.

```
processImage(event.media, function(processResponse) {

    if (processResponse.success) {
        // create the row
        var rowController = Alloy.createController("feedRow",
processResponse.model);

    // add the controller view, which is a row to the table
    if ($.feedTable.getData().length === 0) {
        $.feedTable.setData([]);
        $.feedTable.appendRow(rowController.getView(), true);
    } else {
```

```
        $.feedTable.insertRowBefore(0, rowController.getView(),
true);
        }
    } else {
        alert("Error saving photo " + processResponse.message);
    }
});
```

The final change is to update `controllers/feedRow.js` to support the new object you need to render. The real change here is that the app is now passing the results of the photo being saved to Appcelerator Cloud Services, which means you're working with an `Alloy.Model` object not a plain JavaScript object. There are two approaches to accessing the attributes on the model, and they provide the same results—`model.toJSON()` and `model.attributes`.

```
var model = arguments[0] || {};
//
// this is setting the view elements of the row view
// based on the arguments passed into the controller
//

$.image.image = model.attributes.urls.preview;
$.titleLabel.text = model.attributes.title || '';

// save the model id for use later in app
$.row_id = model.id || '';
```

Figure 5-18 shows the final screenshot of the app with cloud services integration.

List the Saved Photos at Startup

You don't need to make any changes to the app in order for `models/photo.js` to support querying for all objects. You need to update the Appcelerator Cloud Services sync adapter to execute the query when the app needs to read the model or collection objects. The adapter must be intelligent enough to determine whether it is getting one object or a list of objects.

The ACS `ti.cloud.js` library has a method to get one Photo object by the object's ID and another method to query or search for a photo object utilizing additional parameters. See `http://cloud.appcelerator.com/docs/api/v1/photos/show` and `http://cloud.appcelerator.com/docs/api/v1/photos/query` for more information about these methods.

FIGURE 5-18: Application displayed same as before, but now with a photo from ACS.

The following code shows how to update `assets/alloy/sync/acs.js` to support the `read` functionality in `processACSPhotos()`. It checks the parameters for the model passed in to see if it contains an ID, and if so, the program knows it's retrieving an individual object. Otherwise, it assumes it's getting a collection of objects.

```
case "read":
    model.id && (opts.data.photo_id = model.id);

    var method = model.id ? Cloud.Photos.show : Cloud.Photos.query;

    method((opts.data || {}), function(e) {
        if (e.success) {
            model.meta = e.meta;
            if (e.photos.length === 1) {
                opts.success(e.photos[0]);
            } else {
                opts.success(e.photos)
            }
            model.trigger("fetch");
            return;
        } else {
            Ti.API.error("Cloud.Photos.query " + e.message);
            opts.error(e.error && e.message || e);
        }
    });
break;
```

The program uses the ACS library call `Cloud.Photos.show()` when retrieving a single object and uses the method `Cloud.Photos.query()` when retrieving multiple objects.

Adding the loadPhotos() Method to the Controller

The following code updates `controllers/feed.js` to display a collection of photos returned from ACS sync adapter using the `fetch` method on the collection. The `fetch` method callbacks work the same as the `save` method callbacks on the model object in regards to responding to success and error response from the cloud services API. This code processes the results of the `fetch` by looping through the collection and adding each of the model objects to the table view. It then utilizes `controllers/feedRow.js` to create the rows for the table view. You will use this method to initialize the view with the photos saved in the cloud whenever the application starts up.

```
$.initialize = function(){
    loadPhotos();
}

  // Add the above code for the function initialize to feed.js

function loadPhotos() {
    var rows = [];

    // creates or gets the global instance of photo collection
    var photos = Alloy.Collections.photo ||
  Alloy.Collections.instance("Photo");

    // be sure we ignore profile photos;
    var where = {
        title : {
            "$exists" : true
        }
    }

    photos.fetch({
        data : {
            order : '-created_at',
            where : where
        },
        success : function(model, response) {
            photos.each(function(photo) {
                var photoRow = Alloy.createController("feedRow",
  photo);

                rows.push(photoRow.getView());
            });
            $.feedTable.data = rows;
            Ti.API.info(JSON.stringify(data));
        },
        error : function(error) {
            alert('Error loading Feed ' + e.message);
            Ti.API.error(JSON.stringify(error));
        }
    });
}
```

Add the previous code to `feed.js` to supporting loading photos.

Next, you need to update `controllers/index.js` to display the recent photos when the application starts. You do this by calling the `initialize` method on the feed controller. You gain access to the public methods in the feed controller by using `$.feedController.initialize()`, which is why the code adds the ID to the `require` objects when they were included in the view `views/index.xml`.

Here is the `index.xml` file exposing the other controllers through their IDs:

```
<Alloy>
    <TabGroup>
        <!-- Tabs included via <Require> tag -->
        <Require id="feedController" src="feed"/>
        <Require id="friendsController" src="friends"/>
        <Require id="settingsController" src="settings"/>
    </TabGroup>
</Alloy>
```

The initialization method, which is accessed from `controllers/index.js`, calls the `loadPhotos` method discussed previously.

```
// when we start up, create a user and log in
var user = Alloy.createModel('User');

// we are using the default administration account for now
user.login("wileytigram_admin", "wileytigram_admin",
  function(_response) {
    if (_response.success) {

        // open the main screen
        $.index.open();

        // pre-populate the feed with recent photos
        $.feedController.initialize();

    } else {
        alert("Error Starting Application " + _response.error);
        Ti.API.error('error logging in ' + _response.error);
    }
});
```

Summary

This chapter covered a lot of complex and new concepts, so feel free to return to it in the future. You will continue to add features in the application, but they will all require updates to the sync adapter to add new model objects. You will also always add view and controller pairs like you did here with the feed view and feed controller.

You also started working with the Appcelerator Cloud Services API to interact with the cloud services and predefined objects. The documentation links provided in this chapter are very thorough—they explain all of the parameters as well as how to utilize them in various scenarios.

Here's a summary of the concepts that this chapter covered:

- Alloy project creation

- Photo and user model creation

- Extending Alloy model functionality

- Controller creation

- Getting views directly from the controller

- View creation

- Styling objects in Alloy

- Integration with camera and gallery API

- Working with the `TableView` control and creating complex table view rows

- Creating asynchronous adapters

- Using the Appcelerator cloud services library

- Working with Alloy collections

Chapter 6 takes the app to the next level. There, you learn to add functionality to the sync adapter to support the Appcelerator Cloud Service Review object, which you will use to allow the application to support comments on photos. You will follow the same pattern of creating additional models, views, and controller files to support the new feature.

Chapter 6
Integrating Comments

YOU WILL FOLLOW the same process used for creating the controllers in the previous chapter to create a `comment.js` controller and `commentRow.js` controller. The `comment.xml` view will hold a `Titanium.UI.TableView`, which will be a list of comments. The `Titanium.UI.TableViewRow` will be represented as the `commentRow.xml` views. This pattern is the exact same one you used in the previous chapter, so I will move quickly through the content.

Creating the Comment Table View Layout

You'll first create the `comment.xml` view file, similar in layout to the `feed.xml` with some different button functionality. Here, I have added a `newCommentButton`, which will be used for creating new comments. You connect that functionality to the controller later in the chapter, but for now I am focusing on listing the comments associated with the photo selected.

I also have created the `commentTable` that will hold the list of comments added to the application and associated it with the `currentPhoto`.

```
<Alloy>
    <Window id="commentWindow" title="Comments">
        <RightNavButton>
            <Button id="newCommentButton">Comment</Button>
        </RightNavButton>
        <TableView id="commentTable"></TableView>
    </Window>
</Alloy>
```

Since you are building a cross-platform solution, you need to account for the differences in the Android solution. This code will work fine on iOS, but there are a few changes needed to support Android.

First, you do not have the concept of navigation buttons on Android so you will need to add the platform identifier for iOS to make sure the button code is included only when building for that platform. The next change is to add an event listener when the window opens so the application can construct the menu and title bar for Android.

The modified `comment.xml` file with cross-platform support should look similar to the following code listing:

```
<Alloy>
    <Window id="commentWindow" title="Comments" onOpen="doOpen">
        <RightNavButton platform="ios">
            <Button id="newCommentButton">Comment</Button>
        </RightNavButton>
        <TableView id="commentTable"></TableView>
    </Window>
</Alloy>
```

Rendering the Rows Using a Different View and Controller

Along with the `comment.xml` view, you will use the `commentRow.xml` view to separate out the user interface and the functionality associated with the rows in the table.

In the row, you will show the user profile photo for the person who created the comment, the username and the timestamp of the comment, and finally the comment text.

You also keep track of the comment model ID so when you need to manipulate the model, you can retrieve the ID from the row object.

The following code is for the `commentRow.xml` view file, which is the XML representation of each row that you will render in the table.

```
<Alloy>
    <TableViewRow id="row" comment_id="">
        <View class="container">
            <ImageView id="avatar" />
            <View class="textContainer">
                <View class="userInfo" layout="horizontal">
                    <Label id="userName" />
                    <Label id="date" />
                </View>
                <Label id="comment"></Label>
            </View>
```

```
        </View>
    </TableViewRow>
</Alloy>
```

Styling the Views to Match the Mockups

You have not done much styling at this point in the book, but there is a need to do some layout here to get the rows to render the way they were designed in the original mockups. The way you apply styles in the view files is through the commentRow.tss style file and you use the .CSS format to specify classes for the elements and also apply specific styles to the elements.

```
"#row" : {
    selectedBackgroundColor : 'transparent',
    width : Ti.UI.FILL,
    height : Ti.UI.SIZE,
    horizontalWrap: false
},
".container": {
    backgroundColor : 'white',
    width : Ti.UI.FILL,
    height : Ti.UI.SIZE,
    top : 0,
    layout : 'horizontal',
    horizontalWrap: false,
},
".textContainer": {
    backgroundColor : 'white',
    width : Ti.UI.FILL,
    height : Ti.UI.SIZE,
    top : 0,
    bottom : '5dp',
    layout : 'vertical',
},
"#avatar" : {
    top : '5dp',
    left : '5dp',
    width : '38dp',
    height : '38dp'
},
"#comment" : {
    top : '2dp',
    left : '5dp',
    textAlign : 'left',
```

```
            height : Ti.UI.SIZE,
            width : Ti.UI.FILL,
            font : {
                fontSize : '14dp'
            }
        },
        "#comment[platform=android]" : {
            width : Ti.UI.FILL,
            height : Ti.UI.SIZE,
            bottom : '2dp',
            textAlign : 'left',
            font : {
                fontSize : '14dp'
            }
        },
        ".userInfo" : {
            width : Ti.UI.FILL,
            height : Ti.UI.SIZE,
            horizontalWrap : false,
            bottom : '2dp',
        },
        '#userName' : {
            top : '5dp',
            left : '5dp',
            width : Ti.UI.SIZE,
            height : Ti.UI.SIZE,
            font : {
                fontSize : '14dp',
                fontWeight : 'bold'
            },
        },

        '#date' : {
            top : '5dp',
            right : '5dp',
            width : Ti.UI.FILL,
            height : Ti.UI.SIZE,
            textAlign : 'right',
            font : {
                fontSize : '14dp',
            }
        }
    }
```

Figure 6-1 shows a more detailed mockup of each row, and you can see how the classes and styles are applied to the elements to give the desired outcome. Also notice the use of the platform-specific identifier on the #comment styling entry. Yon can make platform-specific styling selections on specific objects or classes using this approach.

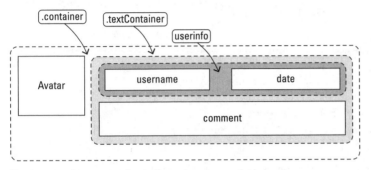

FIGURE 6-1: Design mockup of how the rows are laid out.

Adding Logic to the Controllers

You'll now start to look at the code from the controllers that will pull all this together. The comment.js controller will follow a simple pattern, whereby you will have a function for loading the items into the list, a function for adding a comment to the list, a function for deleting a comment from the list, and of course a function to initialize the view. Remember the objective here is to modularize the business logic into the controllers so that the controller is getting data from models and passing it on to views to render.

Calling the New Controller from feed.js

The first thing you will need to do is pass in some parameters to the comment.js controller when it is created so you know which photo you are working with and where you came from, that is, which controller launched the comment controller. You could create global variables to track this information, but it's better to minimize the use of global variables as a practice and instead pass parameters containing the appropriate information.

So when you create a comment.js controller it will look like the following code; the model and the current controller are passed in as an object parameter. This is how the current controller is passed in by using the $ object. The model object is a local variable representing the photo the user is attempting to create a comment for or view the list of comments associated with it.

The following code is how the new comment controller will be created when called from feed.js:

```
var commentController = Alloy.createController("comment", {
    photo : model,
    parentController : $
});
```

Coding the comment.js Controller

Inside the comment.js controller file you will save the parameters as scope variables, with better names to make the code self-commenting.

```
// Get the parameters passed into the controller
var parameters = arguments[0] || {};
var currentPhoto = parameters.photo || {};
var parentController = parameters.parentController || {};
```

The first thing you need to do is load the comments into the view when the controller is first opened. You can accomplish this through the use of two functions. First, you'll create an initialization function which will be exposed so it can be called to initialize or re-initialized the controller when needed, at this point, the only statement in the $.initialize function will be a call to another function, loadComments. In loadComments, you will query Appcelerator Cloud Services (ACS) to get a list of all of the comments associated with the currentPhoto object passed into the controller.

At this point your comment.js controller should look similar to this:

```
var parameters = arguments[0] || {};
var currentPhoto = parameters.photo || {};
var parentController = parameters.parentController || {};

function loadComments(_photo_id) {
}

$.initialize = function() {
    loadComments();
};
```

Cross-Platform Support in Comment View

When you created the comment view, there were platform-specific components added, specifically the right navigation button that is used to add a new comment. Since the concept of the right navigation button is specific to iOS, you will need an alternative approach for providing that functionality on Android.

On the window open event, you will check for Android and if so, you create the `actionBar` from the window's activity and associate the `menuItem` for a new comment to the `actionBar`.

The code for the doOpen function is listed next and should be added to `comment.js`:

```
function doOpen() {
    if (OS_ANDROID) {
        var activity = $.getView().activity;
        var actionBar = activity.actionBar;

        activity.onCreateOptionsMenu = function(_event) {

            if (actionBar) {
                actionBar.displayHomeAsUp = true;
                actionBar.onHomeIconItemSelected = function() {
                    $.getView().close();
                };
            } else {
                alert("No Action Bar Found");
            }

            // add the button/menu to the titlebar
            var menuItem = _event.menu.add({
                title : "New Comment",
                showAsAction : Ti.Android.SHOW_AS_ACTION_ALWAYS,
                icon : Ti.Android.R.drawable.ic_menu_edit
            });

            // event listener
            menuItem.addEventListener("click", function(e) {
                handleNewCommentButtonClicked();
            });
        };
    }
};
```

If you notice in this code there is a call to a function named `handleNewCommentButton Clicked`. This function will be called from the menu selection and also the `newCommentBtn`, which is displayed on iOS only. You can add the iOS event listener and the function stub now; the code for the function will be presented later in the chapter.

Here is the event listener and function stub added to `comment.js`:

```
OS_IOS && $.newCommentButton.addEventListener("click",
    handleNewCommentButtonClicked);

function handleNewCommentButtonClicked(_event) {
    // FILLED OUT LATER IN CHAPTER
}
```

Coding the commentRow Controller

You will be using the `commentRow.js` controller to generate each of the rows that are rendered in the `tableview`. The controller code will simply take the model's attributes and add them to specific view objects for display.

At this point you should add the following code to the `commentRow.js` controller file to handle the parameters that are passed in when the controller is created. There is one argument required and that is the model representing the comment that will be rendered by this instance of the controller.

You also need to render some information about the user in the comment row, so to make processing the user object easier, you will add a new variable that represents the user, which is an attribute of the photo model passed in.

```
var model = arguments[0] || {};
var user = model.attributes.user;
```

If you recall how you queried Appcelerator Cloud Services in the previous chapter, then all is good because you will follow the exact same pattern thanks to the ACS sync adapter and the model you will create to support comments.

Adding Models and Collections
for Querying Comments

You need to open the model directory and create a new file called `comment.js`; add the following content to the file. The only major changes from the default `model.js` file are the inclusion of the `type` and `collect_name` properties.

```
exports.definition = {

    config : {
        "adapter" : {
            "type" : "acs",
            "collection_name" : "reviews"
        }
    },

    extendModel : function(Model) {
        _.extend(Model.prototype, {});
        return Model;
    },

    extendCollection : function(Collection) {
        _.extend(Collection.prototype, {});
        return Collection;
    },
}
```

For this model, you will be using the Appcelerator Cloud Service object called Reviews. You can get additional information about the object here: http://cloud.appcelerator. com/docs/api/v1/reviews/info.

You are going to go back to the Appcelerator Cloud Services Alloy sync adapter and add some additional code to support working with the new comment model; you will start with the Sync method in the acs.js adapter. Add the processACSComments method to the function so you can work with review objects in the adapter. This example has added an additional condition to the if statement that will check the object_name for the model and then branch, in this case, to the processACSComments function.

```
function Sync(method, model, options) { debugger;
    var object_name = model.config.adapter.collection_name;

    if (object_name === "photos") {
        processACSPhotos(model, method, opts);
    } else if (object_name === "users") {
        processACSUsers(model, method, opts);
    } else if (object_name === "reviews") {
        processACSComments(model, method, opts);
    }
}
```

Now you have a function that you will use to work with the comment model. You have access to the ACS library APIs, which make interacting with these objects pretty straightforward and the abstraction of the model objects through Alloy and Backbone provide a clean consistent interface.

To get all of the reviews/comments for the photo, you'll use the query method; see this documentation for a complete listing of the parameters for the method: http://cloud. appcelerator.com/docs/api/v1/reviews/query.

Inside the processACSComments function, you have a switch statement that maps to the REST functions create, update, read, and delete, so all you have to do is add the appropriate ACS library calls and return the objects the same way you did in the previous chapter when working with photos.

```
function processACSComments(model, method, opts) {

    switch (method) {
        case "create":
        break;
        case "read":
            Cloud.Reviews.query((opts.data || {}), function(e) {
                if (e.success) {
                    model.meta = e.meta;
                    if (e.reviews.length === 1) {
                        opts.success && opts.success(e.reviews[0]);
                    } else {
                        pts.success && opts.success(e.reviews)
                    }
                    model.trigger("fetch");
                    return;
                } else {
                    Ti.API.error("Reviews.query " + e.message);
                    opts.error && opts.error(e.message || e);
                }
            });
        break;
        case "update":
        case "delete":
            break;

    }
}
```

You are using the `Cloud.Reviews.query` method to get all of the comments. You pass parameters into the query using `opts.data` and the method will return the results or an error message if appropriate. You then will need to add the proper callback function in the `comment.js` controller to handle the results and then add them to the `tableView` you created in the previous section.

You will use the same approach for adding the functionality to create a single comment to associate with the photo and for deleting a comment that was previously associated with the photo. The `Cloud.Reviews` object has the corresponding methods of `Cloud.Reviews.create` and `Cloud.Reviews.remove`.

When you create a comment, you will utilize all of the object properties specified in the backbone model as the parameters needed for the `Cloud.reviews.create` method. See `http://cloud.appcelerator.com/docs/api/v1/reviews/create`.

Add the following code to the `switch` statement in the method `processACSComments` to handle the call to the adapter and create a new comment in the application:

```
case "create":
    var params = model.toJSON();

    Cloud.Reviews.create(params, function(e) {
        if (e.success) {
            model.meta = e.meta;
            opts.success && opts.success(e.reviews[0]);
            model.trigger("fetch");
        } else {
            Ti.API.error("Comments.create " + e.message);
            opts.error && opts.error(e.message || e);
        }
    });
    break;
```

When you delete a comment, you will need a comment/review ID and the `photo_id` as the parameters for the `Cloud.reviews.remove` method. See `http://cloud.appcelerator.com/docs/api/v1/reviews/delete`.

Add the following code to the `switch` statement in the method `processACSComments` to handle the call to the adapter and delete an existing comment in the application.

```
case "delete":
    var params = {};
```

```
// look for the review id in opts or on model
params.review_id = model.id || (opts.data && opts.data.id);

// get the id of the associated photo
params.photo_id = opts.data && opts.data.photo_id;

Cloud.Reviews.remove(params, function(e) {
    if (e.success) {
        model.meta = e.meta;
        opts.success && opts.success(model.attributes);
        model.trigger("fetch");
        return;
    }
    Ti.API.error(e);
    opts.error && opts.error(e.error && e.message || e);
});
                                break;
```

Finishing the Comment Controllers

So back in the comment.js controller file, you will set up the collection to use throughout the controller and then add some logic to the loadComments method, which when called will create the list of comments to be displayed in the view.

At the top of the comment.js file, add the following statement to create an instance of the comments collection to be used throughout the controller:

```
var comments = Alloy.Collections.instance("Comment");
```

Next, go to the loadComments function to add the logic. You add objects to the collection by querying Appcelerator Cloud Services using the currentPhoto object's ID property.

You create the parameters for the query using currentPhoto.id, specify that you want the query to return the first 100 comments by setting the per_page property, and finally order the comments by the creation date, which you do by setting the order property.

```
var params = {
    photo_id : currentPhoto.id,
    order : '-created_at',
    per_page : 100
};
```

You will be using the empty collection object comments, and the parameters are set for the query, so all that is left to do is call the `fetch` method on the comment collection object.

Add the following code to the `loadComments` function immediately after the previous lines of code:

```
var rows = [];

comments.fetch({
    data : params,
    success : function(model, response) {
        comments.each(function(comment) {
            var commentRow = Alloy.createController("commentRow",
                                                        comment);

            rows.push(commentRow.getView());
        });
        // set the table rows
        $.commentTable.data = rows;
    },
    error : function(error) {
        alert('Error loading comments ' + e.message);
        Ti.API.error(JSON.stringify(error));
    }
});
```

The commentRow Controller

In the `comment.js` controller file, you can see where the rows are being created for the `$.commentTable` by creating a new `commentRow.js` controller for each of the items from the collection and using the primary view from the `commentRow.js` as the row object. If you take a look at the code from the `commentRow.js` controller, you can see a few things going on there as the code pulls the properties from the `comment` object and constructs the row for the comment, based on the model object passed in as a parameter.

When the `commentRow.js` controller is created by the calling function, it is passed the model object as a parameter. You will access the model properties by using the `model.attributes` property. You will also need to work with the user object associated with the model variable and to make the code easier to read, you can create a variable called `user` and set its value to reflect the properties associated with the comment creator/user. The `commentRow` controller code is made up of statements to get properties from objects and set properties on objects in the `commentRow.xml` view, including the ID of the model that's not displayed but saved in the attribute `$.row.comment_id`. This is done so when the application responds to click events on rows, it can determine the ID of the object by looking at the `comment_id` property.

One of the properties that will be rendered in the view is the date the comment was created. In order to properly format the date in the view, you will need to include a third-party library, moment js, which is distributed with Appcelerator Alloy. To use this library in this controller, you will need to include another `requires` statement at the top of `commentRow.js`.

```
var moment = require('alloy/moment');
```

Add the following code to `commentRow.js` to display the formatted information for the model provided as a parameter:

```
if (user.photo && user.photo.urls) {
    $.avatar.image = user.photo.urls.square_75 ||
  user.photo.urls.thumb_100 || user.photo.urls.original;
}

$.comment.text = model.attributes.content;

// check for first name last name...
$.userName.text = (user.first_name || "") + " " + (user.last_name
  || "");

// if no name then use the username
$.userName.text = $.userName.text.trim().length !== 0 ?
  $.userName.text.trim() : user.username;
$.date.text = moment(model.attributes.created_at).fromNow();


// save the model id for use later
$.row.comment_id = model.id || '';
```

Connecting the Dots . . . Showing the Comment List

Now that you have created the new comment section of the application, you need to provide the method for the user to get access to it. You will do this by connecting the comment button to an event listener that will trigger the whole process when clicked.

Back to the feed and feedRow Controllers

First you need to update the `feed.js` controller so when the user clicks on the `comment Button`, all comments associated with the selected image in the `feed.xml` view will be displayed. Since you are following the Appcelerator Alloy pattern, you will instantiate a new controller `comment.js` and then render the `comment.xml` view of that controller.

If you review the code for the `feedRow.xml`, you can see the `commentButton` added to each row and can see the `row_id` attribute, which is set to the ID of the photo displayed in this row.

```
<!-- file: feedRow.xml -->
<Alloy>
    <TableViewRow id="row" row_id="">
       <View class="container">
       <Label id="titleLabel"></Label>
       <View id="imageContainer">
           <ImageView id="image"></ImageView>
        </View>
        <View id="buttonContainer">
            <Button id="commentButton">Comment</Button>
            <Button id="shareButton">Share</Button>
        </View>
       </View>
    </TableViewRow>
</Alloy>
```

Here is the line in `feedRow.js` controller where the model ID is set.

```
$.row.row_id = model.id || '';
```

In Appcelerator Alloy, events bubble up by default. What this means is that the application can listen for click events at the `Titanium.UI.TableView` level, on the `feedTable` created in the `feed.js` controller, and then determine if the click was done on a specific button from the `feedRow.xml` view.

To do that, create an event listener on the whole table and have a function that is called for each click on the table. Add the following code to the beginning of the `feed.js` controller file.

```
$.feedTable.addEventListener("click", processTableClicks);
```

When the application gets a click event, an event parameter that contains information about the event and the source object of the event is passed as a parameter. In this case, you are looking for a click on the commentButton.

In the processTableClicks function, the application branches on the ID of the object that was clicked, utilizing the object's ID to determine if it was the commentButton or the shareButton. The function handleCommentButtonClicked is added to the feed.js controller file to respond to clicks on the commentButton and create the controller for rendering the comment view.

The following code should be added to the feed.js controller:

```
function processTableClicks(_event) {
    if (_event.source.id === "commentButton") {
        handleCommentButtonClicked(_event);
    } else if (_event.source.id === "shareButton") {
        alert('Will do this later!!');
    }
}
```

```
function handleCommentButtonClicked(_event) {
    var collection = Alloy.Collections.instance("Photo");
    var model = collection.get(_event.row.row_id);

    var controller = Alloy.createController("comment", {
        photo : model,
        parentController : $
    });

    // initialize the data in the view, load content
    controller.initialize();

    // open the view
    Alloy.Globals.openCurrentTabWindow(controller.getView());

}
```

The presence of Alloy.Globals is new in the application; it is a place to store global functions or properties without polluting the global namespace. In this example you will be adding the function openCurrentTabWindow to the application and you want global access to it.

Open `index.js` controller and add the following function to the bottom of the file.

```
Alloy.Globals.openCurrentTabWindow = function(_window) {
  $.tabGroup.activeTab.open(_window);
};
```

So now all of the functions are in place to detect the click on the `commentButton`, create the new controller, and render the table view to list the comments. If you compile and run the code the list should display fine, but with no comments (see Figures 6-2 and 6-3). The next step is to create the functionality for adding comments so you will have something to display in the view.

FIGURE 6-2: Comments list view in iOS.

FIGURE 6-3: Comments list view in Android.

Adding a New Comment to a Photo

The next step is to create the view and the associated controller for adding new comments. This controller will be called from the comment.js controller that you created previously and will be rendered in a completely new window.

In this section, there will be some cross-platform issues you need to address in the application to provide platform-specific functionality; but it will still be much easier than writing two separate code bases.

Creating a New Comment Controller and View

Right-click on the project and select New ⇨ Controller. Name the file commentInput. This command will create the controller, view, and style file to support the object you just created.

The comment input view is quite simple; you need a Save button, a Cancel button, and a text field to hold the contents; the view is laid out as follows.

```
<!-- file: commentInput.xml -->
<Alloy>
    <NavigationWindow id="navWindow" platform="ios">
        <Window id="mainWindow" title="New Comment" onOpen="doOpen" >
            <LeftNavButton >
                <Button id="cancelButton">Cancel</Button>
            </LeftNavButton>
            <RightNavButton>
                <Button id="saveButton">Save</Button>
            </RightNavButton>
            <TextArea id="commentContent"/>
        </Window>
    </NavigationWindow>

    <!-- ANDROID WINDOW -->
    <Window id="mainWindow" title="New Comment" onOpen="doOpen"
                                            platform="android">

        <ScrollView>
          <TextArea id="commentContent"/>
      </ScrollView>
      </Window>
</Alloy>
```

You can see that there are platform attributes added to indicate that the right and left navigation buttons are set on the iPhone only. There is also an event listener called onOpen that is specified in the view file. This event listener will be created in commonInput.js and will set up the menu bar and buttons for the Android version of the application.

You need to do some basic styling here on this view to get the textArea to appear in the proper location on the screen and to ensure you get the appropriate keyboard behavior. There are also some cross platform differences that you will account for in the layout of the window.

The following code is added to commentInput.tss to achieve the desired results in the user interface on iOS:

```
// file: commentInput.tss
"#commentContent" : {
    borderWidth: 2,
    borderColor: '#bbb',
    borderRadius: 5,
    top:'5dp',
```

```
    left:'5dp',
    right:'5dp',
    bottom:'240dp',
    color : 'black',
    font: {
        fontSize:'16dp'
    },
    suppressReturn:false,
    autocapitalization: Ti.UI.TEXT_AUTOCAPITALIZATION_NONE,
    autocorrect: true
}
```

For Android, to get the keyboard to appear properly, you will need to put the `textArea` in a `ScrollView` so the `ScrollView` object and the `TextArea` object need additional properties assigned in the `.tss` file.

```
'#commentContent[platform=android]' : {
    height:'240dp',
},
'ScrollView[platform=android]' : {
    contentHeight:'240dp',
}
```

Properties for `Ti.UI.TextArea` can be found here: `http://docs.appcelerator.com/titanium/latest/#!/api/Titanium.UI.TextArea`.

Most of these properties are pretty self-explanatory, but I do want to mention the `suppressReturn:false` setting. It allows the user to enter newlines in the `textArea`. If you did not set this property on the `textArea` and the user pressed the Return key, the keyboard would close, which is not the desired behavior.

Adding Code to the Comment Input Controller

The controller has to handle a few tricky tasks beyond what you have done in the past. First, you need to get the parameters from the creation of the controller object, which is done by parsing the `arguments[0]` object provided by framework. This is returning a JavaScript hash that is then assigned to the local variable `parameters`. The following code should be added to the beginning of `commentInput.js`.

The first two parameters' purposes should be clear; they represent the photo to associate the comment to and the `parentController` is the controller that instantiated this controller. The last parameter assigned to the local variable `callbackFunction` is the function called when this controller is closing; it is discussed in more detail later.

```
// file: commentInput.js
var parameters = arguments[0] || {};
var currentPhoto = parameters.photo || {};
var parentController = parameters.parentController || {};
var callbackFunction = parameters.callback || null;
```

You need to add the event listeners for the two buttons you have created in the window; one for when the user saves the message, called `saveButton` and one for when the user cancels the action, called `cancelButton`. Since these buttons are included in the user interface only when the application is built for iOS devices, the code checks for the device's OS to be iOS before adding the event listeners to these buttons.

```
OS_IOS && $.saveButton.addEventListener("click",
  handleButtonClicked);
OS_IOS && $.cancelButton.addEventListener("click",
  handleButtonClicked);
```

You also need to add the function for the open window event listener called `doOpen`. In this event listener, you set the focus of the window to the `commentContent`, which is the `textArea` added to the window. Setting the focus of the window to a `textArea` will force the device to display the keyboard when the window is shown.

On Android devices, the event listener has more duties; it will add a `menuItem` to the `actionBar` to save comments when selected. In the event listener you will also connect the menu selection to the same event listener that the `saveButton` on iOS responds to.

When you are working with a window directly and not with the `TabGroup`, you access the `actionBar` through the current window's activity and not through the `TabGroup` activity.

The `doOpen` function does pretty much what I said; it just sets the focus of the comment input window.

```
function doOpen() {
    if (OS_ANDROID) {

        $.getView().activity.onCreateOptionsMenu=function(_event) {

            var activity = $.getView().activity;
            var actionBar = $.getView().activity.actionBar;

            if (actionBar) {
                actionBar.displayHomeAsUp = true;
                actionBar.onHomeIconItemSelected = function() {
```

```
                            $.getView().close();
                    };
            } else {
                alert("No Action Bar Found");
            }

            // add the button to the titlebar
            var mItemSave = _event.menu.add({
                id : "saveButton",
                title : "Save Comment",
                showAsAction : Ti.Android.SHOW_AS_ACTION_ALWAYS,
                icon : Ti.Android.R.drawable.ic_menu_save
            });

            // add save menu item
            mItemSave.addEventListener("click", function(_event) {
                _event.source.id = "saveButton";
                handleButtonClicked(_event);
            });

            var mItemCancel = _event.menu.add({
                id : "cancelButton",
                title : "Cancel",
                showAsAction : Ti.Android.SHOW_AS_ACTION_ALWAYS,
                icon :
            Ti.Android.R.drawable.ic_menu_close_clear_cancel
            });

            // add cancel menu item
            mItemCancel.addEventListener("click",function(_event) {
                _event.source.id = "cancelButton";
                handleButtonClicked(_event);
            });
        };
    }

    // set focus to the text input field, but
    // use set time out to give window time to draw
    setTimeout(function() {
        $.commentContent.focus();
    }, 250);

};
```

The function `handleButtonClicked` supports the event for both buttons in the window since the behavior is very similar. If the `saveButton` is clicked, you call the `callback Function` with the appropriate parameters and then close the window. The `returnParams` object is set with the content from the `textArea` and a `success` property is set to true or false to indicate if the user wanted to cancel the comment input action.

```
// file: commentInput.js
function handleButtonClicked(_event) {
    // set default to false
    var returnParams = {
        success : false,
        content : null
    };

    // if saved, then set properties
    if (_event.source.id === "saveButton") {
        returnParams = {
            success : true,
            content : $.commentContent.value
        };
    }

    // return to comment.js controller to add new comment
    callbackFunction && callbackFunction(returnParams);

}
```

Now that the new controller and view are set up and allow the user to add comments to the photos, you can return to the `comment.js` controller to pull it all together.

Back to the Comment.js Controller

First, you will add the code for the event listener handler, which follows the familiar pattern for creating a controller and passing in some parameters. Remember this function will be called when either the button is clicked or the menu item is selected on an Android device.

```
// file: comment.js
function handleNewCommentButtonClicked(_event) {
    var navWin;
    var inputController = Alloy.createController("commentInput", {
        photo : currentPhoto,
        parentController : $,
        callback : function(_event) {
```

```
        inputController.getView().close();
        inputCallback(_event);
    }
});

// open the window
inputController.getView().open();
}
```

The callback from the `commentInput.js` controller will create the new comment if data is returned successfully from the controller; otherwise an error alert is displayed. As you can see in this function, the `inputCallback` function is passed as a parameter into the `commentInput` controller. The code for `inputCallback` should be added to the `comment.js` file after the `handleNewCommentButtonClicked` function.

See the code for the `inputCallback` function:

```
// file: comment.js
function inputCallback(_event) {
    if (_event.success) {
        addComment(_event.content) ;
    } else {
        alert("No Comment Added");
    }
}
```

Saving the Comment and Updating the Table

If a successful response is received from `inputCallback`, then you create a new comment for the `currentPhoto` by calling a new function called `addComment`. Using the `comment.js` model created earlier in the chapter and the data returned from the controller to create a new comment model, you can begin to structure the function.

The `addComment` function in the `comment.js` controller follows the same pattern for creating a model object and adding it to a table view as was used when creating the photo object in the previous chapter. The function will make a call to the ACS sync adapter using the `backbonejs` save method, and you will then add the row to the `$.commentTable` using the `commentRow.js` controller discussed earlier in the chapter.

The code for the function is as follows:

```
function addComment(_content) {
    var comment = Alloy.createModel('Comment');
    var params = {
        photo_id : currentPhoto.id,
        content : _content,
        allow_duplicate : 1
    };

    comment.save(params, {
        success : function(_model, _response) {
            Ti.API.info('success: ' + _model.toJSON());
            var row = Alloy.createController("commentRow", _model);

            // add the controller view, which is a row to the table
            if ($.commentTable.getData().length === 0) {
                $.commentTable.setData([]);
                $.commentTable.appendRow(row.getView(), true);
            } else {
                $.commentTable.insertRowBefore(0,row.getView(),
                                                            true);

            }
        },
        error : function(e) {
            Ti.API.error('error: ' + e.message);
            alert('Error saving new comment ' + e.message);
        }
    });
};
```

The code does the same check of the table to see if it is empty so the comment can be added to the top of the table or appended to the table.

The parameter photo_id is set by the currentPhoto object passed into the controller when it is instantiated, as discussed earlier in the chapter. The text for the comment is set in the _content parameter and is returned by the commentInputjs controller.. By setting allow_duplicate, you enable users to create more than one comment for the photo. Additional information on the parameters for saving a comment can be found at http://cloud.appcelerator.com/docs/api/v1/reviews/create.

At this point, you should be able to add comments to the photos in your application. The comments should be associated with the photos. When appropriate, clicking on the comment button in the feed view should cause the list of comments to appear and be ordered by date. See Figures 6-4 and 6-5.

FIGURE 6-4: You can now add comments, as shown in this iOS view.

FIGURE 6-5: The Android view of the New Comment feature.

Figures 6-6 and 6-7 show the application with some sample comments entered into it.

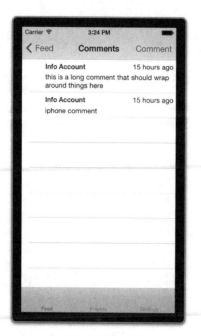

FIGURE 6-6: The Comments list view in iOS.

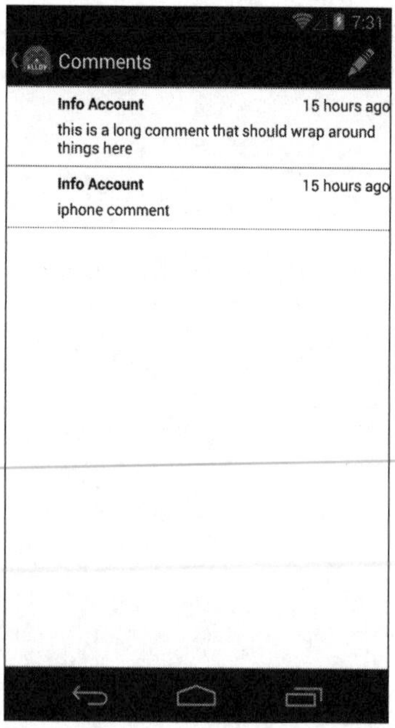

FIGURE 6-7: The Comments list view in Android.

Deleting Comments

Now that you have completed the process of adding a comment to the photo, you will add functionality to delete a comment. This approach will allow the users to delete only the comments that they created. This solution will be implemented on iOS such that the user will swipe the table row to display the ability to delete the item and then make the ACS API call to delete the comment from the system. The Android solution will be to respond to a longpress event on the tableRow.

For this functionality to work, there needs to be some initial setup code added to the comment.js controller. First update the table and set the editable property to true; this will allow the swipe event on the table row to display the delete button.

Next add event listeners for the longpress event on Android and the delete event on the table for supporting iOS.

The setup code to be added to the top of comment.js is listed here; you should add the code near the other event listeners:

```
$.commentTable.addEventListener("delete", handleDeleteRow);
$.commentTable.addEventListener("longpress", handleDeleteRow);
$.commentTable.editable = true;
```

Now in the event handler function called handleDeleteRow, you are provided information on the row clicked from the _event parameter. From there you can get the commentId_ attribute that was added to the tableRow. This ID then can be used to get the selected model from the Comment collection instance. The model object's destroy function is called with the appropriate parameters—the currentPhoto.id from the arguments passed into the controller and the model.id from the comment collection. If the delete is unsuccessful an alert is displayed. In both cases, the table is completely reloaded to ensure the proper models are displayed for the user.

The code for handleDeleteRow is listed next and should be added to the comment.js controller anywhere after the event handlers are added to the file.

```
function handleDeleteRow(_event) {
  var collection = Alloy.Collections.instance("Comment");
  var model = collection.get(_event.row.comment_id);

  if (!model) {
    alert("Could not find selected comment");
    return;
  } else {
```

```
if (OS_ANDROID) {
  var optionAlert = Titanium.UI.createAlertDialog({
    title : 'Alert',
    message : 'Are You Sure You Want to Delete the Comment',
    buttonNames : ['Yes', 'No']
  });

  optionAlert.addEventListener('click', function(e) {
    if (e.index == 0) {
      deleteComment(model);
    }
  });
  optionAlert.show();
} else {
  deleteComment(model);
}
}
}
```

handleDeleteRow calls deleteComment where the ACS adapter is used to delete the comment from the system. The code for deleteCommented is listed here:

```
function deleteComment(_comment) {
  _comment.destroy({
    data : {
      photo_id : currentPhoto.id, // comment on
      id : _comment.id // id of the comment object
    },
    success : function(_model, _response) {
      loadComments(null);
    },
    error : function(_e) {
      Ti.API.error('error: ' + _e.message);
      alert("Error deleting comment");
      loadComments(null);
    }
  });
}
```

Figures 6-8 and 6-9 show what the users will see when they attempt to delete a comment in the application.

FIGURE 6-8: Deleting a comment in iOS.

FIGURE 6-9: The comments delete alert from using the long press in Android.

Summary

In this chapter you extended the functionality of the ACS sync adapter to support an additional model called `comments`, which is important since this pattern will be continued through the book.

The benefits of cross-platform development were demonstrated by how you are able to provide the platform-specific user experience of the `actionBar` on Android and the navigation group title bar pattern on iOS all from the same code base. This approach allows for the development of solutions that do not have a one-size-fits-all approach to interface design.

Chapter 7

Integrating User Accounts with Appcelerator Cloud Services

TO INTEGRATE USER accounts into the mobile application, you will use the Appcelerator Cloud Service user object discussed in Chapter 5 and leverage the built-in social medial functionality from Appcelerator's Facebook module and Appcelerator Cloud Service's ability to link a user object to Facebook credentials.

After you create the user account, you will be able to log in with the user and update the user's information in the Users Settings page, which is covered in Chapter 11.

Adding the Login User Interface

You need to create a few more controller view combinations to support the three new screens—the User Choice, Create User Account, and Login screens. For this application you will integrate all of the screens into one view called the *login view*, which will have an associated controller to interact with the application.

You create the login controller the same as you have created the previous controllers and then open the login.xml view file associated with the controller you just created.

You will start off with the window object as the container for the remainder of the screen elements, but in this case you will also add a ScrollView to the window container. You are adding the ScrollView to the container to help manage the user interface when the keyboard is displayed for the user to enter text into fields. What the ScrollView does is automatically scroll the window contents so the text entry field is visible; this is a nice feature when filling out forms in the mobile application.

```
<Alloy>
  <Window id="index" class="loginContainer" >
    <ScrollView>
    <!-- main content for the screen goes here -->
    </ScrollView>
  </Window>
</Alloy>
```

The views will be constructed by placing all of the objects into the container and hiding and showing the proper container based on the action the users take. For example, when the user clicks the login button, you will hide everything in the view and then fade in the controls and user interface elements for the login action. You will use another one of the Appcelerator built-in libraries called animations.js to easily integrate this functionality.

Next you start to add all the containers to the main loginContainer to create sections that you will hide or show based on the user's actions. You will add a label to display some welcome text to the users so they are aware of the purpose of the page, and then you will add the buttons that represent the choices that user had when launching the application

```
<View id='homeView'>
    <Label id='welcomeText'></Label>
    <View id="hvButtonContainer" >
        <Button id="showCreateAccountBtn" title="Create Account"/>
        <Button id="showLoginBtn" title="Login"/>
        <Button id="showLoginFBBtn" title="Facebook Connect" />
    </View>
</View>
```

You can see the use of view containers to help style and lay out the contents of the page. It is a helpful pattern that you will find useful when trying to get the exact layout and spacing for your user interface. See Figures 7-1 and 7-2.

```
// login.tss
'#homeView' : {
    visible : true,
    top : '90dp',
    layout: 'vertical',
    backgroundColor : 'transparent'
},
```

```
'#hvButtonContainer' : {
    top:'20dp',
    width:'150',
    height:Ti.UI.SIZE,
    layout: 'vertical'
},
'#welcomeText' :{
    text : "Welcome Text Goes Here For the App",
    font:{
        fontSize:'24dp',
        fontWeight : 'bold'
    }
},
```

FIGURE 7-1: The initial home view in iOS.

FIGURE 7-2: The initial home view in Android.

Next you add the container for the login view; here you will include the text fields for the user to enter the username and password. You will set the password type as a property of the password text field to have the password masked when the user enters the text; this code is added to the login.xml file:

```
<View id='loginView'>
    <Label id='loginText'></Label>
    <View id="lvContainer" >
        <TextField id="email" class='tfWrapper' />
        <TextField id="password" class='tfWrapper' />
```

```
        <View class="centerHelper">
            <Button id="doLoginBtn" title="Login" />
            <Button id="cancelLoginBtn" title="Cancel" />
        </View>
        <Button id="forgotPasswordBtn" title="Forgot Password" />
    </View>
</View>
```

You add a similar label as on the previous container so you can display some text to inform the users of the purpose of the page. The last element you will add to the view container is a button for the users to recover the password if they forget. See Figures 7-3 and 7-4.

```
// login.tss
'#loginView' : {
    visible : false,
    width:Ti.UI.SIZE,
    height:Ti.UI.SIZE,
    top : '90dp',
    layout:'vertical',
    borderColor :'transparent'
},
'#loginText' :{
    text : "Login Text Goes Here For the App",
    font:{
        fontSize:'24dp',
        fontWeight : 'bold'
    }
},
'#lvContainer' : {
    top:'20dp',
    width:'280dp',
    height:Ti.UI.SIZE,
    layout:'vertical',
    borderColor :'orange',
    borderWidth :0
},
```

FIGURE 7-3: The app's login view on iOS.

You can see the additional class attributes that are set on some of the fields; this is to provide a basic level of styling and layout to the elements so you can see the functionality in action.

You see the consistent use of the ID attribute assigned to the elements because they are required for accessing the objects from the application controllers when the user clicks on an element or when you need to retrieve a value from a text field or application-level event.

The last section you need to add to the `login.xml` is for the account creation view; this is where you enter the information required to create the user's account in Appcelerator Cloud Services. For this application, you need to provide first and last name and an email address. The password must be entered twice for confirmation.

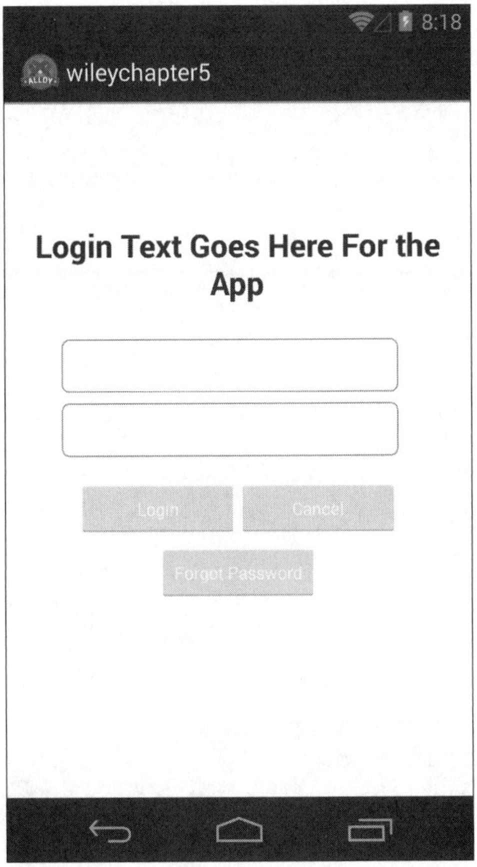

FIGURE 7-4: The app's login view on Android.

```
<View id='createAcctView'>
    <Label id='accountText'></Label>
    <View id="cavContainer" >
        <TextField id="acct_fname" class='tfWrapper' />
        <TextField id="acct_lname" class='tfWrapper' />
        <TextField id="acct_email" class='tfWrapper' />
        <TextField id="acct_password" class='tfWrapper' />
        <TextField id="acct_password_confirmation"
  class='tfWrapper'/>
        <View class="centerHelper">
            <Button id="doCreateAcctBtn" title="Create Account"/>
            <Button id="cancelCreateAcctBtn" title="Cancel" />
        </View>
    </View>
</View>
```

The associated changes to the `login.tss` file are necessary to lay the screens out properly (see Figures 7-5 and 7-6):

```
// General Styles
'.tfWrapper': {
    top: '6dp',
    width: '260dp',
    height: '40dp',
    border: 1,
    borderColor: 'gray'
},
'.centerHelper': {
    top: '10dp',
    height: Ti.UI.SIZE,
    width: Ti.UI.SIZE,
    layout: 'horizontal'
},
ScrollView: {
    contentHeight: Ti.UI.SIZE,
    contentWidth: Ti.UI.SIZE
},
TextField: {
    autocapitalization: Ti.UI.TEXT_AUTOCAPITALIZATION_NONE,
    borderStyle: Ti.UI.INPUT_BORDERSTYLE_NONE,
    autocorrect: false,
    top: '2dp',
    left: '4dp',
    bottom: '2dp',
    right: '4dp',
    paddingLeft: '4dp',
    backgroundColor: 'white',
    color : 'black',

},

// Default Button Style
"Button" : {
    top: '6dp',
    width: '120dp',
    height: '36dp',
    font:{
        fontSize: '13dp'
    }
},
```

```
'#createAcctView' : {
   visible: false,
   width: Ti.UI.SIZE,
   height: Ti.UI.SIZE,
   top: '90dp',
   layout: 'vertical',
   backgroundColor: 'transparent'
},
'#accountText' :{
   text: "Account Text Goes Here For the App",
   font:{
     fontSize: '24dp',
     fontWeight: 'bold'
     }
},
'#cavContainer' : {
   top: '20dp',
   width: '280dp',
   height: Ti.UI.SIZE,
   layout: 'vertical',
},
'#acct_fname' : {
   hintText: 'first name'
},
'#acct_lname' : {
   hintText: 'last name'
},
'#acct_email' : {
   hintText: 'email address'
},
'#acct_password' : {
   passwordMask: true,
   hintText: 'password'
},
'#acct_password_confirmation' : {
   passwordMask: true,
   hintText: 'password confirmation'
},
'#cancelCreateAcctBtn': {
   left: '10dp'
},
```

```
'#doCreateAcctBtn': {
   left: '0dp'
}
```

FIGURE 7-5: The create account view on iOS.

You have created the structure of the user interface that is used to capture input from the user to create an account, log in to an existing account, or log in to an account using your Facebook credentials. The next step is to modify the user model created earlier in the book so you can perform those functions using Appcelerator Cloud Services API calls. Remember that the separation of the user interface from the model enables you to reuse this user model that will support all of the mentioned functions in additional Alloy projects you create.

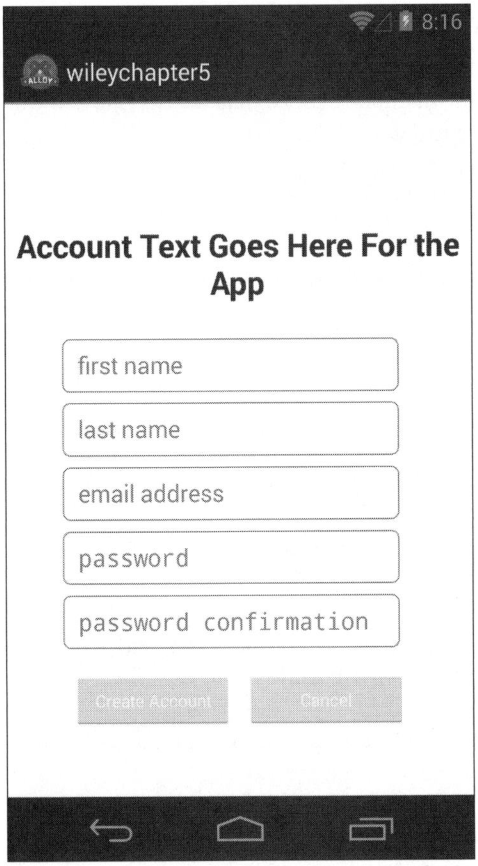

FIGURE 7-6: The create account view on Android.

Updating the User Model

In order to update the user model to support the account creation, you need to create an ability to allow users to login and logout using account credentials and send a forgotten password email when the user needs that hint to log in to the application. You will make additional updates later in the chapter when integrating with Facebook, but for now this will all be Appcelerator Cloud Services integrations. See `http://docs.appcelerator.com/titanium/latest/#!/api/Titanium.Cloud.Users`.

The corresponding methods documented at this link will be integrated into the user model so you can separate the model's behavior directly into the object and not have it spread through the entire application.

User Create Account Method

You will go right below the area where the login function is and add the following code to the user model for creating a new user account. This function is very similar to the one you will find in the official Appcelerator Cloud Services documentation.

```
createAccount: function(_userInfo, _callback) {
    var cloud = this.config.Cloud;
    var TAP = Ti.App.Properties;

    // bad data so return to caller
    if (!_userInfo) {
        _callback && _callback({
            success : false,
            model : null
        });
    } else {
        cloud.Users.create(_userInfo, function(e) {
            if (e.success) {
                var user = e.users[0];
                TAP.setString("sessionId",e.meta.session_id);
                TAP.setString("user",JSON.stringify(user));

                // set this for ACS to track session connected
                cloud.sessionId = e.meta.session_id;

                // callback with newly created user
                _callback && _callback({
                    success: true,
                    model: new model(user)
                });
            } else {
                Ti.API.error(e);
                _callback && _callback({
                    success: false,
                    model: null,
                    error: e
                });
            }
        });
    }
},
```

The _userInfo parameter will be a JavaScript hash of the parameters required by Appcelerator Cloud Services to create a user. You will extract the values from the user interface elements you created in login.xml view and create the object in the controller method you will create soon. The _callback parameter is the same as the login function; it is the method called after the Appcelerator Cloud Services method is completed.

User Logout Method

Logging out the user will disconnect the session with Appcelerator Cloud Services and will keep the user from making API calls that require authentication. You will extend the user object once again to make the Appcelerator Cloud Services call exactly as specified in the official documentation.

```
logout: function(_callback) {
    var cloud = this.config.Cloud;
    var TAP = Ti.App.Properties;

    cloud.Users.logout(function(e) {
        if (e.success) {
            var user = e.users[0];
            TAP.removeProperty("sessionId");
            TAP.removeProperty("user");

            // callback clearing out the user model
            _callback && _callback({
                success: true,
                model: null
            });
        } else {
            Ti.API.error(e);
            _callback && _callback({
                success: false,
                model: null,
                error: e
            });
        }
    });
}
```

Additional User Management Methods

You need a few helper methods to manage the user's session. In Appcelerator Cloud Services, the user's session is maintained for a predetermined amount of time so you don't have to always log in the user. If you noticed in the previous code that on account creation and user login, you save the session ID from Appcelerator Cloud Services. You can later retrieve the session by calling this method `authenticated`, which you can add to the user model with the following code.

```
authenticated : function() {
    var cloud = this.config.Cloud;
    var TAP = Ti.App.Properties;

    if (TAP.hasProperty("sessionId")) {
        Ti.API.info("SESSION ID " + TAP.getString("sessionId"));
        cloud.sessionId = TAP.getString("sessionId");
        return true;
    }
    return false;
},
```

The authenticated function will reset the user session appropriately in order for the application to function properly, but updating the user upon restoring the session will ensure that any updates to the user model are reflected in the application. Adding the following code will call the Appcelerator Cloud Services method to get the user information for the account associated with the current session. Like you did in the previous sections, add this code to the user model to extend its functionality so it can retrieve the user model from the cloud.

```
showMe: function(_callback) {
    var cloud = this.config.Cloud;
    var TAP = Ti.App.Properties;
    cloud.Users.showMe(function(e) {
        if (e.success) {
            var user = e.users[0];
            TAP.setString("sessionId", e.meta.session_id);
            TAP.setString("user", JSON.stringify(user));
            _callback && _callback({
                success: true,
                model: new model(user)
            });
        } else {
            Ti.API.error(e);
```

```
            TAP.removeProperty("sessionId");
            TAP.removeProperty("user");

            _callback && _callback({
                success: false,
                model: null,
                error: e
            });
        }
    });
}
```

You set up the application variables in the successful function of showMe the same way you respond to success of a user login method call.

Updating the Index Controller

The index controller is the starting point for the application. This is where you want to confirm users' statuses and direct them to the proper controller if they are logged in or not. You will first update the index.js controller and then you will set up the login.js controller, which will do most of the heavy lifting in regard to the user status in the application.

Set Up the Basics in the Index Controller

You need to check if the user in logged into the application or has a session saved for the application. You will use the authenticated method created in the user model. You can begin making the changes to the index model by creating a user model and checking to see if there is an existing method.

Replace the existing function to log the user in with the following code in index.js:

```
if (user.authenticated() === true) {
    $.userLoggedInAction();
} else {
    $.userNotLoggedInAction();
}
```

You can see the methods are named such that what you are doing is apparent to the reader. If the application has an existing session, then call the userLoggedInAction method; otherwise, call the userNotLoggedInAction. From this section, you know what you need to do in the `userLoggedInAction`—you need to get the user object since you only have confirmed that there is an active session. The bulk of the code `userLoggedInAction` is for getting the user associated with the session and setting up the app to initialize itself. You use the method `showMe`, which is a new function added to the user model when it was extended, add the following function to the `index.js` controller file:

```
$.userLoggedInAction = function() {
    user.showMe(function(_response) {
        if (_response.success === true) {
            indexController.loginSuccessAction(_response);
        } else {
            alert("Application Error\n " +_response.error.message);
            Ti.API.error(JSON.stringify(_response.error, null, 2));

            // go ahead and do the login
            $.userNotLoggedInAction();
        }
    });
};
```

The `userLoggedInAction` mentions a function you have not seen yet, `loginSuccess Action` it includes everything that must be done to set the application up after the user has been successfully validated. You will call this method after you validate the session of the current user, when creating a new account, and when asking the user to enter a username and password for a valid ACS user account.

```
$.loginSuccessAction = function(_options) {

    Ti.API.info('logged in user information');
    Ti.API.info(JSON.stringify(_options.model, null, 2));

    // open the main screen
    $.tabGroup.open();

    // set tabGroup to initial tab, in case this is coming from
    // a previously logged in state
    $.tabGroup.setActiveTab(0);

    // pre-populate the feed with recent photos
    $.feedController.initialize();

    // get the current user
    Alloy.Globals.currentUser = _options.model;
```

```
    // set the parent controller for all of the tabs, give us
    // access to the global tab group and misc functionality
    $.feedController.parentController = $;
    $.friendsController.parentController = $;
    $.settingsController.parentController = $;

    // do any necessary cleanup in login controller
    $.loginController && $.loginController.close();
};
```

This function requires the callback object with success set to true and a user model specified.

UserNotLoggedInAction is called when the application does not detect a session saved on the device. Since there is no session, you provide the user with options as to what to do next. The functionality of the login process and the create account process is encapsulated in the login controller.

You will first see if there has already been a login controller loaded into memory, if not, you will create the controller, pass it the required parameters for initialization, and save the object. If the login controller exists, you will open the controller to provide the user with the options for starting the application.

Later in the application you will create a settings page for the users to view information about their account and to log out of the application. After the logout process is complete, the application will also call userNotLoggedInAction to reset the user interface for logging in or creating a new account.

```
$.userNotLoggedInAction = function() {

    // open the login controller to login the user
    if (!$.loginController) {
        var loginController = Alloy.createController("login", {
            parentController : $,
            reset : true
        });

        // save controller so we know not to create one again
        $.loginController = loginController;
    }

    // open the window
    $.loginController.open(true);
};
```

Creating the Login Controller

In the controller, you will begin by creating the event handlers for the click events on the buttons in the view. The view was constructed such that to perform specific actions, you will hide and show containers for logging in and for creating accounts. The buttons and the associated event handlers are named to reflect the appropriate actions.

Add the following code to the login.js controller file:

```
$.showLoginBtn.addEventListener('click', showLoginBtnClicked);
$.showCreateAccountBtn.addEventListener('click',
                                        showCreateAccountBtnClicked);
$.cancelCreateAcctBtn.addEventListener('click',
                                       cancelActionButtonClicked);
$.cancelLoginBtn.addEventListener('click',
                                  cancelActionButtonClicked);
```

The next set of handlers respond to the button clicks to perform either the login action or the create account action.

```
$.doLoginBtn.addEventListener('click', doLoginBtnClicked);
$.doCreateAcctBtn.addEventListener('click',
                                   doCreateAcctBtnClicked);
```

The showLoginAction and showCreateAccountAction functions are structured the same; they basically hide and show the appropriate containers, which then provides the user with the appropriate user interface elements for the specific action. In a more advanced, professional application you might include animation effects of sliding in or fading in and out elements, but they are beyond the scope of this book.

```
function showLoginBtnClicked() {
    $.createAcctView.hide();
    $.homeView.hide();
    $.loginView.show();
};
```

You are showing the login container and then hiding everything else. In the case of the create account, you do the same except use the createAccount container.

```
function showCreateAccountBtnClicked() {
    $.createAcctView.show();
    $.homeView.hide();
    $.loginView.hide();
};
```

The last event handler you will add at this time is in response to a click on the Cancel button. Canceling either the create action or the login action should return the users to the initial login controller state.

```
function cancelActionButtonClicked() {
    $.createAcctView.hide();
    $.loginView.hide();

    // set the global login state to false
    Alloy.Globals.loggedIn = false;

    // display only the home state view
    $.homeView.show();
}
```

Logging in the User

When you log in the user, you will be using the user model created previously in the chapter and calling the `login` method you added to the object when extending it. If you recall, the method required the username, password, and a callback method. The user interface you created in the `login.xml` view file will prompt the user for the information, which you will then pass to the login method when the user clicks the login button.

Clicking the login button will execute the login button click handler and execute the following function:

```
function doLoginBtnClicked() {

    // create instance of the user model
    var user = Alloy.createModel('User');

    // call the extended model's function
    user.login($.email.value, $.password.value, function(_resp) {
        if (_resp.success === true) {

            // Do stuff after successful login.
            Alloy.Globals.loggedIn = true;
            Alloy.Globals.CURRENT_USER = _resp.model;

            $.parentController.loginSuccessAction(_resp);

        } else {
```

```
        // Show the error message.
        alert("loginFailed", _response.error.message);

        Alloy.Globals.CURRENT_USER = null;
        Alloy.Globals.loggedIn = false;
      }
    });
};
```

The function is a pretty straightforward use of the login method on the extended user model. You will get the username and password from the interface by accessing the `value` property on the two text fields. When the call is completed, you will have a user model for the logged-in user. There are two global variables created for tracking the user login state and the current user.

You need to set the information on the parent controller so you can execute the login success function. Add this code to the top of the `login.js` controller file:

```
$.parentController = args.parentController;
```

Creating the User Account

Creating the account is very similar to logging in because you will once again use the `value` property on the text fields to get the required parameters for the user model. You will pass in the username, first name, last name, email, and password with confirmation. Once the account is created successfully, you will perform the same actions as when you have a successful login. Since the actions are similar, you can do a slight refactoring of the code.

```
function userActionResponseHandler(_resp) {
    if (_resp.success === true) {

        // Do stuff after successful login.
        Alloy.Globals.loggedIn = true;
        Alloy.Globals.CURRENT_USER = _resp.model;

        $.parentController.loginSuccessAction(_resp);

    } else {
        // Show the error message and let the user try again.
        alert("loginFailed", _resp.error.message);

        Alloy.Globals.CURRENT_USER = null;
        Alloy.Globals.loggedIn = false;
    }
};
```

You can remove the callback code from the login function and create a function of its own. Now the createAccount and the login functions are very clean and simple. They get code from the user interface, make a call to the user module, and then pass the response to be handled by the userActionResponseHandler:

```
function doLoginBtnClicked() {

    var user = Alloy.createModel('User');

    user.login($.email.value, $.password.value,
                                userActionResponseHandler);
};
```

Here is a simple, refactored create account function:

```
function doCreateAcctBtnClicked() {
    if ($.acct_password.value !==
                        $.acct_password_confirmation.value) {
        alert("Please re-enter information");
        return;
    }

    var params = {
        first_name : $.acct_fname.value,
        last_name : $.acct_lname.value,
        username : $.acct_email.value,
        email : $.acct_email.value,
        password : $.acct_password.value,
        password_confirmation : $.acct_password_confirmation.value,
    };

    var user = Alloy.createModel('User');

    user.createAccount(params, userActionResponseHandler);
};
```

Now you need to add some code to initialize the controller when the user needs to log in or create an account. This is done with the open function, which you add to the login.js controller.

```
$.open = function(_reset) {
  _reset && cancelActionButtonClicked();
  $.index.open();
};
```

When the login action or create account action is completed, you will need to clean up the login controller. The `close` function is added for that purpose:

```
$.close = function() {
  $.index.close();
};
```

You can run the code now to see how the interface looks and create a sample account if you like. The screens you see should more or less match the figures shown in the previous sections of this chapter.

Now the code is set up for you to create an account using your email address and a password, but since you may also want to integrate social media into the application, Facebook integration is a great idea. Many people utilize Facebook and feel comfortable logging into applications with those credentials. Appcelerator Cloud Services has made it easy to integrate into your application along with the Appcelerator Facebook module.

Using Facebook for Account Creation

You can find specific details on setting up your app to work with Facebook on the Appcelerator Developer's website. The information provided in the book assumes you have followed the directions and configured your application properly with Facebook. See `http://docs. appcelerator.com/titanium/latest/#!/api/Modules.Facebook`.

Setting Up an Application to Use the Facebook Module

You will add the Facebook setup code to the `alloy.js` file. You can add the Facebook object to the `Alloy.Globals` namespace to access it throughout the application.

```
// Using FB module in the latest release of Appcelerator
Alloy.Globals.FB = require('facebook');
```

Another practice you might find helpful is to set the Facebook `appid` as a property in your `tiapp.xml` file:

```
<property name="ti.facebook.appid">FACEBOOK_APP_ID</property>
```

Facebook Button in the login.xml File

The Facebook button you created in the `login.xml` view will trigger the login process for the application to integrate with Facebook for logging into your application or to launch a web view for logging into your application. You need to get the Facebook Access Token, which is a property returned after a successful login. This property must be provided to Appcelerator Cloud Services for associating the Appcelerator Cloud Services user account with the specified Facebook credentials.

Facebook Method in the User Model

In the user model, you will extend the object once again to make a call to the Appcelerator Cloud Services method `SocialIntegrations.externalAccountLogin`, using the Facebook Access Token to connect the account to Appcelerator Cloud Services. The successful execution of this call will return a user account object the same way the login method and the create account method do.

```
updateFacebookLoginStatus : function(_accessToken, _opts) {
    var cloud = this.config.Cloud;
    var TAP = Ti.App.Properties;

    // if not logged into facebook, then exit function
    if (Alloy.Globals.FB.loggedIn == false) {
        _opts.error && _opts.error({
            success : false,
            model : null,
            error : "Not Logged into Facebook"
        });
        alert('Please Log Into Facebook first');
        return;
    }

    // we have Facebook  access token so we are good
    cloud.SocialIntegrations.externalAccountLogin({
        type : "facebook",
        token : _accessToken
    }, function(e) {
        if (e.success) {
            var user = e.users[0];
            TAP.setString("sessionId", e.meta.session_id);
            TAP.setString("user", JSON.stringify(user));
```

```
                // save how we logged in
                TAP.setString("loginType", "FACEBOOK");

                _opts.success && _opts.success({
                    success : true,
                    model : new model(user),
                    error : null
                });
            } else {
                Ti.API.error(e);
                _opts.error && _opts.error({
                    success : false,
                    model : null,
                    error : e
                });
            }
        });
}
```

This function will return a user object just like the login and create account functions. The difference is that there will not be any of the appropriate fields associated with the user object that you get when you create an account through the create account form. Remember you did not enter an email address, a first name, or a last name. You will need to handle that in the login controller.

Facebook Handler in Login Controller

You need to add the event listener to the login.js controller file:

```
$.showLoginFBBtn.addEventListener('click', doFacebookLoginAction);
```

The doFacebookLoginAction function has to do several things:

- It must log in to Facebook and get an access token for Appcelerator Cloud Services to use.

- It must also create a user object and call an extended method to create the ACS user account linked to the Facebook account.

- Finally, it must update the ACS user account with the user information from Facebook; email, first name, and last name.

You can start off with some of the supporting functions that will help the main login action; you need an event handler for the successful response from logging in to Facebook. This function will clean up the event listener so there is no memory leak and it will call doFacebookLoginAction again with the appropriate Facebook credentials and a logged-in Facebook user's access token. See Figure 7-7.

```
function faceBookLoginEventHandler(_event) {

    Alloy.Globals.FB.removeEventListener('login',
                                faceBookLoginEventHandler);

    if (_event.success) {
        doFacebookLoginAction(_event.data);
    } else if (_event.error) {
      alert(_event.error);
    } else {
        _event.cancelled && alert("User Canceled");
    }
};
```

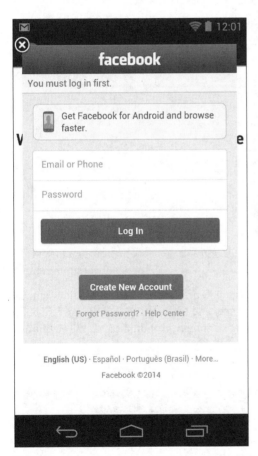

FIGURE 7-7: The Facebook login UI should be consistent on iOS and Android.

When you're testing, you might see the screen in Figure 7-8, which indicates that you have already authenticated Facebook with this application.

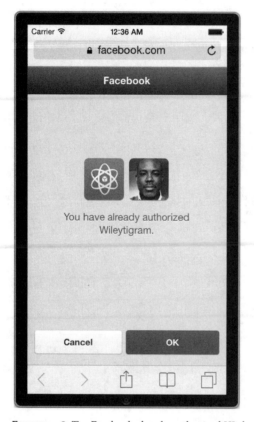

FIGURE 7-8: The Facebook already authorized UI should also be consistent on iOS and Android.

In the doFacebookLoginAction, there are two potential error scenarios—one when the user attempts the initial call to ACS to log in the user and the second when the user model is to be updated with the additional account information. Instead of duplicating the error functionality, you can create a function.

```
function faceBookLoginErrorHandler(_user, _error) {
    // Show the error message somewhere and let the user try again.
    alert("Error: " + _error.code + " " + _error.message);

    Alloy.Globals.loggedIn = false;
    Alloy.Globals.CURRENT_USER = null;
};
```

Now that the supporting functions are in place, you can implement the primary function. This function supports two states—logged in to Facebook and not logged in. The following code shows the not logged in state. When in this state, you will direct the user through the path of authenticating with Facebook through the Appcelerator Facebook module and you will use the faceBookLoginEventHandler method to take the appropriate action based on the user's interaction with the Facebook module.

Add this code to the login.js controller to a new function doFacebookLoginAction:

```
function doFacebookLoginAction(_options) {
    var FB = Alloy.Globals.FB;

    if (FB.loggedIn === false) {

        /// Enabling single sign on using FB
        FB.forceDialogAuth = false;

        // get the app id
        FB.appid = Ti.App.Properties.getString("ti.facebook.appid");

        // set permissions
        FB.permissions = ["read_stream"];

        // login handler with callback
        FB.addEventListener("login", faceBookLoginEventHandler);

        // attempt to authorize user
        FB.authorize();

    } else {
    }
```

If the user has already logged into Facebook, you have the Facebook access token necessary for the Appcelerator Cloud Service's call, so you can call the updateFacebookLogin Status method on the user object to create or authenticate the user.

Add this code to the else condition of the if statement you just added to the doFacebookLoginAction:

```
var user = Alloy.createModel('User');
user.updateFacebookLoginStatus( FB.accessToken, {
    success : function(_resp) {
```

```
Ti.App.Properties.setString("loginType", "FACEBOOK");

Alloy.Globals.loggedIn = true;
Alloy.Globals.CURRENT_USER = _resp.model;

// save the newly created Facebook user
if (!_resp.model.get("username") && _options.email) {
    _resp.model.save({
        "email" : _options.email,
        "username" : _options.username
    }, {
        success : function(_user, _response) {
            $.parentController.loginSuccessAction(_resp);

            Alloy.Globals.CURRENT_USER = _user;
        },
        error : faceBookLoginErrorHandler
    });
} else {
    $.parentController.loginSuccessAction(_resp);
}
},
error : faceBookLoginErrorHandler
});
```

In the login controller you need to update the user object returned with the email address and the first and last name of the user so you have a proper user object. The user account created by default from the Appcelerator Cloud Services method will not include those fields. You can get those fields as part of the data returned from the successful Facebook login method you called to get the access token. You will use those fields and perform an update on the user model returned from Appcelerator Cloud Services. The account should then be all ready to go.

Updating User with Facebook Information

When the user account is created through Facebook, the user does not enter her email address or username, in fact the user doesn't enter any information at all. The application is built so that on successful Facebook login, you will get the additional information you need for the user from the Facebook account information.

The first step is to update the `acs.js` sync adapter to update the user objects. Add the following code to the sync adapter in the `processACSUsers` function:

```
function processACSUsers(model, method, options) {
  switch (method) {
    case "update":
      var params = model.toJSON();
      Cloud.Users.update(params, function(e) {
        if (e.success) {
          model.meta = e.meta;
          options.success && options.success(e.users[0]);
          model.trigger("fetch");
        } else {
          Ti.API.error("Cloud.Users.update " + e.message);
          options.error &&
                   options.error(e.error && e.message || e);
        }
      });
      break;

  }
}
```

When you save the user object after successfully logging in with Facebook in the function
updateFacebookLoginAction you will used the fields from Facebook to update the user
object. See the following code from the updateFacebookLoginAction:

```
_resp.model.save({
   "email" : _options.email,
   "username" : _options.username
}, {
   success : function(_user, _response) { },
   error : faceBookLoginErrorHandler
});
```

The _options parameter holds all of the information returned from the successful Facebook
login.

Check for Facebook Authentication on Startup

The Facebook module provided by Appcelerator provides a method to determine if the user
has logged in with Facebook and if there is a valid session you can use within the application.
In this specific scenario, you do not need to check for a specific Facebook login because the
Appcelerator Cloud Services session is the one that matters.

Logging Out of Facebook

You should call the Facebook logout whenever the user logs out of the application and the login type global variable is set to indicate the user logged in with Facebook. You should also call the logout method whenever the user attempts to log in using Facebook to ensure you are working with a clean slate and have eliminated any lingering Facebook session information.

Summary

In this chapter you moved away from using the default test account to allowing users of the application to create their own accounts with their own usernames and passwords or by leveraging an existing Facebook account.

You have added code for the users to log in with the new account with the custom extensions that were written for the user model. You also learned how to extend the functionality of the `acs.js` sync adapter to work with user models.

Finally, you learned how to add the "remember me" functionality, whereby the application saves the user and session information. This enables a more seamless user experience because, after the user has logged in to the application once, there is no requirement to log in again.

Chapter **8**
Working with Friends and Followers

APPCELERATOR CLOUD SERVICES comes with a robust set of predefined objects, many of which you have used already to build your application. The next one you will use is the `Friends` object. This object allows you to create relationships between users so you can create followers just like with Facebook and Twitter. In the application you are building, you will allow the users of the application to select users to follow so they can view pictures of all of the people they follow. The pictures will automatically be added to the feed.

In this chapter, you will create new models, views, and controllers to support the `Friends` functionality and also update other areas of the application to support the `Friends` functionality. See `http://docs.appcelerator.com/cloud/latest/#!/api/Friends`.

Before you get started with friends and followers, you need to create a library to provide the activity indicator. This will let users know that there is some sort of network or long activity happening and that the application is not locked up. This also gives you an opportunity to see how `CommonJS` libraries can be integrated into your application, potentially repurposing old non-Alloy-based code that you believe is still valuable in your development toolset.

Creating the CommonJS Library in Alloy

Go to the folder `app/ lib`; in that directory, create a new file called `progressWindow.js`.

In this file, you can write plain old JavaScript code with plain old objects, the way you did before Alloy came along. You will create a set of functions to hide or show a progress window and export those functions so this library can be used throughout your application.

In this example, you will use the pre-Alloy window and user interface creation functions; once again, this is to demonstrate the flexibility of Alloy and to show how you can mix the old and new together to create your application.

Adding the Code

The variables that are within the scope of this library are created first. You have variables for the user interface components and variables to let you know if a progress window is displayed or not.

```
var activityIndicator, showingIndicator, activityIndicatorWindow,
  progressTimeout;
var progressIndicator = null;
```

Next you will create the two functions, one to show the activity window and one to hide the activity window. This code is very similar to the code provided in the documentation on the `Titanium.UI.ActivityIndicator` at `http://docs.appcelerator.com/titanium/3.0/#!/api/Titanium.UI.ActivityIndicator`.

Here is the code for showing the `activityIndicator`:

```
exports.showIndicator = function(_messageString) {
    Ti.API.info('showIndicator: ' + _messageString);

    activityIndicatorWindow = Titanium.UI.createWindow({
        top : 0,
        left : 0,
        width : "100%",
        height : "100%",
        backgroundColor : "#58585A",
        opacity : .7
    });

    activityIndicator = Ti.UI.createActivityIndicator({
        style : OS_IOS ? Ti.UI.iPhone.ActivityIndicatorStyle.DARK :
Ti.UI.ActivityIndicatorStyle.DARK,
        top : "10dp",
        right : "30dp",
        bottom : "10dp",
        left : "30dp",
        message : _messageString || "Loading, please wait.",
        color : "white",
```

```
        font : {
            fontSize : 16,
            fontWeight : "bold"
        },
        style : 0
    });
    activityIndicatorWindow.add(activityIndicator);
    activityIndicatorWindow.open();
    activityIndicator.show();
    showingIndicator = true;

    // safety catch all to ensure the screen eventually clears
    // after 25 seconds
    progressTimeout = setTimeout(function() {
        exports.hideIndicator();
    }, 35000);
};
```

Here is the code for hiding the `activityIndicator`:

```
exports.hideIndicator = function() {

    if (progressTimeout) {
        clearTimeout(progressTimeout);
        progressTimeout = null;
    }

    Ti.API.info('hideIndicator');
    if (!showingIndicator) {
        return;
    }
    activityIndicator.hide();

    activityIndicatorWindow.remove(activityIndicator);
    activityIndicatorWindow.close();
    activityIndicatorWindow = null;

    // clean up variables
    showingIndicator = false;
    activityIndicator = null;
};
```

Notice the `exports` reserved word used in the beginning of the two functions; this allows the functions to be exported as part of the `CommonJS` library you have just created. So now you need to require the library so that it can be used throughout your application.

You can open the `alloy.js` file in the root of your application directory. At the top of this file, in the comments section, it explains how this file is run before anything else in your application and how it is a great place to include globals and global functions. This is what you are going to do.

Add the following code to the `alloy.js` file:

```
Alloy.Globals.PW = require('progressWindow');
```

This code will create an instance of the `progressWindow` library that you can now use throughout your application and that you will start to use when querying for friends and followers in this chapter.

Adding the Friends User Interface

You created a basic window when you started the application so that you could move through the application tabs. Now is the time to add some new functionality to the window.

You will also get to work with some new concepts and a new user interface element called a `Titanium.UI.ListView` in this section. First off the `Titanium.UI.ListView`. The `Titanium.UI.ListView` provides a better user interface for displaying and managing lists of objects in the interface on your mobile application. The `Titanium.UI.ListView` will provide noticeable scrolling speed improvements over the `Titanium.UI.TableView` on iOS and will probably address troublesome bugs you found when implementing complex rows on Android.

The other new concept introduced in this chapter is *data binding*. Data binding allows you to create views that will update automatically based on changes in the underlying model or collection that you bind to the view. In this chapter, you will bind the collection of users from the friends model to the `Titanium.UI.ListView`, but it is possible to also bind a single model to a view.

The `Titanium.UI.ListView` is made up of the `Titanium.UI.ListView`, `Titanium.UI.ItemTemplate`, `Titanium.UI.ListSection`, and `Titanium.UI.ListItem`, all of which can be configured in the view file and the `.tss` style file with no code required in the controller file. The Appcelerator documentation has a thorough overview of the differences between the `Titanium.UI.ListView` and the `Titanium.UI.TableView`, so I cover only the basics required for the application you are building.

The user interface for the friends view is quite simple; it is a window with a list comprised of list rows that contain an image from the specific users profile, the user's name, and a button to make the user your friend or to end the friendship. At the top of the window is a `Titanium.UI.TabbedBar` on iOS devices for toggling between the different user lists. On Android, you will use the `Titanium.UI.Picker` control to perform the same function.

Open the file `friends.xml` in the `views` folder and add the following code. You will begin by laying out the high-level objects; I'll cover `Titanium.UI.ListView` specifics later in this section.

```xml
<Alloy>
    <Tab title="Friends">
        <Window title="Friends" id="friendsWindow">
            <!-- used to toggle between different types of users -->
            <View id="filterContainer">
                <TabbedBar id="filter" platform="ios">
                    <Labels>
                        <Label>Users</Label>
                        <Label>Friends</Label>
                    </Labels>
                </TabbedBar>
                <View id="androidPickerContainer"
                                    platform="android">
                    <Picker id="filter">
                        <PickerColumn id="column1">
                            <PickerRow title="Users"/>
                            <PickerRow title="Friends"/>
                        </PickerColumn>
                    </Picker>
                </View>
            </View>
            <ListView>
                <Templates>
                    <ItemTemplate/>
                </Templates>
                <ListSection>
                    <ListItem />
                </ListSection>
            </ListView>
        </Window>
    </Tab>
</Alloy>
```

The first thing you might notice at the top is the creation of the `Titanium.UI.TabbedBar` and the `Titanium.UI.Picker` controls. Since you are using the `platform` attribute in the XML file, you can control which user interface elements get compiled into the build based on the platform. This allows you to create the cross-platform application, yet provide platform-specific user interface elements, all from the same code base. Both of these elements respond to events that will let you know which item is clicked and is active. You will use this to control which group of users is rendered in the `Titanium.UI.ListView`.

The user interface styling for the `Titanium.UI.TabbedBar` and the `Titanium.UI.Picker` controls are pretty straightforward. You will use the platform-specific attribute in the `friends.tss` file to control the differences in the style elements based on platform. There is the style of the `Titanium.UI.TabbedBar` that's OS-specific. On Android, the dimension of the control and additional non-iOS attributes are required.

The contents of your `friends.tss` file should look similar to the following in order to render the page properly to match the original wireframes.

```
".container": {
  backgroundColor: "white"
}
"#friendsWindow" : {
    layout: "vertical"
},
"#filterContainer" : {
    top: "5dp",
    height: Ti.UI.SIZE,
    width: "70%"
},
"#androidPickerContainer" : {
    height: Ti.UI.SIZE,
    width: Ti.UI.SIZE,
    backgroundColor : 'gray'
},
"#filter[platform=ios]" : {
    style: Ti.UI.iPhone.SystemButtonStyle.BAR,
    height: 30,
    width: "86%"
},
"#filter[platform=android]" : {
    height: "38dp",
    width: "70%",
    selectionIndicator: true
},
```

To round out the `Titanium.UI.Picker` and `Titanium.UI.TabbedBar` functionality, you can open up the `friends.js` controller file and start to enter the code for handling events on the control for selecting the type of users in the list. Since the `ListView` and the models are not created yet, you will create stub methods to fill in later with the actual functionality.

The first thing after the basic setup code is to include the code for handling the events:

```
// EVENT LISTENERS
// on android, we need the change event not the click event
$.filter.addEventListener(OS_ANDROID ? 'change' : 'click',
  filterClicked);

$.friendsWindow.addEventListener("androidback",
  androidBackEventHandler);

/**
 * called when the back button is clicked, we will close the
 * window and stop event from bubbling up and closing the app
 *
 * @param {Object} _event
 */
function androidBackEventHandler(_event) {
    _event.cancelBubble = true;
    _event.bubbles = false;
    Ti.API.debug("androidback event");
    $.friendsWindow.removeEventListener("androidback",
  androidBackEventHandler);
    $.friendsWindow.close();
}
```

The interesting code here is once again changes added to support both platforms from the same code base. When using the `Titanium.UI.Picker` on Android, when the user selects the specific item, a `change` event is triggered. When the `Titanium.UI.TabbedBar` is changed, the event you want to listen for is the `click` event. Luckily, both events return the information required to take the appropriate action so you only need one function to handle the logic for both platforms.

The `filterClicked` function responds to the event and calls the appropriate functions for displaying the users. The _event generated provides the index that you need in a different property, `index`, or `rowIndex`, depending on the specific platform you are building for; the conditional statement at the start of the function handles that for you to keep the rest of the code straightforward.

```
function filterClicked(_event) {
    var itemSelected;
    itemSelected = ! OS_ANDROID ? _event.index : _event.rowIndex;

    // clear the ListView display
    $.section.deleteItemsAt(0, $.section.items.length);

    // call the appropriate function to update the display
    switch (itemSelected) {
        case 0 :
            getAllUsersExceptFriends();
            break;
        case 1 :
            loadFriends();
            break;
    }
}
```

The next step is to return to the `friends.xml` file to discuss the `Titanium.UI.ListView` element for rendering the list of users.

As stated earlier, there is a thorough explanation of the `Titanium.UI.ListView` and its many options in the Appcelerator documentation. This is a simple example that you will probably use multiple times in your application development experience, but please read the documentation because there is so much more functionality available in this element.

`Titanium.UI.ListView` renders a section containing items based on a specific template. In this example, the template for all of the list items are the same based on the selected picker item. You will configure most of the element's information in the `.xml` and `.tss` files.

First you add an id to the `Titanium.UI.ListView` element so it can be accessed in the controller.

```
<ListView id="listView">
```

Next, you set the `Titanium.UI.ItemTemplate`; since you can have multiple `Titanium.UI.ItemTemplates`, there is a container element in the XML called `Titanium.UI.Templates`. You will add two templates to the XML file, one for users you are following and one for users you are not following. You can see in the following code that the elements look very similar to how you set up the complex `Titanium.UI.TableViewRow` earlier in the book.

```
<Templates>
  <ItemTemplate name="fullItem" height="40dp" width="Ti.UI.FILL">
    <View id="userView">
      <ImageView bindId="userAvatar" id="userAvatar"/>
      <Label bindId="userName" id="userName"/>
    </View>
    <Button title="Follow" class="actionBtn"
                                onClick="followBtnClicked"/>
  </ItemTemplate>
  <ItemTemplate name="friends" height="40dp" width="Ti.UI.FILL">
    <View id="userView">
      <ImageView bindId="userAvatar" id="userAvatar"/>
      <Label bindId="userName" id="userName"/>
    </View>
    <Button title="UnFollow" class="actionBtn"
                                onClick="followingBtnClicked"/>
  </ItemTemplate>
</Templates>
```

A few points to notice here. You are specifying the event handler of the button in the template; this is required because there is no access to the specific button element from the controller. Later in the chapter you will create the `followBtnClicked` and `followingBtnClicked` functions in the controller to respond to the button click to follow or un-follow a user.

The `Titanium.UI.ListSection` is very similar to `Titanium.UI.TableViewSection`. Here in the view.xml file, you specify the `Titanium.UI.ListSection` with the `Titanium.UI.ListItem` element. The `List` section requires an ID attribute so it can be accessed from the controller; for the `Titanium.UI.ListItem`, we will leave that blank for now since most of the attributes are specific to data-binding.

```
<ListSection id="section" >
    <ListItem />
</ListSection>
```

Finishing Up the ListView with Style

The `friends.tss` file now needs to be updated to properly format the list view to reflect the functionality described in the wireframes presented earlier in the book. Open the `friends.tss` file and add the following code.

```
"#listView" : {
    background : "white",
    separatorColor : '#CCC',
```

```
        width: Ti.UI.FILL,
        height: Ti.UI.FILL
    },
    "#userAvatar" : {
        width: "36dp",
        height:  "36dp",
    },
    "#userName" : {
     left : "8dp",
        width: Ti.UI.SIZE,
        height: Ti.UI.SIZE,
        font: {
            fontSize: '15dp'
        }
    },
    "#userView" : {
        top : "2dp",
        left : "4dp",
        background : "white",
        width: Ti.UI.FILL,
        height: Ti.UI.FILL,
        layout : "horizontal"
    },
    ".actionBtn[platform=android]" : {
        right : "8dp",
        width: "90dp",
        height: "34dp",
        font: {
            fontSize: '14dp'
        }
    }
    ".actionBtn[platform=ios]" : {
        right : "8dp",
        width: "90dp",
        height: "26dp",
        font: {
            fontSize: '14dp'
        }
    }
}
```

There are once again some platform-specific sections to account for device difference, but there should be nothing new here.

You can add the two functions to respond to the button clicks as placeholders so the code can compile and you can verify the user interface is correct. Add the following code to the `friends.js` controller file.

```
function followBtnClicked(_event) {}
function followingBtnClicked(_event) {}
```

Now you can run the application and click on the Friends tab. The application should look like Figure 8-1 or 8-2, depending on your platform.

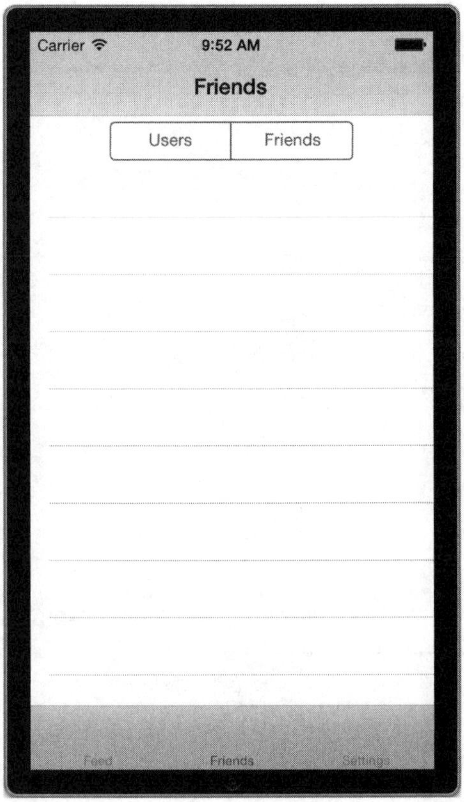

FIGURE 8-1: Basic user list view that is used for displaying users and friends on iOS.

Before you can go any further with the user interface, you need to have some data to render. Next you will start to create the models necessary for the friends functionality and then you will begin to fill in the stub methods created earlier when working with the `friends.js` controller.

FIGURE 8-2: Basic user list view that is used for displaying users and friends on Android.

After the models and the associated methods are in place, you will return to the `friends.xml` view file to bind the data to the view by making a few more edits.

Introduction to Appcelerator Cloud Services Friends Object

The basic model template is similar to how the model file has been created in the past. You just need to set the adapter type to `acs` and the `collection_name` to friends.

friend.js

```
exports.definition = {
```

```
    config : {
       "adapter" : {
           "type" : "acs",
           "collection_name" : "friends",
       }
    },

    extendModel : function(Model) {
       _.extend(Model.prototype, {});
       // end extend
       return Model;
    },

    extendCollection : function(Collection) {
       _.extend(Collection.prototype, {});
       // end extend
       return Collection;
    }
};
```

Modifying the ACS Sync Adapter to Support User Queries

The application needs to display a list of all of the users in the application so that the user can select other users they would like to follow. Following other users allows you to see other photos from users.

In this chapter, you add the functionality to get the list of users. To support querying users, you will add code to the `switch` statement to support the `read` functionality. This approach is very similar to how the other Appcelerator Cloud Services objects were added to the adapter. See `http://docs.appcelerator.com/cloud/latest/#!/api/Users`.

To query the list of users, add the following code to the `switch` statement in `processAC SUsers` in the `acs.js` sync adapter:

```
case "read":

    opts.data = opts.data || {};
    _model.id && (opts.data.user_id = _model.id);

    var readMethod = _model.id ? Cloud.Users.show :
  Cloud.Users.query;
```

```
readMethod((opts.data || {}), function(e) {
    if (e.success) {
        _model.meta = e.meta;
        if (e.users.length === 1) {
            opts.success(e.users[0]);
        } else {
            opts.success(e.users);
        }
        _model.trigger("fetch");
        return;
    } else {
        Ti.API.error("Cloud.Users.query " + e.message);
        ;
        opts.error(e.error && e.message || e);
    }
});

break;
```

The code follows the function provided by the Appcelerator Cloud Services documentation, but you are combining querying for a list of users with querying or showing one user. The trick is model_id. If there is a model_id present, then you will call the function Cloud. Users.show because you want a specific user. If there is no ID specified, then you are looking for a list of users and then will call Cloud.Users.query.

This one switch condition can return a single user as a model object or multiple users as a collection of user model objects.

Modifying the ACS Sync Adapter to Support Friends

To wire up the friends support in the sync adapter, you will follow the same pattern as when adding support for the other ACS objects. First, you create the stub function for the specific object type and then provide a handler for create, read, update, and delete.

```
function processACSFriends(model, method, opts) {
    switch (method) {
        case "create" :
            break;
        case "read" :
            break;
        case "delete" :
            break;
    }
}
```

Next you need to ensure the adapter branches when `object_name` equals `friends`; see the following updated code:

```
function Sync(method, model, opts) {
    var object_name = model.config.adapter.collection_name;

    if (object_name === "photos") {
        processACSPhotos(model, method, opts);
    } else if (object_name === "users") {
        processACSUsers(model, method, opts);
    } else if (object_name === "reviews") {
        processACSComments(model, method, opts);
    } else if (object_name === "friends") {
        processACSFriends(model, method, opts);
    }
}
```

Now you need to start to fill out the functions for each of the CRUD options in the `process ACSFriends` function. This approach is very similar to how the other Appcelerator Cloud Services objects were added to the adapter. See `http://docs.appcelerator.com/ cloud/latest/#!/api/Friends`.

The corresponding methods documented at this link will be integrated into the adapter so you can separate the model's behavior indirectly into the object and not have it spread through the entire application.

Creating the Friend Relationship

This code is straight from the documentation sample, but modified to support the Backbone model it will need to return. The code follows the Backbone.js pattern of determining parameters by looking on the provided option parameter of the model. In the case of the create/add method, the required parameters are passed in the model provided. Since the Appcelerator Cloud Service method does not return an object, but only success or failure, you will just return an empty object upon success.

```
case "create":
    var params = model.toJSON();

    Cloud.Friends.add(params, function(e) {
        if (e.success) {
            model.meta = e.meta;
            opts.success && opts.success({});
```

```
        model.trigger("fetch");
        return;
    }
    Ti.API.error(e);
    opts.error && opts.error(e.error && e.message || e);
    model.trigger("error");
});
break;
```

Finding Friend Relationships Based on a User's ID

This code is straight from the documentation sample but modified to support the Backbone model it will need to return. The function determines its parameters by looking on the provided options parameter of the function. This code is implemented to look for the userid in either the options.data or as part of the model, specifically the model.id property. This function will return all friends of the selected user as a collection of user objects you created in the last chapter.

```
case "read":
    opts.data = opts.data || {};
    _model.id && (opts.data.user_id = _model.id);

    Cloud.Friends.search((opts.data || {}), function(e) {
        if (e.success) {
            _model.meta = e.meta;
            opts.success(e.users);
            _model.trigger("fetch");
            return;
        } else {
            Ti.API.error("Cloud.Friends.query " + e.message);
            opts.error(e.error && e.message || e);
            _model.trigger("error");
        }
    });
        break;
```

Removing Friend Relationships from a User

This function can take multiple user IDs that will be removed from the relationship with the current user. The function determines its parameters by looking on the provided options parameter of the function. This code is implemented to look for the user_ids in the options.data property. This function does not return a model, but only a success or failure.

```
case "delete":
    Cloud.Friends.remove({
        user_ids : opts.data.user_ids.join(",")
    }, function(e) {
        Ti.API.debug(JSON.stringify(e));
        if (e.success) {
            _model.meta = e.meta;
            opts.success && opts.success({});
            _model.trigger("fetch");
            return;
        }
        Ti.API.error("Cloud.Friends.remove: " + e);
        opts.error && opts.error(e.error && e.message || e);
        _model.trigger("error");
    });
    break;
```

Extending the User Model to Support User-Specific Friends Functionality

Since the friends are associated in a relationship with a specific user, in this application you will be extending the user object to provide the necessary function for utilizing the friends objects you just created. This is about creating an application structure with objects that interact like real world objects, meaning you will ask the user to provide a list of her friends, you will ask a user to follow another user, and finally you will ask a user to un-follow another user.

You will create the corresponding function by extending the user object and use the `Friend` object you just created. The process of extending a Alloy model is covered in previous chapters, so the essential code is provided here only.

Since the `getFollowers` function will also be leveraged to support `getFriends`, you will set the parameters such that the results are either followers or friends. To get the Appcelerator Cloud Services function to return friends, you set the `followers` parameter to false.

Get the current user's list of followers as a `Friend` collection; pass the current user's ID, `this.id`, in as the parameter for `user_id`.

```
getFollowers : function(_callback, _followers) {

    var followers = Alloy.createCollection("Friend");
    followers.fetch({
        data : {
            per_page : 100,
```

```
            q : " ",
            user_id : this.id,
            followers : _followers || "true"
        },
        success : function(_collection, _response) {
            _callback && _callback({
                success : true,
                collection : _collection
            });
        },
        error : function(_model, _response) { debugger;
            _callback && _callback({
                success : false,
                collection : {},
                error : _response
            });
        }
    });

},
```

To get the user's friends, you just call the same function with the parameter set to false. You can add the following function as a helper and to create some self-documenting code.

```
getFriends : function(_callback) {
    this.getFollowers(_callback, false );
}
```

To follow a user and become the user's friend, the Appcelerator Cloud Services method requires the ID of the new friend, user_ids, which is provided as a model property along with the approval_required flag set to false. Additional information on the approval_required parameter can be found in the Appcelerator Cloud Services documentation.

```
followUser : function(_userid, _callback) {
    // create properties for friend
    var friendItem = {
        "user_ids" : _userid,
        "approval_required" : "false"
    };

    var friendItemModel = Alloy.createModel('Friend');
    friendItemModel.save(friendItem, {
```

```
        success : function(_model, _response) {
            _callback({
                success : true
            });
        },

        error : function(_model, _response) {
            _callback({
                success : false
            });
        }
    });
},
```

To un-follow a user and end the friend relationship, the Appcelerator Cloud Services method requires the ID of the friend to be removed, user_ids, which is provided as an options. data property.

```
unFollowUser : function(_userid, _callback) {

    var friendItemModel = Alloy.createModel('Friend');

    // MUST set the id so Backbone will trigger the delete event
    friendItemModel.id = _userid;

    // destroy/delete the model
    friendItemModel.destroy({
        data : {
            "user_ids" : [_userid]
        },

        success : function(_model, _response) {
            _callback({
                success : true
            });
        },
        error : function(_model, _response) {
            _callback({
                success : false
            });
        }
    });
},
```

Now that the models are all created and you can create friend relationships and you have extended the user object so the code flows in a more natural manner, you can now start the final step, which is to bind the data to the user interface.

Integrating ListView Data-Binding with Friends Collections

With the features of Backbone and Alloy, you can easily keep the user interface synchronized with the data models through binding the data to the view. Earlier in the chapter, you created the basic `ListView`, which you will now bind to a list of users for the application users to select as someone to follow, a list of followers for the user to see, and a list of followers for the user to select and un-follow.

Revisiting the friends.xml File

Since you are going to bind this view to a collection of users, you need to create a local instance of the collection; in this example you create that in the `friends.xml` by adding this line of code right after the Alloy opening tag:

```
<Collection src="user" instance="true" id="friendUserCollection">
```

Now when the application instantiates this view/controller combination, a user collection named `friendUserCollection` will be created automatically. This collection must be created immediately since in the current implementation of Alloy; the view is rendered before any user functions are executed and the bound collection for the view must exist.

The next change is to bind that collection to the `Titanium.UI.ListSection`; remember the section will be displayed in the `Titanium.UI.ListView` so the contents will be visible when the view is rendered.

Finally, you need to bind the model objects from the `friendUserCollection` to the specific `Titanium.UI.ListSection` in the `Titanium.UI.ListView`; basically each model in the collection will be represented as an individual `Titanium.UI.ListItem`.

Here is the complete code for the updated `ListSection`:

```
<ListSection id="section" dataCollection="$.friendUserCollection"
                          dataTransform="doTransform"
                          dataFilter="doFilter">
    <ListItem template="{template}"
              userName:text="{title}"
```

```
                    userAvatar:image="{image}"
                    modelId="{modelId}"/>
</ListSection>
```

The `dataCollection` attribute is the name of the variable, `$.friendUserCollection`, which holds the collection to be rendered in the view.

The `dataTransform` and `dataFilter` functions are added to the controller to modify the model object that is passed to the `Titanium.UI.ListItem` as a JavaScript object and the `dataFilter` is used to filter the collection of objects that is rendered in the view. These are optional functions; however, you will be utilizing both functions in the updated `friends.js` controller code.

The `Titanium.UI.ListItem` has the properties that actually bind the model's attributes to the list to be rendered. Notice that the attribute names match the `bindId` property values that were specified in the templates you created in the first section on working with the `friends.xml` view. The attributes in the curly braces map to the model attributes that are provided by the collection, which is in turn bound to the view.

Integrating ListView Data-Binding with the Friends Controller

Back to the controller to fill in the stubs you created earlier in the chapter, there were three primary views—All Users, All Friends, and All Followers. This section begins with All Users.

When this view is first displayed, it will show all of the users in the system who you are not following. So the first step is to get the list of users you are following and then get all of the users. The initialization code for the `friends.js` controller is listed next, and it's called when the view gets focus.

```
function initialize() {
    $.filter.index = 0;

    Alloy.Globals. opts.showIndicator("Loading...");

    updateFollowersFriendsLists(function() {
        Alloy.Globals.PW.hideIndicator();

        // get the users
        $.collectionType = "fullItem";
```

```
        getAllUsersExceptFriends();

    });

};
```

You need to fetch the content when the view gains focus not on open, so you create this event listener for the controller. You also specify the `$.collectionType` variable so the `Titanium.UI.ListView` knows which template to use when rendering the list.

```
$.getView().addEventListener("focus", function() {
    !$.initialized  && initialize();
    $.initialized = true
});
```

Displaying All Users

The method to support finding all users in called `getAllUsersExceptFriends`, which will do exactly what it says, but it requires some help. We need a list of the user IDs of the current user's friends so they can be excluded from the collection; that can be accomplished with the function `updateFollowersFriendsLists`.

`updateFollowersFriendsLists` gets the list of friends and followers and then using the underscore `_.pluck` method removes just the user IDs and saves them in an location array `$.followersIdList`.

```
function updateFollowersFriendsLists(_callback) {
    var currentUser = Alloy.Globals.currentUser;

    // get the followers/friends id for the current user
    currentUser.getFollowers(function(_resp) {
        if (_resp.success) {
            $.followersIdList =
                _.pluck(_resp.collection.models, "id");

            // get the friends
            currentUser.getFriends(function(_resp) {
                if (_resp.success) {
                    $.friendsIdList =
                        _.pluck(_resp.collection.models, "id");
                } else {
                    alert("Error updating friends and followers");
                }
```

```
            _callback();
        });
    } else {
        alert("Error updating friends and followers");
        _callback();
    }

    });
}
```

Now you have the list of IDs to exclude from the all users list, since this is just the list of people you are not already following, you need to construct a query for the `friendUserCollection` collection to make this happen. Notice the use of the Appcelerator Cloud Services where query functionality to exclude the user IDs that match the IDs in the provided array.

```
function getAllUsersExceptFriends() {
    var where_params = null;

    // which template to use when rendering listView
    $.collectionType = "fullItem";

    Alloy.Globals.PW.showIndicator("Loading Users...");

    // remove all items from the collection
    $.friendUserCollection.reset();

    if ($.friendsIdList.length) {
    // set up where parameters using the $.friendsIdList
    // from the updateFollowersFriendsLists function call
        var where_params = {
            "_id" : {
                "$nin" : $.friendsIdList, // means NOT IN
            },
        };
    }


    // set the where params on the query
    $.friendUserCollection.fetch({
        data : {
            per_page : 100,
            order : '-last_name',
            where : where_params && JSON.stringify(where_params),
        },
```

```
        success : function() {
            // user collection is updated into
            // $.friendUserCollection variable
            Alloy.Globals.PW.hideIndicator();
        },
        error : function() {
            Alloy.Globals.PW.hideIndicator();
            alert("Error Loading Users");
        }
    });
}
```

The last step to get the binding working is to create the doFilter and doTransform functions you specified in the view.xml file. You can start with the doFilter function since it is pretty straightforward. You do not want to display yourself or the admin accounts in any of the views so filter the collection and extract users with your ID and end user object that comes back as an admin.

```
function doFilter(_collection) {
    return _collection.filter(function(_i) {
        var attrs = _i.attributes;
        return ((_i.id !== Alloy.Globals.currentUser.id) &&
                    (attrs.admin === "false" || !attrs.admin));
    });
};
```

Next for the dataTransform, you need to return an object with the properties that match the values specified in the curly braces from the ListSection in view.xml. So here you will transform the data from the original model in the collection into a JavaScript object containing the appropriate properties to match the user interface and pass the object, modelParams as the return. See Figures 8-3 and 8-4.

```
function doTransform(model) {

    var displayName, image, user = model.toJSON();

    // get the photo
    if (user.photo && user.photo.urls) {
        image = user.photo.urls.square_75 ||
                user.photo.urls.thumb_100 ||
            user.photo.urls.original ||
            "missing.gif";
    } else {
```

```
        image = "missing.gif";
    }

    // get the display name
    if (user.first_name || user.last_name) {
        displayName =
            (user.first_name || "") + " " + (user.last_name || "");
    } else {
        displayName = user.email;
    }

    // return the object
    var modelParams = {
        title : displayName,
        image : image,
        modelId : user.id,
        template : $.collectionType
    };

    return modelParams;
};
```

Displaying the Friends List

This is a straightforward call to the getFriends method added to the extended user model. It will return a list of user objects that will be assigned to the $.friendUserCollection collection.

This assignment will trigger the data binding to update the Titanium.UI.ListView and display the friends. Also notice the assignment of the collectionType that will control the template user to display the list items.

```
function loadFriends(_callback) {
  var user = Alloy.Globals.currentUser;

  Alloy.Globals.PW.showIndicator("Loading Friends...");

  user.getFriends(function(_resp) {
    if (_resp.success) {
      if (_resp.collection.models.length === 0) {
        $.friendUserCollection.reset();
      } else {
```

```
      $.collectionType = "friends";
      $.friendUserCollection.reset(_resp.collection.models);
      $.friendUserCollection.trigger("sync");
    }
  } else {
    alert("Error loading followers");
  }
  Alloy.Globals.PW.hideIndicator();
  _callback && _callback();
});
};
```

FIGURE 8-3: The iOS version of the basic user list view that is used for displaying users, friends, and followers.

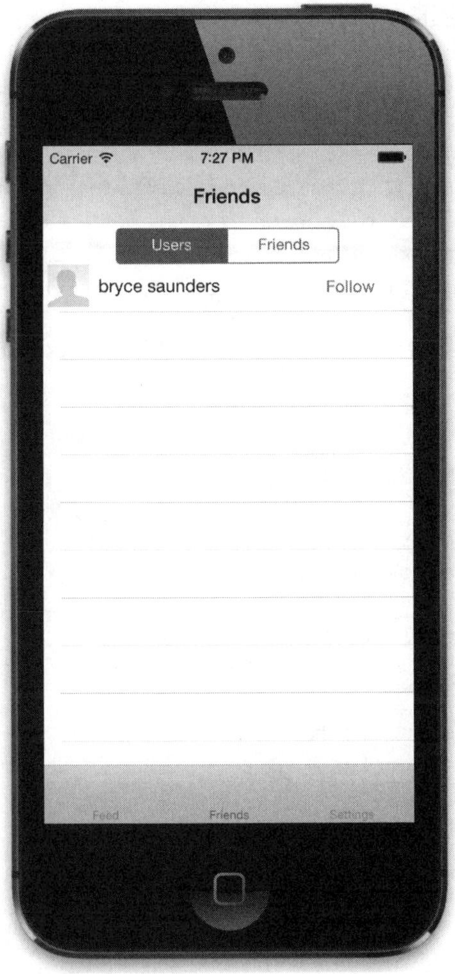

FIGURE 8-4: The Android version of the basic user list view that is used for displaying users, friends, and followers.

Working with User and Friends Lists

When selecting a user from the all users list to add as a friend, you will be following the event handler pattern that should be familiar to you by now, with a slight change for list views. At the time of the writing of this book, `Titanium.UI.ListView` must have the event handler defined in `view.xml` and not in the controller. So if you remember from earlier in this chapter, you added the `onClick` attribute to the button in the `Titanium.UI.ItemTemplate` in the `Titanium.UI.ListView`.

The following code responds to the click on the button and calls the function `followUser` that was added to the extended user model to create a friend relationship between two users. The function will add the selected user to the current user's friend's list. When the call is completed successfully you then call the function `updateFollowersFriendsLists` to update the current list of friends and followers so you have the proper list of user IDs to exclude from the lists. Remember you do not want to display users in the list who are already friends. After the function completes, you then need to update `$.friendUserCollection` by calling `getAllUsersExceptFriends`. Since you used data binding, as soon as the `$.friendUserCollection` is updated, the application will respond to the updated event and update the user interface for you.

Replace the method stub for `followBtnClicked` in `friends.js` controller file with this code:

```
function followBtnClicked(_event) {

  Alloy.Globals.PW.showIndicator("Updating User");

  var currentUser = Alloy.Globals.currentUser;
  var selUser = getModelFromSelectedRow(_event);

  currentUser.followUser(selUser.model.id, function(_resp) {
    if (_resp.success) {

      // update the lists IF it was successful
      updateFollowersFriendsLists (function() {

        // update the UI to reflect the change
        getAllUsersExceptFriends(function() {
          Alloy.Globals.PW.hideIndicator();
          alert("You are now following " + selUser.displayName);
        });
      });
    } else {
      alert("Error trying to follow " + selUser.displayName);
    }
    Alloy.Globals.PW.hideIndicator();

  });

  _event.cancelBubble = true;
};
```

The helper function `getModelFromSelectedRow` used in the previous code encapsulates functionality needed to get the model and the specific display name from a list element. Using the `model.id` specified in the model transformation function and added as an attribute on each `Titanium.UI.ListItem`, you can then do a local query on the collection to get the entire model object. The function returns the model and the display name to be displayed in the list.

```
function getModelFromSelectedRow(_event) {
    var item = _event.section.items[_event.itemIndex];
    var selectedUserId = item.properties.modelId;
    return {
        model : $.friendUserCollection.get(selectedUserId),
        displayName : item.userName.text,
    };
}
```

Figure 8-5 shows the alert that tells users they are now following a new friend.

FIGURE 8-5: The Android version of the alert.

Removing a Friend from the Friends List

To remove a user from the current user's friends list, you will use the functions previously added to the user object to call the underlying methods on the `friends` object. Utilizing the helper method to get the model from the row that was clicked, you then pass that ID to the `unfollowUser` function. If the function executes successfully, you will need to update the local variable holding the `friendsList` since that is required for the proper filtering of the display and then finally call `loadFriends` to reset the `$.friendUserCollection` and trigger the data binding to update the view.

```
function followingBtnClicked(_event) {

  Alloy.Globals.PW.showIndicator("Updating User");

  var currentUser = Alloy.Globals.currentUser;
  var selUser = getModelFromSelectedRow(_event);

  currentUser.unFollowUser(selUser.model.id, function(_resp) {
    if (_resp.success) {
      // update the lists
      updateFollowersFriendsLists(function() {

        // update the UI to reflect the change
        loadFriends(function() {
          Alloy.Globals.PW.hideIndicator();
          alert("You're no longer following " +
                                  selUser.displayName);
        });
      });

    } else {
      alert("Error unfollowing " + selUser.displayName);
    }
    Alloy.Globals.PW.hideIndicator();

  });
  _event.cancelBubble = true;
};
```

At this point, you should have completed all of the functions associated with the `filter Clicked` event handler so when the user is running the application, he can toggle between various user lists and followers.

You can also experiment with following users and then unfollowing them to see how the user interface performs.

Updating the Application to Be Friend- and Location-Aware

These additional functions are added to personalize the user's experience with the application. Since you have now added the ability to select friends; you will now only show photos in the feed from the friends or from the current user.

The code searches for photos except for the inclusion of the _user.getFriends method, which gets the current user's friends list. This list of user IDs is needed to add to the collection query's where clause to ensure only photos from the current user and the user's friends are included.

Updated function to add to the photo.js model file included here; be sure to add the code to the collection and not the model:

```
findMyPhotosAndWhoIFollow : function(_user, _options) {
  var collection = this;

  // get all of the current users friends
  _user.getFriends(function(_resp) {
    if (_resp.success) {

      // pluck the user ids and add current users id
      var idList = _.pluck(_resp.collection.models, "id");
      idList.push(_user.id);

      // set up where parameters using the user list
      var where_params = {
        "user_id" : {
          "$in" : idList
        },
        title : {
          "$exists" : true
        }
      };
      // set the where params on the query
      _options.data = _options.data || {};
      _options.data.order = '-created_at';
```

```
      _options.data.per_page = 25;
      _options.data.where = JSON.stringify(where_params);

      // execute the query
      collection.fetch(_options);
    } else {
      Ti.API.error('Error fetching friends');
      _options.error();
    }
  });
},
```

Summary

This chapter covered a lot of material around the data-view binding, which is a powerful concept that you should be aware of when creating your applications. The underlying Backbone.js event functionality is an important concept, so you are encouraged to review the Backbone documentation along with the Appcelerator Alloy documentation.

The `Titanium.UI.ListView` is a must-use in most situations because of the performance gains. At the time of writing this book, `Titanium.UI.ListView` has been recently released and there are still issues being resolved. However, it should not stop you from starting with `Titanium.UI.ListView` anyplace you would normally use a `Titanium.UI.TableView`.

Appcelerator Cloud Services pre-built objects once again save a lot of time by providing functionality out of the box. In this example you implemented two-way friends with no approval required. The Appcelerator Cloud Services API allows for you to create friend relationships that require an approval. All of the functions are there for you to use; take a look at the documentation to see if there is a better fit for your implementation.

Chapter 9

Working with Maps and Locations

APPCELERATOR TITANIUM PROVIDES excellent support for most of your geolocation needs. This is not the complete demonstration of the functionality, but serves as more of an introduction. You should review the documentation provided on the website; the wiki has a separate section on using geolocation. Also review the Q&A forums, where you might find that someone has run into the same problem you are facing and the community has provided a solution.

See `http://docs.appcelerator.com/titanium/latest/#!/guide/Location_ Services` for more information.

Associating GPS Information When Saving a Photo

Associating GPS information when you're saving a photo involves the following steps, which are outlined in the following sections:

- Modifying the photo model
- Getting GPS information from a device
- Creating a `CommonJS` library for geolocation
- Updating the feed controller to add location to a photo

Modifying the Photo Model

No changes are required to the photo model to support saving geolocation information with the object. Appcelerator Cloud Services provides custom fields for storing this information. The way you have implemented the photo model allows for additional fields to be passed as parameters to the Save method of the photo model. That is the only change that's required.

Getting GPS Information from a Device

To get geolocation information from the device, Appcelerator has provided a fair bit of functionality out of the box in its location services library. You will be integrating the `Ti.Geolocation` library with your app to get the user's location. This location will be saved with the photo when the user takes the photo. You will use the function once again when you need to find the user's current location in order to display photos near the user.

Since you will be utilizing this functionality in multiple places in the application, it is a good example of where you can integrate a `CommonJS` library for geolocation-related functionality.

Creating a CommonJS Library for Geolocation

You need to create a new file called `geo.js` and save it in the folder called `lib`. The `lib` folder should be inside of the `app` folder in the project directory.

In the `geo.js` file you create a function called `getCurrentLocation` with one parameter, which is a callback. This is the method that will be called when the device completes the request for the current location. If the request is successful, the current geo-coordinates will be returned as a JSON object, similar to the following code:

```
{
    "accuracy": 100,
    "altitude": 0,
    "altitudeAccuracy": null,
    "heading": 0,
    "latitude": 40.493781233333333,
    "longitude": -80.056671,
    "speed": 0,
    "timestamp": 1318426498331
}
```

In the `locationCallbackHandler` function, you want to have your code handle error conditions properly. In order to do that, you will check for the callback returning the `_location` object since that is where you will find the latitude and longitude coordinates. The check first makes sure there was no error from location services, and then checks the location and the location coordinates object for values. If no values are found, an error is returned and the `_location` object is set to null.

Here is the code for the `locationCallbackHandler`. This code will be called whenever the device generates a location event.

```
function locationCallbackHandler(_location) {

  // remove event handler since event was received
  Ti.Geolocation.removeEventListener('location',
                                locationCallbackHandler);

  if (!_location.error && _location && _location.coords) {

    var lat, lng;

    lat = _location.coords.latitude;
    lng = _location.coords.longitude;

    reverseGeocoder(lat, lng, function(_title) {
      locationCallback({
        coords : _location.coords,
        title : _title
      }, null);
      locationCallback = null;
    });
  } else {
    alert('Location Services Error: ' + _location.error);
    _callback(null, _location.error);
  }
}
```

Along with the latitude and longitude values from the device, you can also retrieve a more descriptive name of the location. The Appcelerator framework provides a function for reverse geolocation lookup. You provide the function with the coordinates and it will return a list of locations that match the coordinates. The following code incorporates this functionality so you will have both the coordinates and a descriptive name of the location to save with the photo.

The geolocation function incorporating the reverse lookup is listed next. The function will return a JavaScript object in the callback containing the geo-coordinates and a title string for the location. These values are used when saving the photo.

Here is the reverse geolocation function code that should be added to geo.js:

```
function reverseGeocoder(_lat, _lng, _callback) {
  var title;

  Ti.Geolocation.purpose = "Wiley Alloy App Demo";
```

```
    // callback method converting lat lng into a location/address
    Ti.Geolocation.reverseGeocoder(_lat, _lng, function(_data) {
      if (_data.success) {

        Ti.API.debug("reverseGeo "+JSON.stringify(_data, null, 2));

        var place = _data.places[0];
        if (place.city === "") {
          title = place.address;
        } else {
          title = place.street + " " + place.city;
        }
      } else {
        title = "No Address Found: " + _lat + ", " + _lng;
      }
      _callback(title);
    });
}
```

In the latest version of Appcelerator, the geolocation module has been updated to support better information when running on the Android OS. To get the customized functionality you will need to use the `Titanium.Geolocation.Android`. There is additional information available on the Appcelerator documentation site at `http://docs.appcelerator.com/titanium/3.0/#!/api/Titanium.Geolocation.Android`.

The `getCurrentLocation` function in `geo.js` is in the next code snippet. Notice the exports in the beginning of the function name; they allow you to call the library function when you require the library elsewhere in your code.

This function will create the location event listener that will respond to the device providing the GPS data. The callback handler mentioned previously will process the data and do the reverse geo lookup for additional information on the photo's location.

Add this code to `geo.js`:

```
exports.getCurrentLocation = function(_callback) {

  if (!Ti.Geolocation.getLocationServicesEnabled()) {
    alert('Location Services are not enabled');
    _callback(null, 'Location Services are not enabled');
    return;
  }
```

```
// save in global for use in locationCallbackHandler
locationCallback = _callback;

Ti.Geolocation.purpose = "Wiley Alloy App Demo";
Ti.Geolocation.accuracy = Ti.Geolocation.ACCURACY_HIGH;
Ti.Geolocation.distanceFilter = 10;
Ti.Geolocation.addEventListener('location',
                            locationCallbackHandler);
};
```

Be sure to add the global variable `locationCallback` to the top of the file also.

Here's an example callback response object:

```
{
    "coords": {
        "timestamp": 1374430154064,
        "altitude": 0,
        "speed": -1,
        "latitude": 38.35954666137695,
        "longitude": -75.07244873046875,
        "accuracy": 5,
        "altitudeAccuracy": -1,
        "heading": -1
    },
    "title": "31st Street, Ocean Bay City, Maryland, 21842"
}
```

Updating the Feed Controller to Add Location to a Photo

The feed controller will now need to update the process image function and pass the geolocation information to the photo model when it is saved. This information will be saved with the other the information when the photo is saved to Appcelerator Cloud Services.

The change you will make to the `feed.js` is to first include the new geo library you created by adding the `require` line to the beginning of the file.

```
// load Geolocation library
var geo = require("geo");
```

Now that the library is accessible in `feed.js`, you can call the method to get the current location. Remember that since it is an asynchronous call, you must place the process image functionality inside the `getCurrentLocation` callback.

Since there is a possibility of the `getCurrentLocation` function not being able to successfully return `_coords`, you must account for the error condition in the code. In this case, you will allow for the image to be saved without the `_coords` field set, but you must check for the condition here. You will check for it later when attempting to display the location of the image in the map view.

```
function processImage(_mediaObject, _callback) {

    geo.getCurrentLocation(function(_coords) {

        var parameters = {
            "photo" : _mediaObject,
            "title" : "Sample Photo " + new Date(),
            "photo_sizes[preview]" : "200x200#",
            "photo_sizes[iphone]" : "320x320#",
            // Since we are showing the image immediately
            "photo_sync_sizes[]" : "preview",
        };

        // if we got a location, then set it
        if (_coords) {
            parameters.custom_fields = {
                coordinates : [_coords.coords.longitude,
                                _coords.coords.latitude],
                location_string : _coords.title
            };
        }

        var photo = Alloy.createModel('Photo', parameters);

        photo.save({}, {

            success : function(_model, _response) {
                Ti.API.debug('success: ' + _model.toJSON());
                _callback({
                    model : _model,
                    message : null,
                    success : true
                });
            },
```

```
        error : function(e) { debugger;
            Ti.API.error('error: ' + e.message);
            _callback({
                model : parameters,
                message : e.message,
                success : false
            });
        }
    });
});
}
```

The new function takes the _coords parameter and passes the values as custom fields to the Appcelerator Cloud Services photo object. Appcelerator Cloud Services supports geolocation queries against photo objects so you can find photos using this information stored in the custom fields of the photo. See the Appcelerator Cloud Services for additional information on custom fields at http://docs.appcelerator.com/cloud/latest/#!/guide/ customfields-section-5.

Displaying the Photo Location on a Map

Create the .js controller choosing File ⇨ New ⇨ Alloy Controller from the context menu. Add the code to the mapView.js file. You will display a thumbnail of the photo along with the tile and the location of the image in the header.

You can see that the code takes the args.photo object that is passed and gets the appropriate properties from the object to display in the user interface. You use the predefined image transformation "preview" from Appcelerator Cloud Services and the custom_fields saved with the object to provide an informative display.

You will need the proper layout information included in the style file for the application to create the proper user interface.

Android Support for Google Maps v2

To include support for the new Google Maps in your Android project, you need to follow the directions here on the Appcelerator website on updating your tiapp.xml configuration after setting up the Google service. See http://docs.appcelerator.com/titanium/ latest/#!/guide/Google_Maps_v2_for_Android.

After those changes are made you need to add the map module to your project in tiapp. xml. Add the module to the project the same way you added the Facebook module.

Create the global map object that you will use in this section by adding the following line to the bottom of `alloy.js`:

```
Alloy.Globals.Map = require('ti.map');
```

Add this code to the new controller file you created in `mapView.js`:

```
var args = arguments[0] || {};

// get the photo object from the parameters
var coords = args.photo.get("custom_fields").coordinates[0];
var locationString = args.photo.get("custom_fields").location_
  string;

// create annotation
var annotation = Alloy.Globals.Map.createAnnotation({
    latitude : Number(coords[1]),
    longitude : Number(coords[0]),
    title : args.photo.get("title"),
    subtitle : locationString,
    myid : args.photo.id
    //leftView : imageView,
    // animate : true
});
// set the header
$.thumb.image = args.photo.get("urls")["preview"];
$.title.text = args.photo.get("title");
$.location.text = locationString;

// add them to map
$.mapview.setAnnotations([annotation]);

// set the region around the photo
$.mapview.setRegion({
    latitude : annotation.latitude,
    longitude : annotation.longitude,
    latitudeDelta : 0.040,
    longitudeDelta : 0.040
});
```

Android Support for ActionBar in MapView

Since you are building a cross-platform solution, additional changes are required to support the Android back button and the ActionBar/Title Bar on the Android OS.

The code you need to add will handle the user clicking on the back button; add this code to the end of the `mapView.js` controller file:

```
// detect click on back button
$.getView().addEventListener("androidback",
                                androidBackEventHandler);


// handle the event and close the window
function androidBackEventHandler(_event) {
  _event.cancelBubble = true;
  _event.bubbles = false;
  $.getView().removeEventListener("androidback",
  androidBackEventHandler);
  $.getView().close();
}
```

To get the application to properly respond to a click on a menu icon to go back in the application, add this code to the end of the `mapView.js` controller file:

```
$.getView().addEventListener("open", function() {
  OS_ANDROID && ($.getView().activity.onCreateOptionsMenu =
  function() {
    var actionBar = $.getView().activity.actionBar;
    if (actionBar) {
      actionBar.displayHomeAsUp = true;
      actionBar.onHomeIconItemSelected = function() {
        $.getView().removeEventListener("androidback",
                                      androidBackEventHandler);
        $.getView().close();
      };
    }
  });
});
```

Adding the Map Component to MapView XML

The map view uses a different namespace than the standard Titanium modules so you need to add the ns attribute to the XML element when placing it in the view file. You add a basic window as the container for the map and place the map in the window. There is some basic styling applied to the map object in the `mapview.tss` file.

You can also add text fields to provide more information, such as a title and location of the photo.

```
<Alloy>
    <Window id="mainWindow">
        <View id="header">
            <ImageView id="thumb"></ImageView>
            <View id="textContainer" >
                <Label id="title"></Label>
                <Label id="location"></Label>
            </View>
        </View>
        <View ns="Alloy.Globals.Map" id="mapview" ></View>
    </Window>
</Alloy>
```

Here are the styles, which are added into `mapview.tss` for the layout of the map view and the associated header information. The main objects are the map view and the header. The header contains the thumb, the title, and the location that is laid out separately from the map view.

```
"#mainWindow" : {
    backgroundColor: "white",
    title: "Location Detail",
    top: "0dp",
    layout: "vertical",
    width: "100%",
    height: "100%"
},
"#mapview" : {
    width: "90%",
    height: "290dp" ,
    top: "5dp",
    borderColor: "gray",
    borderWidth: 1
},
```

```
"#thumb" : {
    top: '5dp',
    width: '38dp',
    height: '38dp'
},
"#header" : {
    width: "90%",
    height: Ti.UI.SIZE,
    layout: "horizontal"
},
'#title' : {
    top: '2dp',
    left: '2dp',
    width: Ti.UI.SIZE,
    height: Ti.UI.SIZE,
    textAlign: 'left',
    font: {
        fontSize: '13dp'
    }
},
'#location' : {
    top: '2dp',
    left: '2dp',
    width: Ti.UI.SIZE,
    height: Ti.UI.SIZE,
    textAlign: 'left',
    font: {
        fontSize: '10dp'
    }
},
"#textContainer" : {
    left :"5dp",
    width: Ti.UI.FILL,
    height: Ti.UI.SIZE,
    layout: "vertical"
}
```

The list of photos in the feed view did not originally contain a button to view the location of the photo on the map. The following changes will add a button for the user to view a map.

```
<Alloy>
    <TableViewRow id="row" row_id="">
        <View class="container">
```

```
        <Label id="titleLabel"></Label>
        <View id="imageContainer">
            <ImageView id="image"></ImageView>
        </View>
        <View id="buttonContainer">
            <Button id="commentButton">Comment</Button>
            <Button id="shareButton">Share</Button>
            <Button id="locationButton">Location</Button>
        </View>
    </View>
  </TableViewRow>
</Alloy>
```

Minor modifications to the feedRow.tss file are added to account for the new button added. You will see that the button size has been adjusted to approximately 30% of the width of the view, which allows for some spacing between the buttons. You will also need to adjust the font size some so that the button titles appear properly in the windows.

```
"#commentButton" : {
 width: '30%',
 left: '6dp',
 height: '32dp'
},
"#shareButton" : {
 left: '6dp',
 width: '30%',
 height: '32dp'
}
"#locationButton" : {
 left: '6dp',
 width: '30%',
 height: '32dp'
}
"#commentButton[platform=android]" : {
  height : '42dp'
},
"#shareButton[platform=android]" : {
  height : '42dp'
},
"#locationButton[platform=android]" : {
  height : '42dp'
},
```

Add another event listener to respond to the button click in the feed view. This button click will execute the handler to display the map view. You add the following code to the feed.js controller file.

```
// EVENT HANDLERS
function processTableClicks(_event) { debugger;

    if (_event.source.id === "commentButton") {
        handleCommentButtonClicked(_event);
    } else if (_event.source.id === "locationButton") {
        handleLocationButtonClicked(_event);
    } else if (_event.source.id === "shareButton") {
        alert('Will do this later!!');
    }
}
```

Now you'll add a handler to open the map view in response to the user clicking on the location button when there is a location. Since there is the possibility that a location was not saved when the photo was taken, you need to check the custom_fields returned from the photo for the coordinates object. If there is no field, the detail view with the map will not be displayed and the user will be alerted.

```
function handleLocationButtonClicked(_event) {

    var collection = Alloy.Collections.instance("Photo");
    var model = collection.get(_event.row.row_id);

    var customFields = model.get("custom_fields");

    if (customFields && customFields.coordinates) {
        var mapController = Alloy.createController("mapView", {
            photo : model,
            parentController : $
        });

        // open the view
  Alloy.Globals.openCurrentTabWindow(mapController.getView());
    } else {
        alert("No Location was Saved with Photo");
    }
}
```

If you run your application, you should see there are now three buttons on each row under the photo. The new Location button has been added. If you clicked it right now it would display an alert saying that no location is found. Figures 9-1 and 9-2 show the new row and alert in iOS and Android, respectively.

FIGURE 9-1: The new feedRow with a Location link on iOS.

FIGURE 9-2: The new feedRow with a Location button on Android.

Now take a photo on your device and wait for the view to update and display the new photo on your feed list. After the photo appears on your feed list, click the Location button. You should see a view of the map showing where the photo was just taken. The Location Detail page should look similar to Figures 9-3 and 9-4.

FIGURE 9-3: Photo location detail view on iOS.

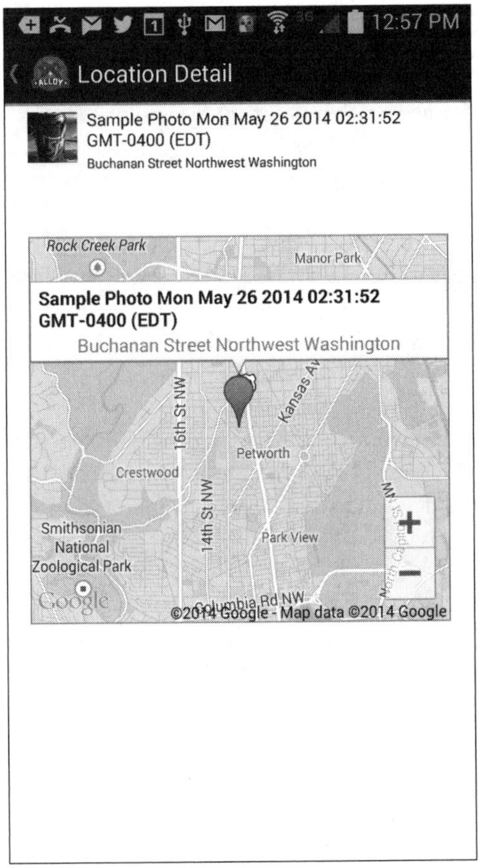

FIGURE 9-4: Photo location detail view on Android.

Displaying a Map of Photos Near Your Location

You have created a view that shows the location of the one photo on the map; the next feature will show all of the photos in the existing list in a map view. This example will try to keep things simple by just showing the first 25 images, but a more complex example could potentially update the map view as the user scrolls into new regions and adds additional image locations.

Querying ACS Photo Objects Using Your Current Location

Appcelerator Cloud Services provides support for geolocation-based queries on objects that contain the `custom_field` coordinates. Earlier in the chapter, you added that support to the photos that were saved so you should have data ready to be queried.

You will need to update the photo model in `photo.js` with a custom function to execute this query. This function could be incorporated in the `feeds.js` controller, but adding it to the photo model separates the functionality by placing it in a more appropriate place. This also allows for the query to be used in other places of the application without duplicating code. See `http://docs.appcelerator.com/cloud/latest/#!/guide/search_query`.

The new function will convert the `distance` parameter to radians since the Appcelerator Cloud Services API needs the parameter converted. Finally, the function will execute the collection's `fetch` function to return the photos the desired distance from current location.

Add the following code to the `photos.js` model as a function to extend the collection object. Be sure to add the code to the collection and not the model.

```
findPhotosNearMe :function(_user, _location, _distance, _options) {
  var collection = this;

  // convert distance to radians if provided
  var distance = _distance ? (_distance / 3959) : 0.00126;

  if (_location === null) {
    _options.error("Could Not Find Photos");
    return;
  }
  // get all of the current users friends
  _user.getFriends(function(_resp) {
    if (_resp.success) { debugger;

      var idList = _.pluck(_resp.collection.models, "id");
      idList.push(_user.id);

      // first we get the current location
      var coords = [];
      coords.push(_location.coords.longitude);
```

```
      coords.push(_location.coords.latitude);

      // set up where parameters
      var where_params = {
        "user_id" : {
          "$in" : idList
        },
        "coordinates" : {
          "$nearSphere" : coords,
          "$maxDistance" : distance // 5 miles in
          // radians
        }
      };
      // set the where params on the query
      _options.data = _options.data || {};
      _options.data.per_page = 25;
      _options.data.where = JSON.stringify(where_params);

      // execute the query
      collection.fetch(_options);
    } else {
      _options.error("Could Not Find Photos");
      return;
    }
  });
}
```

Remember to do the proper error-checking in case there is an issue getting the device's current location. The function does check to see if the `_location` parameter is valid; otherwise, it returns an error.

Updating the User Interface to Show a Map View

For the user interface, you will add a map view to the main feed tab and toggle the view between a list of items and a map view showing the photos closest to your current location.

In the `feed.xml` view file you will add a section for the tabbed button on iOS, which will be used to toggle between the two views. This code should be added directly above the location in the file where the table view is created.

Since you are building a cross-platform solution, you need to account for the differences between iOS and Android devices. The following code is added to support the selection of the view to be either the list of photos or the map view of the photos closest to the current location.

```
<View id="filterContainer" >
    <TabbedBar id="filter" platform="ios" >
        <Labels>
            <Label>List</Label>
            <Label>Map</Label>
        </Labels>
    </TabbedBar>
</View>
```

Now for Android support, you use the `Picker` control, adding it to the same `filterContainer` element just below the iOS `TabbedBar` control. After the Android or iOS code is added, the `filterContainer` should look similar to the following code.

```
<View id="filterContainer" >
    <TabbedBar id="filter" platform="ios">
        <Labels>
            <Label >List</Label>
            <Label >Map</Label>
        </Labels>
    </TabbedBar>
    <View id="androidPickerContainer" platform="android">
      <Picker id="filter" selectionIndicator="true">
        <PickerColumn id="column1">
            <PickerRow title="List"/>
            <PickerRow title="Map"/>
        </PickerColumn>
      </Picker>
    </View>
</View>
```

You will need to add the associated changes to the `feed.tss` file to properly layout the `tabbedbar` on the `feedWindow`. You are laying out these larger view objects vertically so they will appear in the screen from top to bottom.

```
"#feedWindow" : {
    layout: "vertical"
},
"#filterContainer" : {
    top: "5dp",
    height: Ti.UI.SIZE,
    width: "70%"
},
"#filter[platform=ios]" : {
    style: Ti.UI.iPhone.SystemButtonStyle.BAR,
    height: 30,
    width: "70%"
}
"#filter[platform=android]" : {
    height: "38dp",
    width: "70%"
},
'#androidPickerContainer' : {
    height: Ti.UI.SIZE,
    width: Ti.UI.SIZE,
    backgroundColor : '#A3A3A3'
},
"#mapview" : {
    width: "90%",
    height: Ti.UI.FILL,
    top: "5dp",
    bottom: "5dp",
    borderColor: "gray",
    borderWidth: 1,
    visible: false
},
"#feedTable" : {
    width: Ti.UI.FILL,
    height: Ti.UI.FILL
}
```

The map view will be shown when the user selects the item on the `tabbedBar` by hiding the `tableView` and showing the map view. The `tableView` will be displayed when the user clicks the list item on the `tabbedBar`. See Figures 9-5 and 9-6.

FIGURE 9-5: The new tabbed button on an iOS screen.

The `feed.xml` view will be changed to place both the `tableView` and the `mapView` on top of one another on the view. You will need to replace the code in the `feed.xml` file where the table is currently created, and replace it with the following code.

```xml
<View id="viewContainer">
    <TableView id="feedTable"></TableView>
    <View ns="Alloy.Globals.Map" id="mapview" ></View>
</View>
```

FIGURE 9-6: The new picker on an Android screen.

Changes in the feed.js Controller

The controller will have quite a few changes, but they are pretty straightforward and similar to code you have written already. First, you need to create the listener, handler pair to respond to the click on the tabbedBar buttons or to the UI.Picker on Android that you added in the feed.xml view.

```
$.filter.addEventListener( OS_IOS ? 'click':'change',
                        filterTabbedBarClicked);
```

Next is the handler function, where the `filterTabbedBarClicked` method is passed an event object that contains the index of the button item clicked in the `tabbedBar` or the `rowIndex` of the item clicked in the `UI.Picker`. You will then use the value called `itemSelected` to take the appropriate action and update the user interface by showing either the map view or the list view.

```
function filterTabbedBarClicked(_event) {
    var itemSelected = OS_IOS ? _event.index : _event.rowIndex;
    switch (itemSelected) {
        case 0 :
            // List View Display
            $.mapview.visible = false;
            $.feedTable.visible = true;
            break;
        case 1 :
            // Map View Display
            $.feedTable.visible = false;
            $.mapview.visible = true;
            showLocalImages();
            break;
    }
}
```

You have seen the functions used to display the list view from earlier in the book; now you will add two functions to the `feed.js` controller to display the same information in a map view relative to the current location of the user.

The first function you will create is `showLocalImages`. This function will call the extended method you added to the photo model to find all images within a specified distance from the user. The method follows the familiar pattern of creating the collection, setting the query parameters, and then handling the success or error conditions. Add the following function to the `feed.js` controller file:

```
function showLocalImages() {
    // create new photo collection
    $.locationCollection = Alloy.createCollection('photo');

    // find all photos within five miles of current location
    geo.getCurrentLocation(function(_coords) {
        var user = Alloy.Globals.currentUser;

        $.locationCollection.findPhotosNearMe(user, _coords, 5, {
```

```
    success : function(_collection, _response) {
      Ti.API.info(JSON.stringify(_collection));

      // add the annotations/map pins to map
      if (_collection.models.length) {
        addPhotosToMap(_collection);
      } else {
        alert("No Local Images Found");
        filterTabbedBarClicked({
          index : 0,
          rowIndex : 0,
        });

        if (OS_ANDROID) {
          $.filter.setSelectedRow(0, 0, false);
        } else {
          $.filter.setIndex(0);
        }
      }
    },
    error : function(error) {
      alert('Error loading Feed ' + e.message);
      Ti.API.error(JSON.stringify(error));
    }
  });
});
}
```

If the query is successful, the response will be a collection of images, which will be passed to the next function called `addPhotosToMap`. This function will use the geo-coordinates in the photo model to create map annotations to place on the map. The use of these Appcelerator Framework API calls for map functionality should be familiar by now. There is one difference in that now you will create an array of annotations and place them all on the map at once.

```
function addPhotosToMap(_collection) {
  var annotationArray = [];
  var lastLat;

  // remove all annotations from map
  $.mapview.removeAllAnnotations();

  var annotationRightButton = function() {
```

```
    var button = Ti.UI.createButton({
      title : "X",
    });
    return button;
  };

  for (var i in _collection.models) {
    var mapData = _collection.models[i].toJSON();
    var coords = mapData.custom_fields.coordinates;
    var annotation = Alloy.Globals.Map.createAnnotation({
      latitude : Number(coords[0][1]),
      longitude : Number(coords[0][0]),
      subtitle : mapData.custom_fields.location_string,
      title : mapData.title,
      //animate : true,
      data : _collection.models[i].clone()
    });

    if (OS_IOS) {
      annotation.setPincolor(Alloy.Globals.Map.ANNOTATION_RED);
      annotation.setRightButton(Titanium.UI.iPhone.SystemButton.
      DISCLOSURE);
    } else {
      annotation.setRightButton(annotationRightButton);
    }
    annotationArray.push(annotation);

  }

  // calculate the map region based on the annotations
  var region = geo.calculateMapRegion(annotationArray);
  $.mapview.setRegion(region);

  // add the annotations to the map
  $.mapview.setAnnotations(annotationArray);
}
```

You can see in this code that you are first ensuring there are no annotations on the map by removing them all, and then creating an array of the new annotations to add to the map.

There is another helper function that was added to geo.js library that calculates the region of the map based on the annotations that are being added. See Figures 9-7 and 9-8 for the end result.

FIGURE 9-7: Map view with pins for local images on iOS.

FIGURE 9-8: Map view with pins for local images on Android.

Responding to Clicks on Map Annotations

When the user clicks on the map annotations, you want to show a detail screen of the image similar to what the user would see if the image was scrolled on the list view. It would be ideal to reuse the code from the list view for this purpose.

Changes to `feed.js` will require an additional event listener and handler pair to capture the click on the map and the map annotation.

```
$.mapview.addEventListener('click', mapAnnotationClicked);
```

Next is the function called `mapAnnotationClicked`, which responds to the event. In the function, you will look for a click on the `rightbutton` of the map annotation to indicate the user's desire to show the details for the image represented by the map pin.

The `click` event function receives the event with the annotation object and a `clicksource` property, which lets you know if the `rightbutton` was selected. If the `rightbutton` was selected, you will open a new `mapDetail.js` controller and pass it the necessary information for displaying and handling clicks in the window.

```
function mapAnnotationClicked(_event) {
  // get event properties
  var annotation = _event.annotation;
  //get the Myid from annotation
  var clickSource = _event.clicksource;

  var showDetails = false;

  if (OS_IOS) {
    showDetails = (clickSource === 'rightButton');
  } else {
    showDetails =
      (clickSource === 'subtitle' || clickSource === 'title');
  }

  if (showDetails) {

    // load the mapDetail controller
    var mapDetailCtrl = Alloy.createController('mapDetail', {
      photo : annotation.data,
      parentController : $,
      clickHandler : processTableClicks
    });

    // open the view
    Alloy.Globals.openCurrentTabWindow(mapDetailCtrl.getView());

  } else {
    Ti.API.info('clickSource ' + clickSource);
  }
};
```

There is some interesting reuse of code here. Notice you are passing in the `clickHandler` for the `tableRow`, `processTableClicks`. If you remember, the click handler for the table row handles the clicks on the `comment`, `share`, and `location` buttons. In this map detail view, the application needs to respond to those clicks and perform the appropriate actions. The application will be reusing this functionality in the `mapDetail` controller by passing the event object back to the parent controller to execute the proper actions for displaying comments and sharing information on the photo.

For this to work properly, the application will need to be modified to handle the different event objects that will be sent from the `mapDetail` view. The `processTableClicks` function passes control to the specific button handler based on the button ID; each of these functions is changed to add a condition for detecting if the event came from the `tableRow` or if it came from the `mapDetail` controller. If the click did not come from the `tableRow`, the application will expect to find the event information in the data field as opposed to attempting to retrieve it from the collection on the page.

The changes to the `feed.js` controller `handleCommentButtonClicked` is listed here:

```
function handleCommentButtonClicked(_event) {
  var collection, model = null;

  // handle call from mapDetail or feedRow
  if (!_event.row) {
    model = _event.data;
  } else {
    collection = Alloy.Collections.instance("Photo");
    model = collection.get(_event.row.row_id);
  }

  var controller = Alloy.createController("comment", {
    photo : model,
    parentController : $
  });

  // initialize the data in the view, load content
  controller.initialize();

  // open the view
  Alloy.Globals.openCurrentTabWindow(controller.getView());

}
```

Now you will create the new controller named `mapDetail`. Starting with the `mapDetail.xml` view file, you will create the interface.

```
<Alloy>
    <Window id="mainWindow"  fullscreen="false" >
        <View class="container">
            <Label id="titleLabel"></Label>
            <View id="imageContainer">
                <ImageView id="image"></ImageView>
            </View>
            <View id="buttonContainer">
                <Button id="commentButton">Comment</Button>
                <Button id="shareButton">Share</Button>
            </View>
        </View>
    </Window>
</Alloy>
```

The `mapDetail.tss` style file is very similar to the `feedRow.tss` style except for the removal of the location button since it is not needed in the map detail. See Figures 9-9 and 9-10.

```
'.container': {
  layout: 'vertical',
  width: '90%'
},
'#buttonContainer': {
  layout: 'horizontal',
  width: Ti.UI.FILL,
  height: '42dp'
},
'#image': {
  top: '5dp',
  left: '14dp',
  width: '270dp',
  height: '270dp'
},
'#imageContainer': {
  width: '300dp',
  height: '284dp'
},
'#commentButton': {
  left: '26dp',
  width: '40%',
```

```
    height: '32dp'
  },
  '#shareButton': {
    left: '10dp',
    width: '40%',
    height: '32dp'
  }
  '#commentButton[platform=android]': {
    height: '42dp'
  },
  '#shareButton[platform=android]': {
    height: '42dp'
  }
```

FIGURE 9-9: Selected pin on iOS; user expects to see detail when clicked.

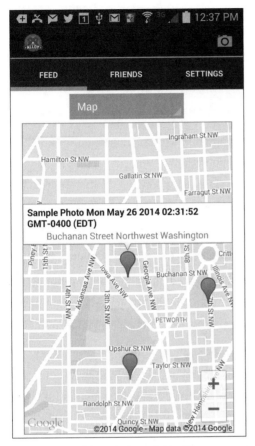

FIGURE 9-10: Selected pin on Android; user expects to see detail when clicked.

Creating the controller for `mapDetail.js` is very similar to the code used in `feedRow.js` except for how the application will handle clicks events on the view. The application uses the parameters passed in on creation of the controller to set the image and the labels appropriately. The interesting code is how the events are handled on the view.

The `eventListener` assigned to the `buttonContainer` gets the model objects that were passed into the view and adds them to the event object. The event object is then passed on to the `clickHander` that was provided to the controller when it was created. This is the `clickHandler processTableClicks` that was created in `feed.js`.

```
// Get the parameters passed into the controller
var parameters = arguments[0] || {};
var currentPhoto = parameters.photo || {};
```

```
var parentController = parameters.parentController || {};

$.image.image = currentPhoto.attributes.urls.preview;
$.titleLabel.text = currentPhoto.attributes.title || '';

// get comment count from object
var count = currentPhoto.attributes.reviews_count !== undefined ?
  currentPhoto.attributes.reviews_count : 0;

// modify the button title to show the comment count
// if there are comments already associated to photo
if (count !== 0) {
  $.commentButton.title = "Comments (" + count + ")";
}

$.buttonContainer.addEventListener('click', function(_event) {
  // add the model information as data to event
  _event.data = currentPhoto;
  parameters.clickHandler(_event);
});

$.getView().addEventListener("androidback",
  androidBackEventHandler);

function androidBackEventHandler(_event) {
  _event.cancelBubble = true;
  _event.bubbles = false;
  $.getView().removeEventListener("androidback",
  androidBackEventHandler);
  $.getView().close();
}

// Set up the menus and actionBar for Android if necessary
$.getView().addEventListener("open", function() {
  OS_ANDROID && ($.getView().activity.onCreateOptionsMenu =
    function() {
      var actionBar = $.getView().activity.actionBar;
      if (actionBar) {
        actionBar.displayHomeAsUp = true;
        actionBar.onHomeIconItemSelected = function() {
          $.getView().removeEventListener("androidback",
                                androidBackEventHandler);
```

```
        $.getView().close();
    };
  }
 });
});
```

The application should now display the map pins indicating where you or your friends took pictures. Remember you will most likely need to take new photos on your device to get the locations saved with the photos.

Once you click on the map annotations, the application should display a photo detail page that looks similar to Figure 9-11 or 9-12, depending on your platform.

FIGURE 9-11: Detail view displayed when annotation is clicked on iOS.

FIGURE 9-12: Detail view displayed when annotation is clicked on Android.

Summary

This chapter covered the integration of maps and geolocation. Location-aware applications are well suited for mobile devices since the GPS is integrated into the operating system. The combination of the ease of use provided by the Appcelerator Titanium map module and the Appcelerator Cloud Services location-based queries open up tremendous possibilities of what can be accomplished very quickly with the Appcelerator toolset.

Chapter 10
Sharing via Facebook, Email, and Twitter

APPCELERATOR TITANIUM PROVIDES excellent support for sharing using the Facebook module and also for sharing via email if it is properly configured on the device. There are more options for sharing, specifically Twitter, but that is not currently incorporated into the framework although there are various open source solutions to support that functionality.

In this chapter, you will integrate sharing to the Facebook wall, sharing the photo to the user's Facebook photo album, sharing the photo on Twitter, and finally sharing the photo as an attachment through email.

The examples here use the Facebook module and custom code from Appcelerator Alloy social.js module for Twitter integration. There are open source modules to integrate social media using the native APIs and the IOS 6 native integration of Facebook and Twitter that can be found in the Appcelerator Marketplace and on Github.

Creating the CommonJS Library for Sharing Functions

To get started, you need to create a new file called sharing.js and add it to the lib folder created previously. In the sharing.js library file you will start off by ensuring that the Facebook module has been loaded. Add the following code to the top of the sharing.js library file:

```
// if facebook not loaded, then load it
if (!Alloy.Globals.FB) {
  Alloy.Globals.FB = require('facebook');
}

// Enabling single sign on using FB
Alloy.Globals.FB.forceDialogAuth = false;
```

```
// get the app id
Alloy.Globals.FB.appid =
        Ti.App.Properties.getString("ti.facebook.appid");
```

The application will provide the users with three choices for sharing:

- Posting a message to the user's Facebook wall.

- Posting the picture to the user's Facebook Album.

- Sharing the image through the user's email.

The Appcelerator Titanium Framework has an option dialog that's used to allow the user to select the method of sharing (see Figures 10-1 and 10-2). Once the user selects a share method, the application will verify the Facebook permission, if necessary, and then call the appropriate function from the share library.

FIGURE 10-1: Sharing options for sharing a photo on iOS.

FIGURE 10-2: Sharing options for sharing a photo on Android.

```
exports.sharingOptions = function(_options) {

  var dialog, params;

  if (OS_ANDROID) {
    params = {
      options : ['Facebook Feed', 'Facebook Photo', 'Email'],
      buttonNames : ['Cancel'],
      title : 'Share Photo'
    };
  } else {
    params = {
      options : [
```

```
        'Facebook Feed', 'Facebook Photo',
        'Email', 'Cancel'
      ],
      cancel : 3,
      title : 'Share Photo'
    };
  }

  dialog = Titanium.UI.createOptionDialog(params);
  // add event listener
  dialog.addEventListener('click', function(e) {

    // user clicked cancel
    if ( OS_ANDROID && e.button) {
      return;
    }

    if (e.index === 0) {
      prepForFacebookShare(function() {
        shareWithFacebookDialog(_options.model);
      });
    } else if (e.index === 1) {
      prepForFacebookShare(function() {
        shareFacebookPhoto(_options.model);
      });
    } else if (e.index === 2) {
      shareWithEmailDialog(_options.model);
    }
  });

  // show the dialog
  dialog.show();

};
```

There are a few things you should notice. The sharingOptions method is the only method exported from this library; all of the other functions are accessible only from this library. The dialog is created with the options and the event listener determines which button was clicked.

Facebook Permissions and Reauthorization

The new Facebook module for Appcelerator supports the latest Facebook SDK requirements for separating logging in to Facebook from requesting specific permissions for posting to the user's wall or feed. In order to properly allow users to share the photos in the application, the application must first check if the user has logged in to Facebook and then confirm that the user has provided the application with the proper permissions. See `http://docs.appcelerator.com/titanium/latest/#!/api/Modules.Facebook` for more information.

Since the user in the application can create an account through Facebook or with an email and a password, the application needs to verify the user's login status before verifying permission. The following code is the first step in allowing sharing from the app.

Facebook's new authorization process allows you to reauthorize the user to verify permissions. The initial login for a user's account can only request the minimum access; the following code checks to see if the users have given the app the proper permission to post photos to their stream.

Add this code to `sharing.js`:

```
function checkPermissions(_permissions, _callback) {
  var FB = Alloy.Globals.FB;
  var query = "SELECT " + _permissions + " FROM permissions WHERE
uid = me()";
  FB.request("fql.query", {
    query : query
  }, function(resp) {
    try {
      resp.result = JSON.parse(resp.result);
      _callback(resp);
    } catch (e) {
      _callback(resp);
    }
  });
};
```

This code uses the Appcelerator Facebook module to perform a Facebook query against the users account to see if the specified permission is available on the account. The Facebook module for Appcelerator supports the Facebook Query Language, the Facebook Graph API, and specific Facebook dialogs; you will use the Facebook Share dialog in the next section.

In the function `prepForFacebookShare`, the application checks the logged in status. If the user is not logged in, it provides the user the opportunity to log in using the Facebook authorize method. At this point the application flow is handled by the login event callback function `loginCB`. If the user successfully logs in to Facebook, the application flow will then call the function `prepForFacebookShare` again, this time with the appropriate credentials.

When the application calls `prepForFacebookShare` with the appropriate appID and settings, the application will first check if the permission is available using the `checkPermissions` function. If permission is not available, it will reauthorize the user with the new permission request and then move on. If the user approves the authorization for the additional permissions, then the application is now prepared for sharing on Facebook. The code for the function is listed here, and should be added to `sharing.js`:

```javascript
function prepForFacebookShare(_callback) {

  var FB = Alloy.Globals.FB;

  var loginCB = function(e) {
    if (e.success) {
      prepForFacebookShare(_callback);
    } else if (e.error) {
      alert(e.error);
    }
    // remove event listener now that we are done
    FB.removeEventListener('login', loginCB);
    return;
  };

  // if not logged in then log user in and then try again
  if (FB.loggedIn === false) {
    FB.addEventListener('login', loginCB);
    FB.authorize();
  } else {

    // First make sure this permission exists for user
    checkPermissions('publish_stream', function(_response) {
      var hasPermission=(_response.result[0].publish_stream === 1);
      if (_response.success && hasPermission) {
        _callback();
      } else {
        // if not try and get the permission
        FB.reauthorize(['publish_stream'], 'me', function(e) {
          if (e.success) {
```

```
            _callback();
        } else {
            alert('Authorization failed: ' + e.error);
        }
    });
  }
});
}
}
```

Sharing to the Facebook Wall

All of the sharing starts with clicking the Share button on the `feed.xml` or `mapDetail.xml` view. Since the application responds to click events on the Share button in the `feed.js` controller, the code changes will begin there.

Feed.js Controller Changes

The first change to the application is to include the new library called `share.js` in the controller file for the feed. At the top of the `feed.js` controller file, add this line:

```
// load sharing library
var sharing = require("sharing");
```

Next update the `handleShareButtonClicked` function to support the click on the `shareButton`. A click on the `shareButton` will call the new function called `handleShareButtonClicked`.

```
function processTableClicks(_event) {
  if (_event.source.id === "commentButton") {
    handleCommentButtonClicked(_event);
  } else if (_event.source.id === "locationButton") {
    handleLocationButtonClicked(_event);
  } else if (_event.source.id === "shareButton") {
    handleShareButtonClicked(_event);
  }
}
```

The function `handleShareButtonClicked` is structured the same as `handleComment ButtonClicked`; retrieve the proper model that is associated with the click and call the appropriate function to perform the action. In this case, I introduce a new CommonJS library to handle all of the sharing functionality for the application.

Here is the code for the `handleShareButtonClicked` function:

```
function handleShareButtonClicked(_event) {
  var collection, model;

  if (!_event.row) {
    model = _event.data;
  } else {
    collection = Alloy.Collections.instance("Photo");
    model = collection.get(_event.row.row_id);
  }

  // commonjs library for sharing
  sharing.sharingOptions({
    model : model
  });
}
```

For sharing to the user's wall, the application will use the Appcelerator Titanium Framework Facebook module, which provides access to the Facebook dialog API. See the specific Appcelerator documentation at `http://docs.appcelerator.com/titanium/latest/#!/api/Modules.Facebook`.

Add this code to `sharing.js`:

```
function shareWithFacebookDialog(_model) {

  var data = {
    link : _model.attributes.urls.original,
    name : "tiGram Wiley Sample App",
    message : " ACS Alloy Sample App and the photo",
    caption : _model.attributes.title,
    picture : _model.attributes.urls.preview,
    description : "None"
  };

  Alloy.Globals.FB.dialog("feed", data, function(e) {
    if (e.success && e.result) {
      alert("Success!");
    } else {
      if (e.error) {
```

```
        alert(e.error);
      } else {
        alert("User canceled dialog.");
      }
    }
  });
}
```

So you can test the functions as you move through the chapter, add the other two functions from the `shareOptions` method as empty stubs so the application can compile. Add the stubbed-out methods to `sharing.js`:

```
function shareFacebookPhoto(_model) {}
function shareWithEmailDialog(_model) {}
```

Using the Facebook Feed dialog the application sets up the parameters for the function from the photo model that is passed into the method from the click event handler. The application provides the URL for the original image upload, which should be the larger of the images. The application also provides a title from the model and the preview URL for a smaller version of the image to display in the feed.

Run the application and select the Facebook Feed option to see the image uploaded to your Facebook Feed. If you have not logged in with Facebook yet, the application will prompt you to and request the appropriate permissions. See Figure 10-3; note that the screens look very similar so only the iOS version is presented here.

Sharing to the Facebook Album

Sharing to the photo album is a bit more complex since the Facebook module requires the image blob, not an URL for uploading the image. An additional share library function can be added to download the file from Appcelerator Cloud Services and then you can pass the image blob to the Facebook module for sharing.

Image Download Helper Function

The function takes an URL to download and a path to save the file. Since in some scenarios, there is no need to save the file, the application just needs the blob. The function will return the blob only if there is no _path specified when calling the function. The object returned from the callback will contain success as true and a property blob, which will contain the image.

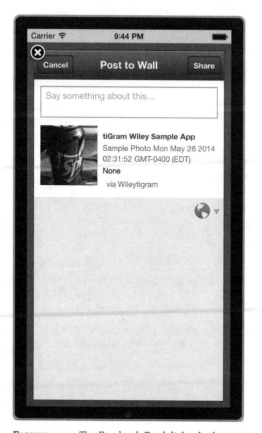

FIGURE 10-3: The Facebook Feed dialog looks pretty much the same on both platforms.

The function itself makes an HTTP request to download the file. If the `http.onload` method is called, the function will write the response data to the file created based on the `_path` parameter and the `applicationDataDirectory`. If the application does not specify a `_path` parameter, the response data will be returned as a blob.

Add this code to the `sharing.js` library file:

```
function downloadFile(url, _path, _callback) {
  Alloy.Globals.PW.showIndicator("Downloading File", true);
  _path && Ti.API.debug("downloading " + url + "  as " + _path);

  var f, fd, http;

  http = Ti.Network.createHTTPClient({
    ondatastream : function(e) {
      // update the caller with information on download
```

```
    if (e.progress > 0) {
      Alloy.Globals.PW.setProgressValue &&
Alloy.Globals.PW.setProgressValue(e.progress);
    }
  }
});

http.open("GET", url);

http.onload = function() {

  if (_path) {
    if (Ti.Filesystem.isExternalStoragePresent()) {
      fd = Ti.Filesystem.externalStorageDirectory;
    } else {
      // No SD or iOS
      fd = Ti.Filesystem.applicationDataDirectory;
    }

    // get the file
    f = Ti.Filesystem.getFile(fd, _path);

    // delete if already exists
    if (f.exists()) {
      f.deleteFile();
      f = Ti.Filesystem.getFile(fd, _path);
    }

    // write blob to file
    f.write(http.responseData);
    Alloy.Globals.PW.hideIndicator();

    _callback && _callback({
      success : true,
      nativePath : f.nativePath
    });

  } else {
    Alloy.Globals.PW.hideIndicator();
    // if no path, the just return the blob
    _callback && _callback({
      success : true,
      nativePath : null,
      blob : http.responseData
    });
```

```
    }
  };
  // if error return information
  http.onerror = function(e) {
    Alloy.Globals.PW.hideIndicator();
    _callback && _callback({
      success : false,
      nativePath : null,
      error : e
    });

  };

  http.send();
};
```

Revisiting and Refactoring the Progress Window Library

If you look carefully you will see that there is a new parameter added to the `Alloy.Globals.PW.showIndicator` function; that parameter indicates if you want to display a progress bar in the view along with the message. The progress bar is used to provide feedback to the users when the file is being downloaded from the server. When sharing images to social media, the application is using a higher-resolution image than what is displayed on the devices, so there will be a noticeable delay in the application. Providing the users with a visual cue that there is a long-running task is just good design.

To support this new parameter, you will need to make some changes to the `progress Window.js` library. When the parameter is set to true, you will display the progress bar instead of just loading a message. To support the progress bar, you also need to include a method to update the progress as the file is downloaded; the `setProgressValue` method is provided for that purpose.

Replace the contents of the file with the following listing; the change to the library impacted all the methods:

```
var activityIndicator, showingIndicator,
    activityIndicatorWindow, progressTimeout;
var androidContainer = null;

exports.showIndicator = function(_messageString, _progressBar) {
```

```
// if Android, we need a container for the progress bar to
// make it more visible
if (OS_ANDROID) {
  androidContainer = Ti.UI.createView({
    top : "200dp",
    width : Ti.UI.FILL,
    height : Ti.UI.SIZE,
    opacity : 1.0,
    backgroundColor : 'black',
    color : 'black',
    visible : true
  });
}

activityIndicatorWindow = Titanium.UI.createWindow({
  top : 0,
  left : 0,
  width : "100%",
  height : "100%",
  backgroundColor : "#58585A",
  opacity : .7,
  fullscreen : true
});

if (_progressBar === true) {
  // adjust spacing, size and color based on platform
  activityIndicator = Ti.UI.createProgressBar({
    style : OS_IOS && Titanium.UI.iPhone.ProgressBarStyle.PLAIN,
    top : ( OS_IOS ? "200dp" : '10dp'),
    bottom : ( OS_ANDROID ? '10dp' : undefined),
    left : "30dp",
    right : "30dp",
    min : 0,
    max : 1,
    value : 0,
    message : _messageString || "Loading, please wait.",
    color : "white",
    font : {
      fontSize : '20dp',
      fontWeight : "bold"
    },
    opacity : 1.0,
    backgroundColor : ( OS_ANDROID ? 'black' : 'transparent')
```

```
    });
  } else {
    activityIndicator = Ti.UI.createActivityIndicator({
      style : OS_IOS ? Ti.UI.iPhone.ActivityIndicatorStyle.BIG :
  Ti.UI.ActivityIndicatorStyle.BIG,
      top : "10dp",
      right : "30dp",
      bottom : "10dp",
      left : "30dp",
      message : _messageString || "Loading, please wait.",
      color : "white",
      font : {
        fontSize : '20dp',
        fontWeight : "bold"
      },
    });
  }

  // if Android, you need to account for a container when
  // setting up the window for display
  if (OS_ANDROID) {
    androidContainer.add(activityIndicator);
    activityIndicatorWindow.add(androidContainer);
    activityIndicatorWindow.open();
  } else {
    activityIndicatorWindow.add(activityIndicator);
    activityIndicatorWindow.open();
  }

  activityIndicator.show();
  showingIndicator = true;

  // safety catch all to ensure the screen clears
  // after 25 seconds
  progressTimeout = setTimeout(function() {
    exports.hideIndicator();
  }, 35000);
};

exports.setProgressValue = function(_value) {
  activityIndicator && activityIndicator.setValue(_value);
};
```

```
exports.hideIndicator = function() {

  if (progressTimeout) {
    clearTimeout(progressTimeout);
    progressTimeout = null;
  }

  if (!showingIndicator) {
    return;
  }

  activityIndicator.hide();

  // if android, you need to account for a container when
  // cleaning up the window
  if (OS_ANDROID) {
    androidContainer.remove(activityIndicator);
    activityIndicatorWindow.remove(androidContainer);
    androidContainer = null;
  } else {
    activityIndicator &&
  activityIndicatorWindow.remove(activityIndicator);
  }
  activityIndicatorWindow.close();
  activityIndicatorWindow = null;

  // clean up variables
  showingIndicator = false;
  activityIndicator = null;
};
```

Sharing to a Facebook Album

Now that the application has a way to get the image as a blob, the way to upload the image to the user's Facebook account is simply to call the proper Facebook Graph API calls.

```
function shareFacebookPhoto(_model) {

  var dataModel = _model.attributes;
  var message;

  // get image as blob, null passed for _path
  downloadFile(dataModel.urls.original, null, function(_data) {
```

```
if (_data.success === false) {
  alert("Error downloading file for sharing");
  return;
}

message = dataModel.title;
message += "\nfrom ACS & Alloy Sample App";

var data = {
  message : message,
  picture : _data.blob,
};

Alloy.Globals.PW.showIndicator("Uploading File to Facebook",
false);

// Now post the downloaded photo
Alloy.Globals.FB.requestWithGraphPath('me/photos', data,
'POST', function(e) {
  Alloy.Globals.PW.hideIndicator();
  if (e.success) {
    alert("Success! From Facebook: ");
  } else {
    if (e.error) {
      alert('Error Posting Photo to Album ' + e.error);
    } else {
      alert("Unknown result");
    }
  }

});
});
};
```

Sharing an Image as an Email Attachment

Sharing the image as an email attachment requires that there is an email account configured on the device.

The Appcelerator Titanium Framework provides API access to an email dialog box that will present the user with the platform-specific interface for sending email messages. Using this API, the application will prepopulate the mail message with some content from the photo model and provide the attachment of the original photo along with a link to the photo.

This email dialog requires that the device is configured for mail, so the first check is to confirm mail is available.

The application will send HTML-formatted mail so when the `emailDialog` is initialized the HTML property is set to `true`.

The download helper function discussed in the previous section will be utilized in this attachment function since the attachment is read from a file to be associated with the email.

All of the additional fields are retrieved from the photo model that is passed to the function from the click event handler.

```
function shareWithEmailDialog(_model) {

  var dataModel = _model.attributes;

  var emailDialog = Ti.UI.createEmailDialog({
    html : true
  });

  if (emailDialog.isSupported() === false) {
    alert("Email is not configured for this device");
    return;
  }

  emailDialog.subject = " Wiley ACS & Alloy Sample App";
  emailDialog.messageBody = '<html>' + dataModel.title + '<br/>';
  emailDialog.messageBody += '<a href="' + dataModel.urls.original;
  emailDialog.messageBody += '">Link to original image</a>';
  emailDialog.messageBody += '</html>';

  downloadFile(_model.attributes.urls.original, "temp.jpeg",
  function(_data) {

    if (_data.success === false) {
      alert("Error downloading file\n Image not shared!");
      return;
    }

    var f = Ti.Filesystem.getFile(_data.nativePath);
    emailDialog.addAttachment(f);

    emailDialog.addEventListener("complete", function(_event) {
      if (e.result === emailDialog.SENT) {
```

```
        alert('Message Successfully Sent!');
      }
   });

   emailDialog.open();

 });
```

When you run the code for the email attachment, the iOS experience looks similar to Figure 10-4.

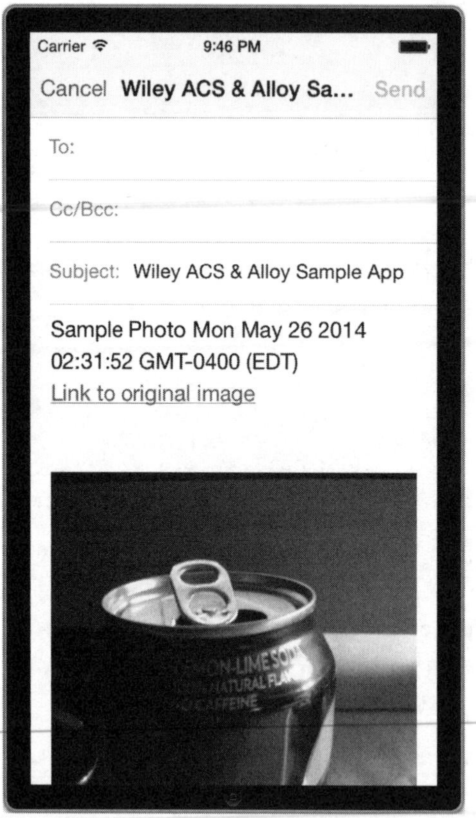

FIGURE 10-4: Adding an email attachment looks pretty much the same on both platforms.

The experience on Android is a bit different since the API is using intents, so you are given a list of applications that support sharing of the image. If you select the email options, your experience should be similar to Figures 10-5 and 10-6.

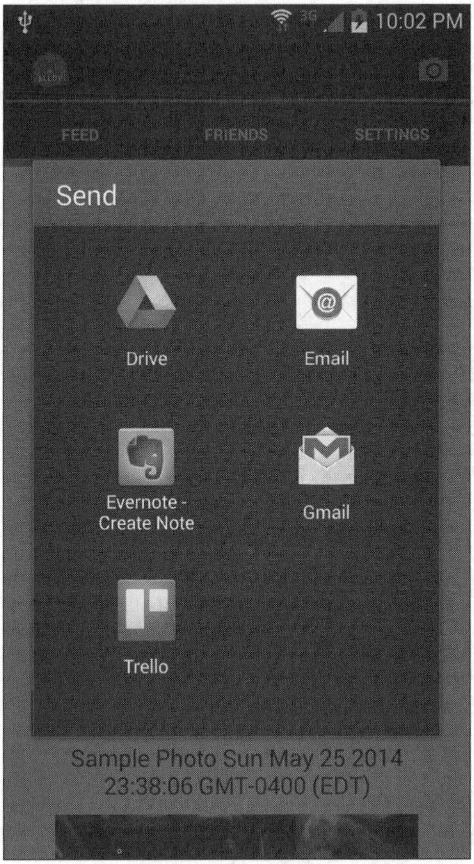

FIGURE 10-5: Email sharing experience on Android.

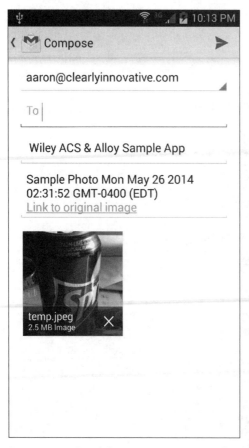

FIGURE 10-6: Email sharing experience on Android when Gmail is selected.

Twitter Integration with the social.js Module

When Alloy was first released, there was a sample application written for Appcelerator's Developer Conference CODESTRONG 2012, which demonstrated the early potential of the Alloy Framework. In that application there was a module called `social.js`, which demonstrated Twitter integration with Appcelerator using the REST APIs from Twitter. Since the release of that application, Twitter has changed the way images are posted to its service, so the module no longer works.

In the following section, code is presented that will allow for the `social.js` module to be modified to support uploading images to Twitter. This section is not intended to be a comprehensive overview of the code in the `social.js` library, but to demonstrate integrating Twitter in an Appcelerator Titanium Alloy application using JavaScript APIs.

Setting Up Your Twitter Developer Account

To create a Twitter Developer Account, log in to `https://dev.twitter.com/` and select Create a New App. Follow the instructions and create your application. Take note of the keys generated by the application. You will need to use the consumer key and secret key to add to your `tiapp.xml`, because this is how the application will interact with Twitter to validate the user's credentials and provide access to the Twitter API on the user's behalf. Copy the keys and paste the credentials to `tiapp.xml` as follows:

```
<property name="twitter.consumerKey">wNuaWTd7whh43kjHGA</property>
<property name="twitter.consumerSecret">Al0unUGyANSLEpU</property>
```

Adding social.js to Your Project

The `social.js` library can be found in the Appcelerator Alloy Github repository located at `https://github.com/appcelerator/alloy/blob/master/Alloy/builtins/social.js`. Download the file to the library directory of your project and save.

> I suggest renaming the `social.js` library file so you know you are working with a modified copy; in this example, the file has been renamed `social_wiley.j`. **TIP**

Android issues with `social_wiley.js` animation were resolved by making additional changes to the file. Change the code on line 510 to the following:

```
opacity : Ti.Android ? 1 : 0,
```

Change the code on line 560 to the following:

```
!Ti.Android && animation.popIn(window);
```

Adding the shareImage Function

The current version of `social.js` does not support uploading images with Twitter, so this is the new functionality that you will be adding. The application needs to implement the image upload API call from the Twitter v1 SDK. The full documentation on the API call is available at `https://dev.twitter.com/docs/api/1.1/post/statuses/update_with_media`.

You should add the following code to the `social_wiley.js` file in the `lib` directory of your application. The code will create the proper oAuth POST request to the Twitter servers to upload the image for sharing using your Twitter credentials.

```
this.sendTwitterImage = function(options) {
    var pUrl =
 "https://api.twitter.com/1.1/statuses/update_with_media.json";
    var pTitle = options.title;
    var pSuccessMessage = options.onSuccess;
    var pErrorMessage = options.onError;
    if (accessToken == null || accessTokenSecret == null) {
        Ti.API.debug("The client doesn't have an access token");
        return;
    }
    accessor.tokenSecret = accessTokenSecret;
    var message = createMessage(pUrl);

    message.parameters.push(["oauth_token", accessToken]);
    message.parameters.push(["oauth_timestamp",
                                        OAuth.timestamp()]);
    message.parameters.push(["oauth_nonce", OAuth.nonce(42)]);
    message.parameters.push(["oauth_version", "1.0"]);

    OAuth.SignatureMethod.sign(message, accessor);
    var parameterMap = OAuth.getParameterMap(message.parameters);
    client = Ti.Network.createHTTPClient({
        onload : function() {
            if (client.status == 200) {
                pSuccessMessage && pSuccessMessage(this.responseText)
            } else {
                pErrorMessage && pErrorMessage(this.responseText);
            }
        },
        onerror : function() {
            Ti.API.error("Social.js: FAILED to send a request!");
            Ti.API.error(this.responseText);
            pErrorMessage && pErrorMessage(this.responseText);
        }
    });
    client.open("POST", pUrl);

    header = OAuth.getAuthorizationHeader("", message.parameters);
    client.setRequestHeader("Authorization", header);
    if (!Ti.Android) {
        client.setRequestHeader("Content-Type",
                                        "multipart/form-data");
    }
```

```
        client.send(options.params);
    };
},
```

Next, the library exposes the shareImage function in the same manner that the share function is exposed. The user's authentication status must be verified before the image can be uploaded; library already has the functionality provided through the authorize function, which will display the Twitter mobile web authentication user interface. If authorization is successful, the anonymous callback function will execute the sendTwitterImage function using the values passed in the options parameter.

```
shareImage : function(options) {
    this.authorize(function() {
        adapter.sendTwitterImage({
            params : {
                media : options.image,
                status : options.message,
            },
            title : "Twitter",
            onSuccess : options.success,
            onError : options.error
        });
    });
}
```

Including the social.js Library in the Application

Now that social_wiley.js is properly set up, the application can utilize the functions to share the photos on Twitter. Open the alloy.js file and add the code to load social_wiley.js to the library, right below the code for initializing Facebook.

```
// if twitter is not loaded/initialized
if (!Alloy.Globals.TW) {
  var TAP = Ti.App.Properties;
  Alloy.Globals.TW = require('social_wiley').create({
    consumerSecret : TAP.getString('twitter.consumerSecret'),
    consumerKey : TAP.getString('twitter.consumerKey')
  });
}
```

Adding Functionality to the sharing.js Library

Modify the `sharingOptions` function in the `sharing.js` library to include the Twitter option and connect the `optionsDialog` event to the new `shareTwitterPhoto` function:

```
exports.sharingOptions = function(_options) {

  var dialog, params;

  if (OS_ANDROID) {
    params = {
      options : ['Facebook Feed', 'Facebook Photo',
                 'Twitter', 'Email'],
      buttonNames : ['Cancel'],
      title : 'Share Photo'
    };
  } else {
    params = {
      options : ['Facebook Feed', 'Facebook Photo',
                       'Twitter', 'Email', 'Cancel'],
      cancel : 4,
      title : 'Share Photo'
    };
  }

  dialog = Titanium.UI.createOptionDialog(params);
  // add event listener
  dialog.addEventListener('click', function(e) {

    // user clicked cancel
    if (OS_ANDROID && e.button) {
      return;
    }

    if (e.index === 0) {
      prepForFacebookShare(function() {
        shareWithFacebookDialog(_options.model);
      });
    } else if (e.index === 1) {
      prepForFacebookShare(function() {
        shareFacebookPhoto(_options.model);
      });
    } else if (e.index === 2) {
      shareTwitterPhoto(_options.model);
```

```
    } else if (e.index === 3) {
        shareWithEmailDialog(_options.model);
    }
});

// show the dialog
dialog.show();

};
```

The shareTwitterPhoto function is structured the same as the other sharing photo functions that require the image to be downloaded before sharing to social media. The application downloads the image from the server and then passes the blob—along with the additional text for the status message to be associated with the tweet—to the exposed Twitter API call from the social.js library.

```
function shareTwitterPhoto(_model) {
    var dataModel = _model.attributes;

    var twitter = Alloy.Globals.TW;

    downloadFile(dataModel.urls.iphone, null, function(_data) {

        if (_data.success === false) {
            alert("error downloading file");
            return;
        }
        twitter.shareImage({
            message : dataModel.title + " #tialloy",
            image : _data.blob,
            success : function() {
                Ti.UI.createAlertDialog({
                    title : 'Sample Alloy & ACS App',
                    message : "Tweeted successfully!",
                    buttonNames : ['OK']
                }).show();
            },
            error : function() {
                Ti.UI.createAlertDialog({
                    title : 'Sample Alloy & ACS App',
                    message : 'Unable to post your tweet.',
                    buttonNames : ['OK']
```

```
            }).show();
        }
    })
},
// update the UI progress indicator
function(e) {
    progressIndicator && (progressIndicator.value
                        = e.progress);
});
}
```

Summary

Sharing is an essential feature in many mobile applications; it leverages the network effect to promote the application through popular social media applications and email. The Appcelerator Titanium Framework makes it easy to quickly integrate this sharing functionality with a popular framework like Facebook. The Twitter integration is a bit more challenging, but it shows how flexible the Appcelerator Titanium Framework is in adopting standard REST-based APIs and other JavaScript-based libraries. Also note that this integration is cross-platform and that you have very quickly integrated Twitter and Facebook sharing using JavaScript.

The introduction of some helper functions like the `downloadFile` and the `progress Indicator` supporting functions continue to demonstrate the powerful combination of the Appcelerator Framework and a language like JavaScript.

Chapter 11
Push Notifications

INTEGRATING PUSH NOTIFICATIONS into your application will allow the sending and receiving of messages, called *notifications*, to and from your application. The messages are sent to the specific device, so it does not necessarily require your application to be in the foreground for the message to be received. The application can then take a specific, pre-defined action based on receiving the notification.

iOS and Android mobile operating systems both support this functionality, although their implementations differ. Your application, if iOS-based, will receive notifications from the Apple Push Notifications (APN) service. If your application is Android-based, it will receive push notifications through the Google Cloud Messaging (GCM) service.

- Find more about Google Cloud Messaging (GCM) at `http://developer.android.com/google/gcm/index.html`.

- For more about Apple's push notifications, visit `https://developer.apple.com/library/ios/documentation/NetworkingInternet/Conceptual/RemoteNotificationsPG/Chapters/ApplePushService.html#//apple_ref/doc/uid/TP40008194-CH100-SW9`.

The Appcelerator Cloud Services Push Notifications API provides a user session or a device token-based solution for notifications. In this application, you will be using the push functionality that requires the user to be logged in to receive notifications. You will integrate this into the login process to register for notifications and the logout process for unregistering the user.

Setting Up Push Notifications on Your Development Platform

This section covers the process of setting up push notifications on the Apple and Google development platforms.

Apple Push Notifications Configuration

For configuring your IOS application with Appcelerator Cloud Services for Push Notifications, you need an App ID that has been configured to support push notification services and a SSL Certificate and private key that will be added to the Push Notification server. The Appcelerator Cloud Services App Dashboard will provide the interface to enter the private key information.

Setting up your App ID and obtaining the SSL certificate and private key are beyond the scope of this book and are covered in the Appcelerator documentation. Follow the steps outlined in that documentation and then return here to continue the configuration (see `http://docs.appcelerator.com/cloud/latest/#!/guide/ios-section-push-notification`).

Google Push Notifications Configuration

To configure your Android application with Appcelerator Cloud Services for Push Notifications, you will be using Google Cloud Messaging. To use Google Cloud Messaging, you need a Google Cloud Messaging Project ID and a Google Cloud Messaging API key associated with the Project ID.

Setting up your Google Cloud Messaging Project ID and obtaining the Google Cloud Messaging API key are beyond the scope of this book and are covered in the Appcelerator documentation. Follow the steps outlined in that documentation and then return here to continue the configuration (see `http://docs.appcelerator.com/cloud/latest/#!/api/PushNotifications`).

Configuring Push Notifications in Appcelerator Cloud Services

After you have followed the directions based on the specific platform, your Appcelerator Cloud Services Dashboard should look similar to Figure 11-1. Remember that if you are building an Android application, you are using Google Cloud Messaging in your app, not MqTT.

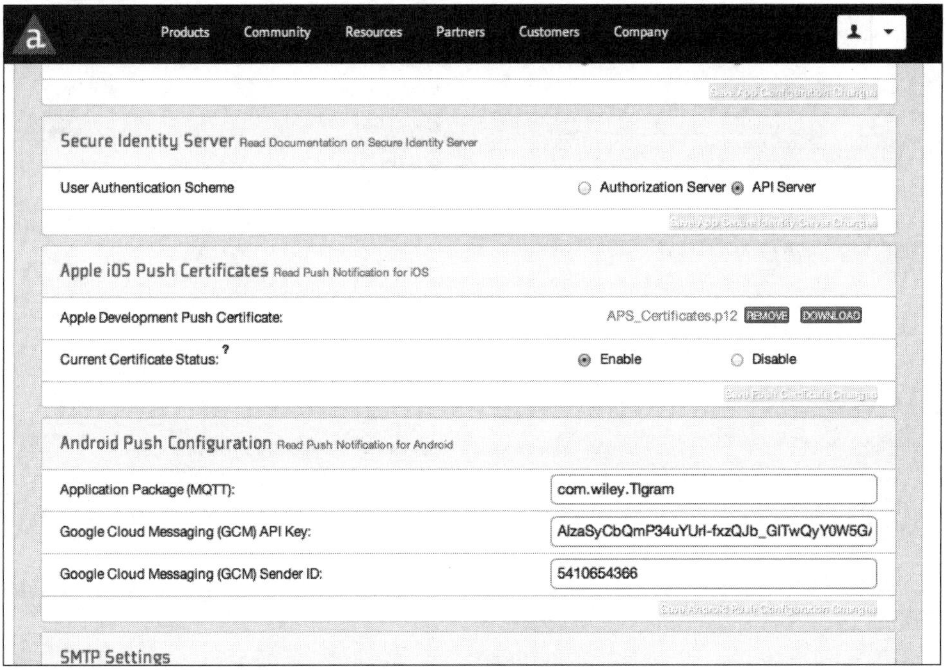

FIGURE 11-1: ACS app console configuration for push notifications.

After this you should be ready to start writing some code.

Creating the Push Notifications Library in an Application

If you are building an Android application, you need to include the `ti.cloudpush` module in your application. To add another module to your application, open your project in Titanium Studio and double-click on the `tiapp.xml` file in the project browser (see Figure 11-2).

Click the green plus to add a new module to the application, then selected the `ti.cloudpush` module from the list of available modules. Figure 11-3 shows the list of available modules.

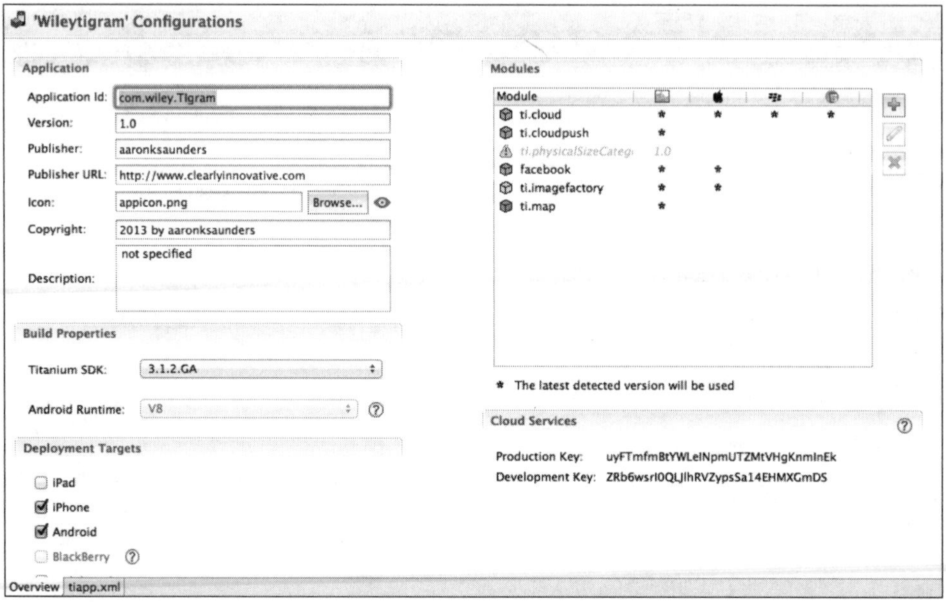

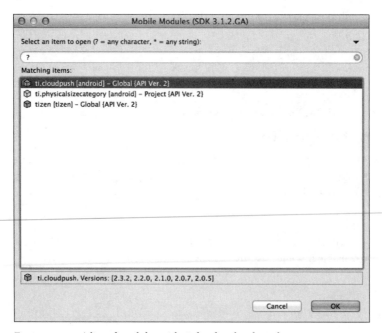

FIGURE 11-2: The tiapp.xml properties editor.

FIGURE 11-3: A list of modules with ti.cloudpush selected.

This module is only used to receive the push notifications, sending notifications is handled by the Appcelerator Cloud services default framework. Additional information on the cloud push module is available at http://docs.appcelerator.com/titanium/latest/#!/api/Titanium.CloudPush.

Creating the pushNotifications.js Library

Create a new library file called pushNotifications.js and add the new file to your project's lib directory; the lib folder should be placed inside of the app folder in the project directory.

The first thing you need to do in your library is provide the cross-platform support by including the Android push library. You will also need to add the Appcelerator Cloud Services library to make the push notification API calls. The Android library is needed for receiving notifications, not sending them.

```
var Cloud = require('ti.cloud');
var AndroidPush = OS_ANDROID ? require('ti.cloudpush') : null;
```

Next you will add the key functions that are needed to support push notifications. You can start with registering the device to receive notifications. To register to receive notifications, you need to get a token from the notification server provided by Appcelerator Cloud Services. Since the IOS and Android approaches are slightly different, they will be covered separately.

Getting the iOS Token

It's important to add a check at the start of the initialization function to alert the users that push notifications work only on a physical device and not in the simulator.

The initialization function requires the user object, since that is how you are implementing push in this application, requiring a user and not token-based push. You are providing a callback method, _pushRcvCallback, to be called when the application receives a push notification; it is in the foreground. The initialization callback, _callback, lets the caller know whether the call was successful or not.

The main call to get the device token on iOS is Ti.Network.registerForPushNotifications.

See http://docs.appcelerator.com/titanium/latest/#!/api/Titanium.Network-method-registerForPushNotifications for more information.

Your pushNotifications.js lib file should look like this after you add the framework code for supporting iOS devices.

```
exports.initialize = function(_user, _pushRcvCallback, _callback) {

  USER_ID = _user.get("id");

  if (Ti.Platform.model === 'Simulator') {
    alert("Push ONLY works on Devices!");
    return;
  }

  // only register push if we have a user logged in
  var userId = _user.get("id");

  if (userId) {

    if (OS_ANDROID) {
      // ANDROID SPECIFIC CODE GOES HERE
    } else {
      Ti.Network.registerForPushNotifications({
        types : [Ti.Network.NOTIFICATION_TYPE_BADGE,
                 Ti.Network.NOTIFICATION_TYPE_ALERT,
                 Ti.Network.NOTIFICATION_TYPE_SOUND
            ],
        success : function(_data) {
          pushRegisterSuccess(userId, _data, _callback);
        },
        error : function(_data) {
          pushRegisterError(_data, _callback);
        },
        callback : function(_data) {
          // what to call when push is received
          _pushRcvCallback(_data.data);
        }
      });
    }
  } else {
    _callback && _callback({
      success : false,
      msg : 'Must have User for Push Notifications',
    });
  }
};
```

Getting the Android Token

The push notification library you included is well documented by Appcelerator at `http://docs.appcelerator.com/titanium/latest/#!/api/Titanium.CloudPush`.

For this application, you will include the same code inside the Android conditional of the `if` statement in the initialization function listed previously. You will perform some additional Android-specific configuration upon success of `retrieveDeviceToken` to properly configure push notifications on the Android devices.

After the Android-specific calls, the application will then call the same callback as the iOS branch conditional. Remember to call `pushRegisterSuccess` the same way you did in the iOS code because the `pushRegisterSuccess` call subscribes the user to the proper channels.

Add the following code to the `pushNotifications.js` file where the comment placeholder currently exists:

```
// reset any settings
AndroidPush.clearStatus();

// set some properties
AndroidPush.debug = true;
AndroidPush.showTrayNotificationsWhenFocused = true;

AndroidPush.retrieveDeviceToken({
  success : function(_data) {
    Ti.API.debug("received device token", _data.deviceToken);

    // what to call when push is received
    AndroidPush.addEventListener('callback', _pushRcvCallback);

    // set some more properties
    AndroidPush.enabled = true;
    AndroidPush.focusAppOnPush = false;

    pushRegisterSuccess(userId, _data, function(_response) {
      // save the device token locally
      Ti.App.Properties.setString('android.deviceToken',
  _data.deviceToken);

      _callback(_response);
    });
  },
```

```
error : function(_data) {
    AndroidPush.enabled = false;
    AndroidPush.focusAppOnPush = false;
    AndroidPush.removeEventListener('callback', _pushRcvCallback);

    pushRegisterError(_data, _callback);
  }
});
```

Registering Callbacks

The pushRegisterSuccess and pushRegisterError functions handle the success or error response from the attempt to get a device token. They are abstracted into separate functions so they can be used to support the Android and the iOS implementation without code duplication.

You can start with the error callback from the call to Ti.Network.registerForPush Notifications since it is quite simple; all you are doing here is responding to the caller with the error information returned from the Appcelerator Cloud Services call and setting the success flag on the returned object.

```
function pushRegisterError(_data, _callback) {
  _callback && _callback({
    success : false,
    error : _data
  });
}
```

The success callback is a bit more complex since you want to accomplish a few other things. With push notifications, the user or device can subscribe to specific channels in the push notification service.

In this application you have two types of channels—the friends channel, which is how you will notify individuals of specific actions taken by their friends and two platform-specific channels that are created for sending platform-specific notifications. The platform channel is included to demonstrate possibilities with this Appcelerator Cloud Service functionality.

The success callback function is passed the data from the Ti.Network.registerFor PushNotifications call and a callback parameter.

Next in the success callback, you will first unsubscribe the user and the device from any channels it was previously subscribed to. This is necessary because Android will continue to generate a unique device token and there will be multiple push notifications sent to the same device.

After the cleanup is completed, you then subscribe the user to the *friend* channel, which is used for the communication between the users of the application.

The code is listed here:

```
function pushRegisterSuccess(_userId, _data, _callback) {

  var token = _data.deviceToken;

  // clean up any previous registration of this device
  // using saved device token
  Cloud.PushNotifications.unsubscribe({
    device_token :
  Ti.App.Properties.getString('android.deviceToken'),
    user_id : _userId,
    type : (OS_ANDROID) ? 'android' : 'ios'
  }, function(e) {

    exports.subscribe("friends", token, function(_resp1) {

      // if successful subscribe to the platform-specific channel
      if (_resp1.success) {

        _callback({
          success : true,
          msg : "Subscribe to channel: friends",
          data : _data,
        });
      } else {
        _callback({
          success : false,
          error : _resp2.data,
          msg : "Error Subscribing to channel: friends"
        });
      }
    });
  });
}
```

This code uses the `exports.subscribe` function to subscribe to push notification channels. The code for this function is pretty straightforward and similar to the Appcelerator Cloud Services documentation for subscribing to a channel, which you can find at `http://docs.appcelerator.com/titanium/latest/#!/api/Titanium.Cloud.Push Notifications`.

There is one difference you will notice, which is that in this code you will be specifying the type when you make the function call. The `type` property will be either `ios` or `gcm`, depending on your platform implementation. The code in the library is written to be cross-platform so following this approach will get you the best results.

```
exports.subscribe = function(_channel, _token, _callback) {
  Cloud.PushNotifications.subscribe({
    channel : _channel,
    device_token : _token,
    type : OS_IOS ? 'ios' : 'android'
  }, function(_event) {

    var msgStr = "Subscribed to " + _channel + " Channel";
    Ti.API.debug(msgStr + ': ' + _event.success);

    if (_event.success) {
      _callback({
        success : true,
        error : null,
        msg : msgStr
      });

    } else {
      _callback({
        success : false,
        error : _event.data,
        msg : "Error Subscribing to All Channels"
      });
    }
  });
};
```

Integrating Push in Your Application

Now that you have created the `pushNotifications.js` library, you can test the configuration after adding the device token and the registration process to the user login functionality. Since Appcelerator Cloud Services application console provides a push notification console, you can send a push to all registered devices as the administrator.

Registering for Push Notifications When the User Logs In

First you need to include the newly created library, pushNotifications, in the index.js file so you can access the initialization function.

You will create a new function to initialize the push and separate out the functionality. You'll add the initializing function to the index.js function called $.loginSuccessAction.

The code should look something like this (the code has been edited for brevity):

```
$.loginSuccessAction = function(_options) {
    initializePushNotifications(_options.model);

    the original code would follow here...
}
```

You add the function called initializePushNotifications, which requires the parameter of the user model from the successful login in the application.

You will create a global variable to hold the device token from the pushNotifications that you can use as a flag to ensure notifications have been initialized. After this setup, you call the function and specify first the callback, which indicates that there was a successful push received, and then the final parameter in the error callback, which is called when an error occurs.

The following example will display a simple alert showing the payload from the test push notification. Add this function to the index.js controller file of your application:

```
function initializePushNotifications(_user) {

  Alloy.Globals.pushToken = null;
  var pushLib = require('pushNotifications');

  // initialize PushNotifications
  pushLib.initialize(_user,
  // notification received callback
  function(_pushData) {
    Ti.API.info('I GOT A PUSH NOTIFICATION');
    // get the payload from the proper place depending
    // on what platform you are on
    var payload;
```

```
    try {
      if (_pushData.payload) {
        payload = JSON.parse(_pushData.payload);
      } else {
        payload = _pushData;
      }
    } catch(e) {
      payload = {};
    }

    // display the information in an alert
    if (OS_ANDROID) {
      Ti.UI.createAlertDialog({
        title : payload.android.title || "Alert",
        message : payload.android.alert || "",
        buttonNames : ['Ok']
      }).show();
    } else {
      Ti.UI.createAlertDialog({
        title : "Alert",
        message : payload.alert || "",
        buttonNames : ['Ok']
      }).show();
    }

  },
  // registration callback parameter
  function(_pushInitData) {
    if (_pushInitData.success) {
      // save the token so we know it was initialized
      Alloy.Globals.pushToken = _pushInitData.data.deviceToken;

      Ti.API.debug("Success: Initializing Push Notifications " +
JSON.stringify(_pushInitData));
    } else {
      alert("Error Initializing Push Notifications");
      Alloy.Globals.pushToken = null;
    }
  });
}
```

Sending Notifications Using the Appcelerator Cloud Services Console

To test the code you have written so far, open the Appcelerator Cloud Services dashboard and go to the application you have created (see `https://my.appcelerator.com/apps`).

Select the app you have created. Make sure you are looking at the development configuration and then click the Send Push Notification button, as shown in Figure 11-4.

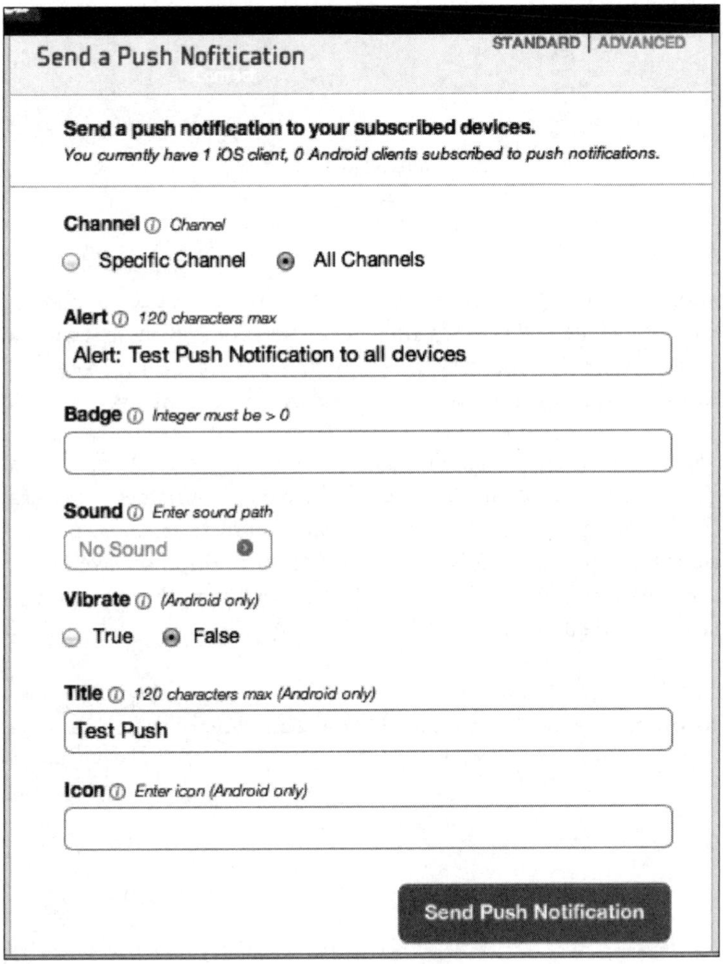

FIGURE 11-4: Console to select push notifications.

Enter information into the displayed form to send a test push notification. To see the same results as the screenshots included, enter the same content. You will only be sending simple text notifications, so make sure the "standard" configuration is set.

Click the Send Push Notification button and your device. If it's running, you should receive a notification alert that looks similar to the one shown in Figures 11-5 and 11-6.

FIGURE 11-5: Screenshot with test notification alert displayed on iOS.

Sending a Push Notification

To send a push notification, you will add another function to the `pushNotifications.js` library. This function will closely follow the documented notify function, which can be found in the Appcelerator Cloud Services documentation—see `http://docs.appcelerator.com/titanium/latest/#!/api/Titanium.Cloud.PushNotifications`.

You will wrap the function so it can support sending notifications to specific user(s) or sending a notification to all users. The `sendPush` function takes a parameter named `_params`, which is a JavaScript hash with specific properties based on the functionality you desire. The `_params` hash contains the specific `user_id` of the user if the notification is only for a specific user. The `_params` hash contains the property `friends` if the notification is to be sent to all users who have subscribed to the friends channel.

The function also verifies there is a valid `deviceToken` set before attempting to send the notification. Add the following code to the `pushNotifications` library so you can send messages based on user actions in the application.

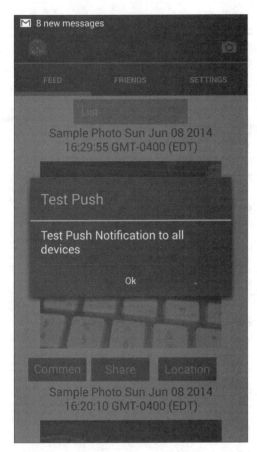

FIGURE 11-6: Screenshot with test notification alert displayed on Android.

```
exports.sendPush = function(_params, _callback) {

  if (Alloy.Globals.pushToken === null) {
    _callback({
      success : false,
      error : "Device Not Registered For Notifications!"
    });
    return;
  }
```

```
// set the default parameters, send to
// user subscribed to friends channel
var data = {
  channel : 'friends',
  payload : _params.payload,
};

// add optional parameter to determine if it should be
// sent to all friends or to a specific friend
_params.friends && (data.friends = _params.friends);
_params.to_ids && (data.to_ids = _params.to_ids);

Cloud.PushNotifications.notify(data, function(e) {
  if (e.success) {
    // it worked
    _callback({
      success : true
    });
  } else {
    var eStr = (e.error && e.message) || JSON.stringify(e);
    Ti.API.error(eStr);
    _callback({
      success : false,
      error : eStr
    });
  }
});
};
```

Sending a Notification When Posting a Photo

When the current user takes a new photo, the application will send a push notification to all of the current user's friends to let them know a new photo has been posted.

For this to work properly, you need to get the friends list from the user so you can send a notification to all of the user's friends. You will use the function getFollowers from the user model for just this purpose. After you have retrieved the user's friends list, you can send the notification message using the exported function.

Add the following function to the feed.js controller:

```
// get all of my friends/followers
function notifyFollowers(_model, _message) {

  var currentUser = Alloy.Globals.currentUser;

  currentUser.getFollowers(function(_resp) {
    if (_resp.success) {
      $.followersList = _.pluck(_resp.collection.models, "id");

      // send a push notification to all friends
      var msg = _message + " " + currentUser.get("email");

      // make the api call using the library
      push.sendPush({
        payload : {
          custom : {
            photo_id : _model.get("id"),
          },
          sound : "default",
          alert : msg
        },
        to_ids : $.followersList.join(),
      }, function(_responsePush) {
        if (_responsePush.success) {
          alert("Notified friends of new photo");
        } else {
          alert("Error notifying friends of new photo");
        }
      });
    } else {
      alert("Error updating friends and followers");
    }
  });

}
```

At the top of the feed.js file, you need to include the following statement to get access to the pushNotifications.js library.

```
var push = require('pushNotifications');
```

In the function `processImage` in the success callback for the `photo.save` function, you can now call the `notifyFollowers` function to let followers know a new photo has been published. Add the function call at the end of the success `if-statement`; the added code should be as follows:

```
notifyFollowers(_photoResp.model, "New Photo Added");
```

Now when the user takes a photo, a push notification will be sent to all her followers. They will receive an alert that looks similar to the one shown in Figure 11-7, if the application is active.

FIGURE 11-7: The Android application alert.

If the application is not active, the user will receive a system notification that looks similar to the one shown in Figure 11-8.

Sending a Notification When Commenting on Photos

When the user comments on a photo, the application will send a push notification to the owner of the photo to let her know that someone has commented on the photo. You need to get the ID of the owner of the photo so you can send a notification to that specific user.

At the top of the `comment.js` file, you will need to include the following statement to get access to the `pushNotifications.js` library:

```
var push = require('pushNotifications');
```

The following code should be added to the `comment.js` controller in the `addComment` function call, where the user saves the comment. In the success callback from saving the new comment model object, you will then send a push notification to the owner of the photo informing her that a new comment has been added.

```
notifyFollowers(_model, currentPhoto, "New comment posted by");
```

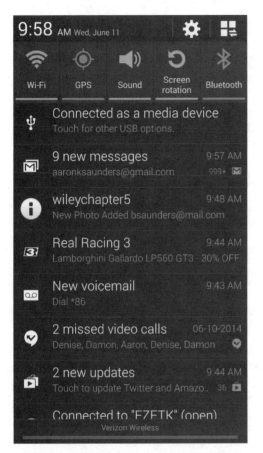

FIGURE 11-8: The Android system notification center.

The `notifyFollowers` function is added to the `comments.js` file to send the push notification about the new comment added, as follows:

```
function notifyFollowers(_model, _photo, _message) {
  var currentUser = Alloy.Globals.currentUser;

  push.sendPush({
    payload : {
      custom : {
        from : currentUser.get("id"),
        commentedOn : _photo.id,
        commentedId : _model.id,
      },
```

```
      sound : "default",
      alert : _message + " " + currentUser.get("email")
    },
    to_ids : _photo.get("user").id
  }, function(_responsePush) {
    if (_responsePush.success) {
      alert("Notified user of new comment");
    } else {
      alert("Error notifying user of new comment");
    }

  });
}
```

Figure 11-9 shows the iOS alert when a comment is added and Figure 11-10 shows the iOS Notification Center.

Sending a Notification When Adding a New Friend

When a user selects a new friend, the application will send a push notification to the new friend to let them know someone is now following their new posts. You need to get the ID of the user who is selected as a friend so you can send a notification to that specific user.

FIGURE 11-9: The iOS alert when a comment is added.

At the top of the friends.js file, you will need to include the following statement to get access to the pushNotifications.js library:

```
var push = require('pushNotifications');
```

To send this notification, add the following code to the friends.js controller inside the followBtnClicked event handler. This code is added to the success callback of the user model's method followUser. You will use the user ID of the user who selected to be followed as the recipient of the push notification by setting the `to_ids` parameter. You can also see in this code that there is a simpler payload being passed in this case, just a string containing the message to be passed.

FIGURE 11-10: The iOS Notification Center when a comment is added.

```
var currentUser = Alloy.Globals.currentUser;

push.sendPush({
  payload : {
    custom : {},
    sound : "default",
    alert : "You have a new friend! " + currentUser.get("email")
  },
```

```
    to_ids : selUser.model.id,
}, function(_responsePush) {
  if (_responsePush.success) {
    alert("Notified user of new friend");
  } else {
    alert("Error notifying user of new friend");
  }
});
```

Figure 11-11 shows the iOS notification when you've been selected as friend.

Alert
You have a new friend!
aaron@clearlyinnovative.com

Ok

FIGURE 11-11: User is being notified in iOS of a new friend.

Unregistering from Push Notifications When Logging Out

When the user logs out of the application, the application will unregister the device from the push notification's server so it will no longer receive notifications.

Create the exported `pushUnsubscribe` function in the `pushNotifications.js` library file in case there is a need to unsubscribe a user from a channel from outside of the library. This function takes a parameter called _data, which is a JavaScript hash comprised of the channel to unsubscribe from and the specific device token. If you look at the Appcelerator documentation, you will see that this is a simple wrapper around the Cloud Services API call.

You use the _callback parameter to return the response data and a response flag of success that is set to true or false.

Add the following code to the `pushNotifications.js` library file; it will be used in Chapter 12, when you attempt to log the user out of the system.

```
exports.pushUnsubscribe = function(_data, _callback) {
```

```
Cloud.PushNotifications.unsubscribe(_data, function(e) {
    if (e.success) {
        Ti.API.debug('Unsubscribed from: ' + _data.channel);
        _callback({
            success : true,
            error : null
        });
    } else {
        Ti.API.error('Error unsubscribing: ' + _data.channel);
        Ti.API.error(JSON.stringify(e, null, 2));
        _callback({
            success : false,
            error : e
        });
    }
});
};
```

Further Integration of Push Notifications in Your Application

Push notifications can send payloads that contact additional information so the application can perform a specific action based on the notification. In the example code provided, you are passing photo_id when the push notification is sent, which indicates that a new photo has been posted. You could potentially modify the application to show the specific photo that has been added to the application. When a new comment notification is received, you could have the application open to the specific photo associated to the comment so the user can see the most recent comments.

These are just two examples of the increased usability that can be added to the application logic to enhance the capabilities of the notifications system within your application. The sample code provided along with this chapter is a good starting point to add similar solutions to the final application you decide to build.

Summary

The addition of push notifications to this sample application allows for interaction between the application's users and gives the users a reason to return to the application, which is critical to the success of your application.

Appcelerator Cloud Services has provided the APIs and cross-platform solution to allow you to seamlessly integrate the functionality into your mobile applications with minimal effort.

Chapter 12
Settings and User Management

THE SETTINGS TAB is the final tab in the application. This tab allows the user to perform the following functions. This is not an exhaustive list of settings for an application like this but it gives you an idea of what can be accomplished using the Appcelerator framework and Appcelerator Cloud Services.

- View and update the photo associated with the account
- View the count of friends and followers
- View the count of photos uploaded
- Turn off friends' push notification
- Log in/out of Facebook
- Log in/out of Twitter

Most of these features will be implemented by enhancing code that has already been written to provide you with additional information. There will be some enhancement to the share library and the push notifications library as well as an introduction to a JavaScript library q that can resolve common issues found when developing code with a lot of asynchronous callbacks.

Getting Started: View, Style, Controller

By now the process for creating windows for applications using the Alloy Framework should be pretty familiar to you. Let's start by opening the `settings.xml` view file and adding the code to construct the user interface to match the wireframes created in the earlier chapters.

Editing the View

First you will need to add the Logout button to the title bar for the iOS version of the application; remember when adding platform-specific code, you will need to specify the platform attribute in the view element. As a child of the window element, you will add the RightButton element.

```
<RightNavButton platform="ios">
    <Button id='logoutBtn'>Logout</Button>
</RightNavButton>
```

After the button element is added, you will start to layout the main containers of the setting window, the header and the mainBody, and those names will correspond to the object IDs you will use in the controller file, which are settings.js and the settings.tss style file. These two elements will be represented with views. The final element at this level of the view hierarchy is the Refresh button, which will be used to update the contents of the window by querying Appcelerator cloud services for the latest information.

After adding the code for the main views, your settings.xml file should look similar to this:

```
<Alloy>
    <Tab title='Settings'>
        <Window title='Settings'>
            <RightNavButton platform='ios'>
                <Button id='logoutBtn'>Logout</Button>
            </RightNavButton>
            <View id='header'>
            </View>
            <View id='mainBody'>
            </View>
            <Button id='refreshBtn'></Button>
        </Window>
    </Tab>
</Alloy>
```

Editing the User Information in the Header Section

First you will get all of the information on the user and display it in the header sections and then you will circle back and add all of the push notifications and social media settings in the view.

In the heading section, you want to display the avatar for the current user, the full name of the user, and Appcelerator Cloud Services information, such as the number of photos they have taken and the number of friends they have. You will add all of the user interface elements in the settings.xml file and then handle the layout and styling in the settings.tss file.

For the avatar, add an `ImageView` element and set the ID to `profileImage`. Next is the Label element, which will hold the full name of the user and then there are labels for the number of photos and the number of friends that are associated with the user. In order to get the labels and the values lined up properly, you will wrap the title and value labels into a view. After adding the code to the `settings.xml`, the contents of the header element should look like this.

```
<ImageView id='profileImage'></ImageView>
<View id='statsBox'>
    <Label id='fullname' class='left4dp top10dp'> </Label>
    <View class='hdrBox left4dp'>
        <Label class='hdrLabel'>Photos:</Label>
        <Label class='hdrCount' id='photoCount'>0</Label>
    </View>
    <View class='hdrBox left4dp bottom10dp'>
        <Label class='hdrLabel'>Friends:</Label>
        <Label class='hdrCount' id='friendCount'>0</Label>
    </View>
</View>
```

Editing the User Information Style

You need to apply some styles to the elements in order to get the UI to match the mockups. You can always add the style information directly to the `settings.xml` file, but it is better to add the information to `settings.tss`.

Open the `settings.tss` file in the styles directory and set some basic style information on the high-level elements:

```
'View' : {
    layout : 'horizontal',
    width : Ti.UI.FILL,
    height : Ti.UI.SIZE,
},
'Window' : {
  layout : 'vertical',
  height : Ti.UI.FILL
},
'Label' : {
  color : '#444'
}
```

Next, you can start to specify specific styles for the elements in the view using their IDs; this is done by creating a style like the following.

```
'#header' : {
    horizontalWrap : false
},
'#logoutBtn' : {
  bottom: '10dp'
},
'#profileImage' : {
    top : '13dp',
    left : '10dp',
    width : '100dp',
    height :'100dp',
    borderColor : '#CCC',
    border : '1dp'
},
'#statsBox' : {
    layout : 'vertical',
    top : '20dp',
    left : '5dp',
    right : '5dp',
    borderColor : '#CCC',
    borderWidth : '1dp',
    horizontalWrap : false
},
// for some reason, the 'right' property is not working on android
// https://jira.appcelerator.org/browse/TIMOB-15525
'#statsBox[platform=android]' : {
    layout : 'vertical',
    top : '20dp',
    left : '5dp',
    width : '65%',
    height : Ti.UI.SIZE,
    borderColor : '#CCC',
    borderWidth : '1dp',
    horizontalWrap : false
},
'#fullname' : {
    bottom : '2dp',
    textAlign : 'left',
        color : '#444',
```

```
    font : {
        fontSize : '18dp',
        fontWeight : 'bold'
    }
}
```

As you can see from this code, we have created an individual style setting for each of the elements in the header section of the page. For the counters, you will use style classes to control the layout instead of using specific styles applied based on object IDs. You will create classes called hdrBox, hdrLabel, and hdrCount that will be applied to the view elements to get the desired outcome. There are also a few helper classes you need to add to settings.tss to properly align the views and labels in the window. See Figures 12-1 and 12-2.

```
'.left4dp' : {
    left :'4dp',
},
'.top10dp' : {
    top :'10dp',
},
'.bottom10dp' : {
    bottom :'10dp',
},
'.hdrBox' : {
},
'.hdrLabel' : {
    left : '0dp',
    textAlign : 'left',
    font : {
        fontWeight : 'bold',
        fontSize : '16dp'
    }
},
'.hdrCount' : {
    font : {
        fontSize : '16dp',
    }
}
```

The refreshBtn is in the settings.xml file, so you can add the styling for that to the settings.tss file since it is only a few properties. You will need to include the platform-specific styling for the height of the button on Android.

```
'#refreshBtn' : {
    top : '50dp',
    width : '80%',
    height : '32dp',
    title : 'REFRESH COUNTS'
},
'#refreshBtn[platform=android]' : {
    height : '42dp',
},
```

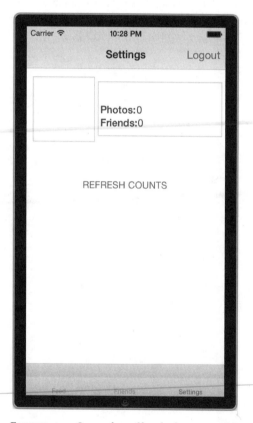

FIGURE 12-1: Screenshot of header layout on iOS.

FIGURE 12-2: Screenshot of header layout on Android.

Handling Logout on Android and iOS

On iOS, the Logout button is available in the navigation bar to allow the users to log out of the application. As you have done on the Feed tab, you need to add some code to set up the menu on the ActionBar when the user views the Settings tab. In this menu, you will enable the users to log out of the application.

Add the following code to the index.js controller file inside of the activity.onCreate OptionsMenu handler in the function doOpen:

```
if ($.tabGroup.activeTab.title === "Settings") {
    menuItem = e.menu.add({
```

```
        title : "Logout",
        showAsAction : Ti.Android.SHOW_AS_ACTION_ALWAYS,
    });
    menuItem.addEventListener("click", function(e) {
        $.settingsController.handleLogoutMenuClick();
    });
} else if ($.tabGroup.activeTab.title === "Feed") {
    // remains same
} else {
    // remains same
}
```

This will add the menu item on the Android ActionBar in the Settings tab and assign the event handler for the menu selection to a function called `handleLogoutMenuClick`. The function `handleLogoutMenuClick` will call the same function as when the user clicks on the Logout button in the Settings tab's navigation bar.

You can now start to add the basic event listeners for the buttons and window actions. To enable users to update their avatars by clicking on their profile images, you need to add an event listener for a click on the `profileImage` view element.

Add the following code to the `settings.js` controller file. You will start to fill out the code as you move through the remainder of the chapter.

```
/* EVENT HANDLERS */
/* in IOS we need to support the button click */
OS_IOS && $.logoutBtn.addEventListener("click",
  handleLogoutBtnClick);

/* listen for click on image to upload a new one */
$.profileImage.addEventListener("click", handleProfileImageClick);

/* listen for close event to do some clean up */
$.getView().addEventListener("close", closeWindowEventHandler);

/* listen for Android back event to do some clean up */
$.getView().addEventListener("androidback",
  androidBackEventHandler);

/* keep state of friends connections */
$.connectedToFriends = false;
```

```
/* keep state of initialization, this prevents the events from
  looping */
$.onSwitchChangeActive = false;

$.handleLogoutMenuClick = function(_event) {
    handleLogoutBtnClick(_event);
};

function handleLogoutBtnClick (argument) {
}

function handleProfileImageClick (argument) {
}


function closeWindowEventHandler (argument) {
}

function androidBackEventHandler (argument) {
}
```

Logging the User Out

Let's start with the primary function of the Settings tab, which is to log out the user. As you can see, you have connected the menu click action on Android to the button click action from iOS. This enables you to put all of the logout functionality into the one function called handleLogoutBtnClick. In this function you will need to do the following:

- Log out of ACS push notification

- Log out of ACS

- Log out of Facebook and Twitter

- Return the application to Login screen

Logging Out of Appcelerator Push Notifications

You will need to import the pushNotifications.js library you used in the previous chapter and call the logout function that was created. This logout function will unsubscribe the user from the friends channel and from the platform-specific channel they were subscribed to when logging into the application.

Logging Out from Appcelerator Cloud Services

Using the current user object global variable, `Alloy.Globals.currentUser`, you will call the extended method logout that was added to the user model. This function will call the Appcelerator cloud service's API to log the user out of the API. The extended function also cleans up some application-specific properties, specifically the `sessionId` and the user object that is saved when the user logs in.

Logging Out from Social Media

You will need to import the `sharing.js` library to log the user out of all social media accounts. The sharing library will be modified to add a new function call named `deauthorize`, which removes the save credentials from the user's device. This will force the user to log in again when restarting the application.

Open `sharing.js` in the `lib` directory and add the function using this code:

```
/**
 * logs out and clears out any social media information
 */
exports.deauthorize = function() {
    Alloy.Globals.TW && Alloy.Globals.TW.deauthorize();
    Alloy.Globals.FB && Alloy.Globals.FB.logout();
};
```

Returning to the Login Screen

Each of the tabs in the application is passed in the parent controller, `index.js`, which gives them access to important functions. One of those functions is `userNotLoggedInAction`. This function will display the login view for a user to log in to the application and is the exact behavior you want after the logout is completed.

Bringing all of this functionality together in the `handleLogoutBtnClick` function, you add the following code to the end of the `settings.js` controller file:

```
function handleLogoutBtnClick(_event) {

  // push logout
  require('pushNotifications').logout(function() {

    Alloy.Globals.currentUser.logout(function(_response) {
      if (_response.success) {
```

```
      Ti.API.debug('user logged out');

      // clear any twitter/FB information
      require('sharing').deauthorize();

      // show login window
      $.parentController.userNotLoggedInAction();

    } else {
      Ti.API.error('error logging user out');
    }
  });
});
};
```

Setting the User's Profile Picture

The view was created earlier in the chapter with a placeholder for the user's profile picture. This picture will be displayed next to comments posted by the user. You will integrate with Appcelerator Cloud Services to associate an image with the user account and use the Appcelerator API to interact with the camera on the device. Most of the code in the controller for working with the camera API should be familiar since it has been covered earlier in the book.

You will create an event handler function handleProfileImageClick so that when the users click on the photo, they can select it from the local device using the API call Ti.Media. openPhotoGallery or take a new photo using Ti.Media.showCamera, which will be saved and associated with the account. Since the view and style information was done already, all that is left is to update the settings.js controller file. Add the following code to the settings.js controller file:

```
function handleProfileImageClick() {
  var dopts = {
    options : ['Take Photo', 'Open Photo Gallery'],
    title : 'Pick Photo Source'
  };

  if (OS_IOS) {
    dopts.options.push('Cancel');
    dopts.cancel = dopts.options.length - 1;
  } else {
    dopts.buttonNames = ['Cancel'];
```

```
    }
    var optionDialog = Ti.UI.createOptionDialog(dopts);

    optionDialog.addEventListener('click', function(e) {
      var options = {
        success : processPhoto,
        cancel : function() {
        },
        error : function(e) {
          Ti.API.error(JSON.stringify(e));
        },
        allowEditing : true,
        mediaTypes : [Ti.Media.MEDIA_TYPE_PHOTO],
      };
      if (e.button) {
        return;
      } else if (e.index == 0) {
        Ti.Media.showCamera(options);
      } else if (e.index == 1) {
        Ti.Media.openPhotoGallery(options);
      }
    });

    optionDialog.show();
}
```

Add the stub for processPhoto function so you can run the app to get an idea of the functionality.

```
function processPhoto(_event) {
}
```

Running the code on iOS, the Settings window and Options dialog should look like Figure 12-3.

Running the code on Android, the Settings window and Options dialog should look like Figure 12-4.

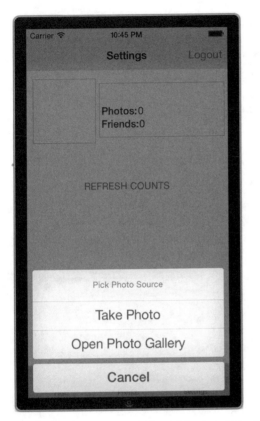

FIGURE 12-3: Screenshot of the iOS Options dialog for Profile Photo Source on Settings tab.

To actually process the photo, you need to get the image media from the camera or the photo gallery and then upload it to Appcelerator Cloud Services. The user object from the Appcelerator Cloud Services has a property called photo that you will use to store the profile picture.

You will need to update the Alloy sync adapter to support the ability to update the user object. This is accomplished by using the Appcelerator Cloud Services API call Cloud. Users.update. The function is implemented in the application in a similar manner as it is presented in the Appcelerator documentation (see http://docs.appcelerator.com/ titanium/latest/#!/api/Titanium.Cloud.Users).

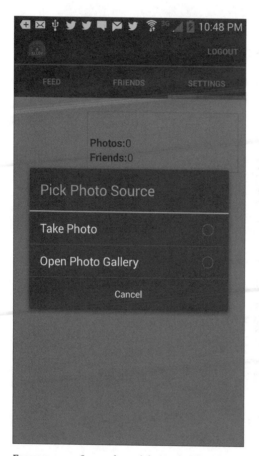

FIGURE 12-4: Screenshot of the Android Options dialog for Profile Photo Source on Settings tab.

Open the `acs.js` file in the `assets/alloy/sync` folder and add the following code to the function `processACSUsers` in the `switch` statement:

```
case "update":
  var params = model.toJSON();
  Cloud.Users.update(params, function(e) {
    if (e.success) {
      model.meta = e.meta;
      options.success && options.success(e.users[0]);
      model.trigger("fetch");
    } else {
      Ti.API.error("Cloud.Users.update " + e.message);
```

```
          options.error && options.error(e.error && e.message|| e);
      }
   });
   break;
```

Using the image from the camera event callback, you can assign the `photo` property on the global variable `Alloy.Globals.currentUser` and save the image. After the image is saved, you will want to assign it directly to the `profileImage` view element so the user gets immediate feedback of the updated image.

Adding a Few Performance Enhancements

Since the cameras on most of the newer phones take high resolution images and you don't need anything like that for the profile picture, there is an Appcelerator native module that we can import to resize the images based on their size. `Ti.ImageFactory` module is a free module that can be downloaded in the Appcelerator Marketplace; download the module and follow the instructions for adding it to your project.

After you install the module, your `tiapp.xml` file should look Figure 12-5.

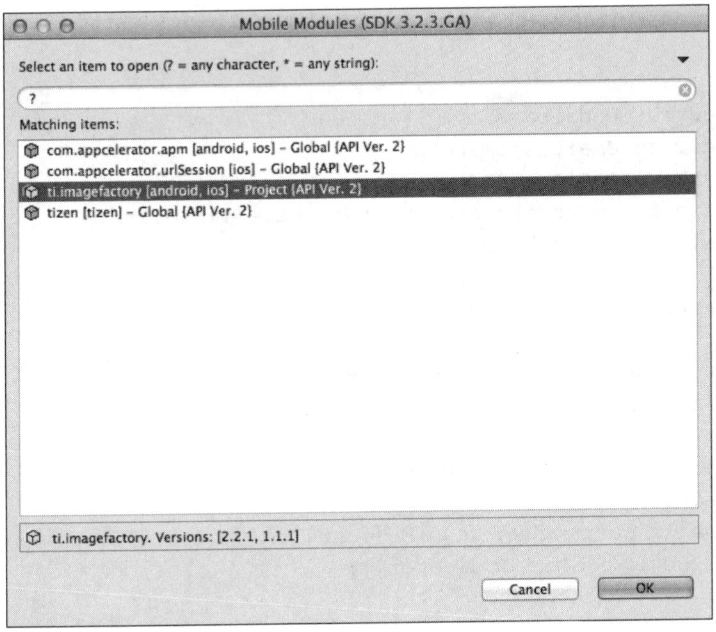

FIGURE 12-5: Screenshot of the tiapp.xml properties page in Titanium Studio showing the ImageFactory module.

Resizing the images before uploading to Appcelerator Cloud Services will provide for a much better user experience since this large image will not get uploaded when only a thumbnail is needed.

Update the function processPhoto with the following code:

```
function processPhoto(_event) {

  Alloy.Globals.PW.showIndicator("Saving Image");
  var ImageFactory = require('ti.imagefactory');

  if (OS_ANDROID || _event.media.width > 700) {
    var w, h;
    w = _event.media.width * .50;
    h = _event.media.height * .50;
    $.currentUserCustomPhoto =
ImageFactory.imageAsResized(_event.media, {
      width : w,
      height : h
    });
  } else {
    // we do not need to compress here
    $.currentUserCustomPhoto = _event.media;
  }

  Alloy.Globals.currentUser.save({
    "photo" : $.currentUserCustomPhoto,
    "photo_sizes[thumb_100]" : "100x100#",
    // We need this since we are showing the image immediately
    "photo_sync_sizes[]" : "thumb_100",
  }, {
    success : function(_model, _response) {

      // take the cropped thumb and display it
      setTimeout(function() {

        // give ACS some time to process image then get
        // updated user object
        Alloy.Globals.currentUser.showMe(function(_resp) {
          Alloy.Globals.PW.hideIndicator();
```

```
        _resp.model && (Alloy.Globals.currentUser = _resp.model);
        if (_resp.model.attributes.photo.processed) {
          $.profileImage.image =
                    _resp.model.attributes.photo.urls.thumb_100;
          alert("Your profile photo has been changed.");
        } else {
          $.profileImage.image =
                    _resp.model.attributes.photo.urls.original;

          alert("Profile photo changed, processing not
                                          complete");
          // clear out values force refresh on next
          // focus if we still dont have an image
          $.currentUserCustomPhoto = null;
          $.initialized = false;
        }
      });
    }, 3000);
  },
  error : function(error) {
    Alloy.Globals.PW.hideIndicator();
    alert("Error saving your profile " + String(error));
    Ti.API.error(error);
    return;
  }
});
}
```

Getting the basic user information for the page to display the avatar photo when it is available is done by calling function `loadProfileInformation` when the window gains focus. To keep the application from making the API calls to Appcelerator Cloud Services every time the window gains focus, you set a flag after the first API call. If the user wants to refresh the information, they can click the Refresh button on the page. The event handler for the Refresh button will be associated with the same function, which is `loadProfileInformation`.

Add the event listener for when the page gains focus to the bottom of the `settings.js` controller file:

```
$.getView().addEventListener("focus", function() {
    setTimeout(function() {
        !$.initialized && loadProfileInformation();
```

```
        $.initialized = true;
    }, 200);
});
```

The function `loadProfileInformation` will perform quite a few other tasks, but for now you will add code to show the user photo when the user opens the Settings tab.

Add this code to get started with the function:

```
function loadProfileInformation() {
  Alloy.Globals.PW.showIndicator("Loading User Information");

  // get the attributes from the current user
  var attributes = Alloy.Globals.currentUser.attributes;
  var currentUser = Alloy.Globals.currentUser;

  Ti.API.debug(JSON.stringify(attributes, null, 2));

  // set the user profile photo
  if ($.currentUserCustomPhoto) {
    $.profileImage.image = $.currentUserCustomPhoto;
  } else if (attributes.photo && attributes.photo.urls) {
    $.profileImage.image = attributes.photo.urls.thumb_100 ||
attributes.photo.urls.original;
  } else if ( typeof (attributes.external_accounts) !==
"undefined") {
    $.profileImage.image = 'https://graph.facebook.com/' +
attributes.username + '/picture';
  } else {
    Ti.API.debug('no photo using missing gif');
    $.profileImage.image = '/missing.gif';
  }

  Alloy.Globals.PW.hideIndicator();
}
```

You can run the code and set up a profile image for a user, as shown in Figures 12-6 and 12-7.

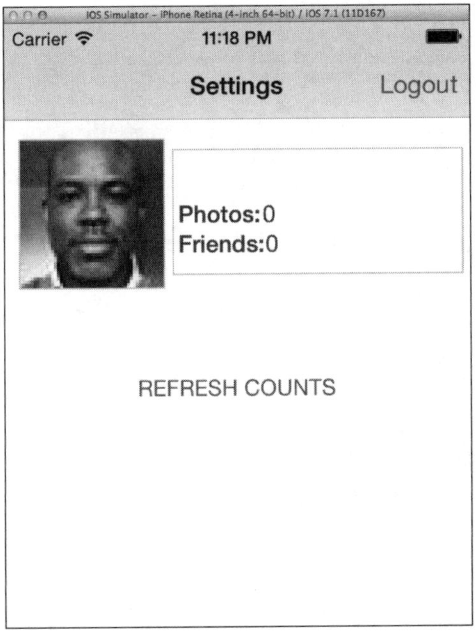

FIGURE 12-6: Screenshot of the iOS User Profile Picture Update on the Settings tab.

Returning to the Feed Controller for Performance and UI Enhancement

This performance enhancement can also be added to your `feed.js` controller. You might have noticed that on high-resolution cameras when running over 3G or LTE that the upload performance of the images is not great. You can add the resizing function to `feed.js` to provide the user with a much better experience.

Replace the success handler in `feed.js` controller file in the `cameraButtonClicked` method; you can see the addition of the indicator to give the user some feedback that there is a process going on. Note also the resizing functionality.

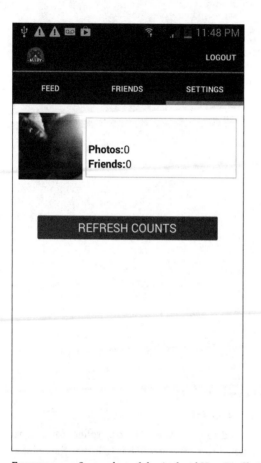

FIGURE 12-7: Screenshot of the Android User Profile Picture Update on the Settings tab.

```
Alloy.Globals.PW.showIndicator("Saving Image", false);
var ImageFactory = require('ti.imagefactory');

if (OS_ANDROID || event.media.width > 700) {
  var w, h;
  w = event.media.width * .50;
  h = event.media.height * .50;
  $.resizedPhoto = ImageFactory.imageAsResized(event.media, {
    width : w,
    height : h
  });
} else {
```

```
    // we do not need to compress here
    $.resizedPhoto = event.media;
}

processImage($.resizedPhoto, function(_photoResp) {

  if (_photoResp.success) {

    // create the row
    var row = Alloy.createController("feedRow", _photoResp.model);

    // add the controller view, which is a row to the table
    if ($.feedTable.getData().length === 0) {
      $.feedTable.setData([]);
      $.feedTable.appendRow(row.getView(), true);
    } else {
      $.feedTable.insertRowBefore(0, row.getView(), true);
    }

    //now add to the backbone collection
    var collection = Alloy.Collections.instance("Photo");
    collection.add(_photoResp.model, {
      at : 0,
      silent : true
    });

    // notify followers
    notifyFollowers(_photoResp.model, "New Photo Added");

  } else {
    alert("Error saving photo " + processResponse.message);
    }
  });
},
```

Additional Information from the User Account

The user has photos and friends; you can utilize the User.showMe method's returned model object to get the latest information on how many photos the user has taken. Getting information about the user's followers requires a separate Appcelerator Cloud Services API.

The displayed name can be the first and last name of the user; if that is not provided you will display the username provided when the account is created. The other information needed is the friend count. Calling the method `User.getFriends`, which was added to the user model in the previous chapter, can give you that information. This can be accomplished with the following code, which you add to the `loadProfileInformation` function in the `settings.js` controller file:

```
// get the name for display
if (attributes.firstName && attributes.lastName) {
    $.fullname.text = attributes.firstName + " " +
  attributes.lastName;
} else {
    $.fullname.text = attributes.username;
}

// get the user object from server and the photo count
currentUser.showMe(function(_response) {
    if (_response.success) {
        $.photoCount.text =
  _response.model.get("stats").photos.total_count;
    } else {
        alert("Error getting user information");
    }

    // get the friends count
    currentUser.getFriends(function(_response2) {
        if (_response2.success) {
            $.friendCount.text = _response2.collection.length;
        } else {
            alert("Error getting user friend information");
        }

        Alloy.Globals.PW.hideIndicator();
    });
});
```

The last thing you'll want to do before working on the next set of data to integrate in the Settings page is to wire up the Refresh Counts button. There might be a more elegant way to implement this feature, but for updating the user information without constant API calls to server, this approach leaves it to the user to initiate the API call. See Figure 12-8 for the completed section.

```
/* listen for click on refreshBtn to refresh data */
$.refreshBtn.addEventListener("click", loadProfileInformation);
```

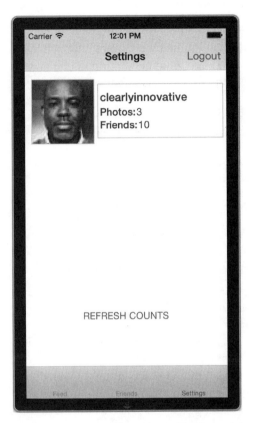

FIGURE 12-8: The Header section of Settings tab is complete.

Adding Content to the Main View in the Settings Tab

The last section to complete on the Settings tab is the content you will be adding to the `mainBody` element in the `settings.xml` view file. In this section, you will be displaying the social media status in Facebook and Twitter and the status of push notifications, on or off.

The way you will lay out the screen is with a section heading, a separator, and then the appropriate switch for the user to turn the functionally on or off. You can add the following code to the `settings.xml` view file for laying out the controls in the window:

```
<View id='mainBody'>
    <Label class='sectionHdr  top20dp'>Social Media</Label>
    <View class='sectionSeparator'/>
    <View class='switchContainer'>
        <Label class='switchLabel'>Facebook Status</Label>
        <Switch id='facebookBtn'
```

```
onChange='onSwitchChange'></Switch>
    </View>
    <View class='switchContainer'>
        <Label class='switchLabel'>Twitter Status</Label>
        <Switch id='twitterBtn' onChange='onSwitchChange'></Switch>
    </View>
    <Label class='sectionHdr top10dp'>Push Notification</Label>
    <View class='sectionSeparator'/>
    <View class='switchContainer'>
        <Label class='switchLabel'>Notifications Status</Label>
        <Switch id='notificationsBtn'
  onChange='onSwitchChange'></Switch>
    </View>
</View>
```

Platform-Specific User Interface for Switch Control

The switch control looks different and requires different properties based on the platform you are using. To address this issue you will be using the platform selectors in the `settings.tss` style file to specify the behavior based on the platform. You can add the following code to the bottom of the `settings.tss` style file for the setting window to get the user interface to look like the mock-ups.

```
'#mainBody' : {
  layout : 'vertical'
},
'.top20dp' : {
    top :'20dp',
},
'.sectionHdr' : {
    width : Ti.UI.FILL,
    height :Ti.UI.SIZE,
    color : '#444',
    font : {
        fontWeight : 'bold',
        fontSize : '16dp',
    }
},
'.sectionSeparator[platform=ios]' : {
    width : '80%',
    height :'1dp',
    backgroundColor : '#CCC'
},
```

```
'.sectionSeparator[platform=android]' : {
    width : '90%',
    height :'1dp',
    backgroundColor : '#CCC'
},
'.switchContainer[platform=ios]' : {
    top : '4dp',
    height : '38dp',
    layout : 'horizontal',
    width : '100%',
},
'.switchContainer[platform=android]' : {
    top : '4dp',
    height : Ti.UI.SIZE,
    layout : 'horizontal',
    width : '100%',
},
'.switchLabel' : {
    textAlign : 'right',
    left : 0,
    right : '30dp',
    width : '60%',
    color : '#444',
    center : {
      y : '50%'
    },
},
'Switch[platform=android]' : {
  titleOn:'Enabled',
  titleOff:'Disabled',
  value:true,
  width: '100dp',
  height:'44dp'
},
'Switch[platform=ios]' : {
    value : true, // mandatory property for iOS
    left : '8dp',
    height : '28dp',
    center : {
      y : '50%'
    },
},
```

You will also need to add the stub for the switch change to the event listener that you added in the `settings.xml` view. You will fill the code in later, but adding the stub now will allow you to run the code to see what the layout looks like. Add this code to `settings.js` controller file.

```
function onSwitchChange(_event) {
}
```

When you run the code, you'll see something like Figure 12-9 on iOS and something like Figure 12-10 on Android.

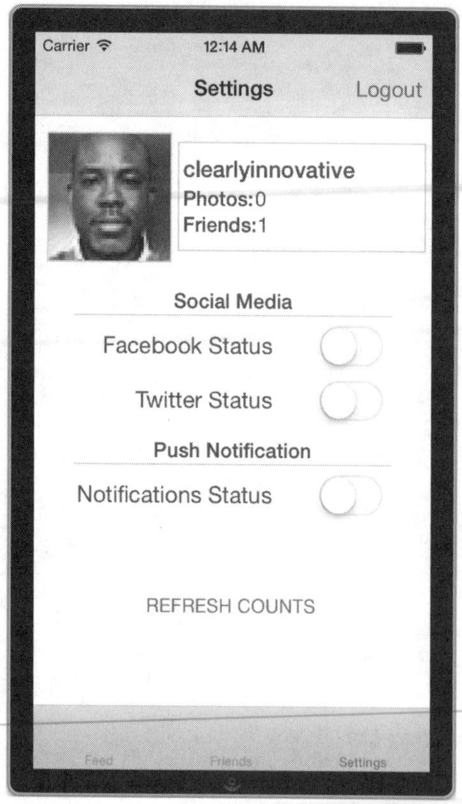

FIGURE 12-9: Final application looks like this on iOS.

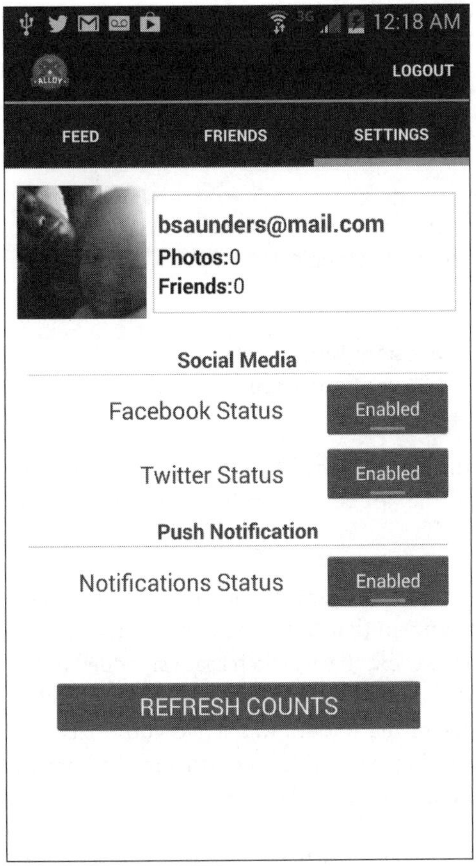

FIGURE 12-10: Final application looks like this on Android.

Handling the Switch Initialization Values

You added the controller variable onSwitchChangeActive to indicate if the switch event listener was activated. You will initialize the value to false when starting the controller so the initial values for all of the switches can be set. You will also set it to false when responding to a user action to make sure the event isn't looping. Add this line of code as the last line in the loadProfileInformation function:

```
$.onSwitchChangeActive = true;
```

Initialize all of the social media switches to false at the top of the settings.js controller file.

```
$.twitterBtn.value = false;
$.facebookBtn.value = false;
```

The `Switch` control in Appcelerator fires the change event whenever the value is changed, even if changed programmatically.

In the `loadProfileInformation` function you created in the previous section, you can add the following code to properly set the Twitter and Facebook status for the current user.

```
// load the social media settings
$.twitterBtn.value = Alloy.Globals.TW.isAuthorized();
$.facebookBtn.value = Alloy.Globals.FB.getLoggedIn();
```

The Twitter check is accomplished by calling the `isAuthorized` method on the Twitter library you included in the social media section. The `getLoggedIn` function is part of the Appcelerator Facebook module.

To activate the social media libraries, you will use the `onSwitchChange` event listener handler; in that function you will create a `switch` statement that will take the appropriate action based on the ID of the control that fired the change event. Each switch that was added to the `settings.xml` view file has a unique identifier based on the social media library it references. The pattern is to check if the specified social media account was active/authorized and if it is when the function is called, then deactivate/logout. Both of the social media libraries can perform the action, so the following code should be self-explanatory.

Add the `sharing.js` library to the `settings.js` controller file:

```
var sharing = require("sharing");
```

Add this code to the `settings.js` controller file:

```
function onSwitchChange(_event) {

    // dont respond to events until initialization is completed
    if ($.onSwitchChangeActive === false) {
        return;
    }

    $.onSwitchChangeActive = false;

    var selItem = _event.source;
```

```
switch (selItem.id) {
    case "notificationsBtn" :
    break;
    case "twitterBtn":
        if (Alloy.Globals.TW.isAuthorized() === false
                            || selItem.value === false) {
            Alloy.Globals.TW.authorize(function(_response) {
                selItem.value =_response.userid ? true:false;
                activateOnSwitchChange();
            });
        } else {
            Alloy.Globals.TW.deauthorize();
            selItem.value = false;
            activateOnSwitchChange();
        }
        break;
    case "facebookBtn":
        if (Alloy.Globals.FB.getLoggedIn() === true) {
            Alloy.Globals.FB.logout();
            selItem.value = false;
            activateOnSwitchChange();
        } else {
            var sharing = require("sharing");
            sharing.prepForFacebookShare(function(_success) {
                selItem.value = _success;
                activateOnSwitchChange();
            });
        }
        break;
    }
}
```

You will also need this helper function to reactivate the listener after the application is done responding to the change event from the user clicking on the switch:

```
function activateOnSwitchChange() {
    setTimeout(function() {
        $.onSwitchChangeActive = true;
    }, 200);
}
```

Displaying Push Notification Status

The push notification status update is the last piece of information that is manageable from this Settings tab. The Appcelerator Cloud Services API does not provide a function in the `ti.cloud.js` library to provide that information, so you will need to leverage the REST API that is provided by Appcelerator Cloud Services. This further demonstrates the overall flexibility of the platform and API; you can extend and customize as needed.

The API call that you will use is the `query.json` endpoint on the `push_notifcation` API. The call is done by using the Appcelerator `Ti.Network.createHTTPClient` function call to make a get request to the API. This request requires the `user.id` and the `client_id` from Appcelerator Cloud Services. The `user.id` you will get from the `currentUser` object and the `client_id` property you will get from the `tiapp.xml` file.

When you enable cloud services in your project on project creation, Titanium Studio will add the production and development keys to the `tiapp.xml` file. Those values are treated a properties and are accessible using the Appcelerator API call `Ti.App.Properties.getString` and then use the key `"acs-api-key-development"` or `"acs-api-key-production"`, depending on the environment you are in.

Now that you can determine the environment appropriately, you can add the following function to the `pushNotifications.js` library file:

```
exports.getChannels = function(_user, _callback) {

  var xhr = Ti.Network.createHTTPClient();

  // create the url with params

  // get the environment specific Key
  var isProduction = Titanium.App.deployType === "production";
  var acsKeyName = "acs-api-key-" +
              ( isProduction ? "production" : "development");

  // construct the URL
  var url =
  "https://api.cloud.appcelerator.com/v1/push_notification/query.
  json?key=";
  url += Ti.App.Properties.getString(acsKeyName);
  url += "&user_id=" + _user.id;

  xhr.open("GET", url);
  xhr.setRequestHeader('Accept', 'application/json');
  xhr.onerror = function(e) {
```

```
    alert(e);
    Ti.API.info(" " + String(e));
  };
  xhr.onload = function() {
    try {
      Ti.API.debug(" " + xhr.responseText);
      var data = JSON.parse(xhr.responseText);
      var subscriptions = data.response.subscriptions[0];
      Ti.API.info(JSON.stringify(subscriptions));

      _callback && _callback({
        success : true,
        data : subscriptions,
      });
    } catch(E) {
      Ti.API.error(" " + String(E));

      _callback && _callback({
        success : false,
        data : null,
        error : E
      });
    }
  };

  xhr.send();
};
```

Now that the function is in place, you will put it to use in the settings.js controller file to set the status of push notification visually through the switch user interface element.

Add the push notification library to beginning of the settings.js controller file:

```
var pushLib = require('pushNotifications');
```

Then in the callback of the controller in loadProfileInformation, add the call to get the channels that the user is subscribed to; you are looking for the friends channel to indicate if the switch should be turned on or off. Add the following code inside the success callback of the currentUser.getFriends function:

```
pushLib.getChannels(currentUser, function(_response3) {
  var friendActive;
```

```
if (_response3.success) {
  $.connectedToFriends = (_.contains(_response3.data.channel,
                                     "friends") !== -1);
  $.notificationsBtn.value = $.connectedToFriends;
} else {
  $.notificationsBtn.value = $.connectedToFriends = false;
}
```

Compile and run your project. You should get visual information regarding push notifications on the friends channel. Next, you will add the functionality to allow the users to turn notifications on and off.

Running the code should look like the previous figures; however, changing the status of the switch from on to off will enable the functionality.

Changing the Push Notification Status

The push notification status indicates whether the user has subscribed to a specific channel. The channel status that you are displaying is the friends channel. In the previous section you made a function that queried Appcelerator Cloud Services to see if the current user is subscribed to the channel. In this section, you will use the ti.cloud.js function to unsubscribe the users from the friends channel when they select the disabled or off status from the push notifications switch.

Add the following code to the notificationsBtn switch in the onSwitchChange function of the settings.js controller file:

```
case "notificationsBtn" :
  if ($.connectedToFriends === true) {
    pushLib.pushUnsubscribe({
      channel : "friends",
      device_token : Alloy.Globals.pushToken
    }, function(_response) {
      if (_response.success) {
        // unsubscribe worked
        selItem.value = $.connectedToFriends = false;
        activateOnSwitchChange();
      }
    });
  } else {
    pushLib.subscribe("friends", Alloy.Globals.pushToken,
    function(_response) {
```

```
    if (_response.success) {
      // subscribe worked
      selItem.value = $.connectedToFriends = true;
      activateOnSwitchChange();
    }
  });
}

break;
```

Calling the `pushUnsubscribe` function, all you have to do is pass the name of the `channel` to unsubscribe from along with the `pushtoken`. The `Alloy.Globals.pushToken` is set when the application configured and connected the user's device to the push notification server.

When the call is completed, you will see that the function updates the value of the switch to reflect the current status of push notifications. When the users unsubscribe from the channel, they will no longer receive notifications, but the notifications will still be sent out.

Summary

This is the last tab in the application, so you should be all done with a functioning cross-platform application using Appcelerator Alloy and Appcelerator Cloud Services. The Settings tab allows you to configure the application and view status of integrations with social media and push notifications.

The Feed tab allows you to list the photos you have taken, comment on the photos, share your photos, and see the location where the photo was taken. The Feed tab also allows you to view photos close to your current location.

The Friends tab shows users who have the app and users you can select to follow.

This app is fully integrated with Appcelerator Cloud Services and is a good start for more advanced functionality and integration with Appcelerator and other third-party systems.

This app follows some of the best practices using the MVC framework Appcelerator Alloy, which will assist you in writing well structured and maintainable cross-platform mobile solutions. Chapter 13 discusses deploying your solution on the iOS App Store and on the Google Play Store.

Chapter 13

Going to Market: Deploying to the App Store and to Google Play

THE DISTRIBUTION PROCESS for deploying your application to the Google Play Store and Apple App Store is pretty well documented on the Appcelerator website. The process is outlined briefly in this chapter, and more detailed step-by-step instructions and FAQs can be found on the Appcelerator site at `http://docs.appcelerator.com/titanium/3.0/#!/guide/Preparing_for_Distribution`.

Process Overview

This chapter describes how to deploy your cross-platform mobile app to the App Store and Google Play. The overall process is similar for both stores and is outlined here.

Registering for a Developer Account

The iOS Developer Program costs $99 per year and a Google Play Developer account costs $25. This barrier to entry is supposed to raise the minimum quality level of app submissions.

Signing Your Application

Signing with a digital certificate proves your identity as the developer of your app. You will create a CSR and sign the application with a certificate to which only you have the private key.

Creating an App Record and Filling Out Metadata

Each store requires certain metadata and image assets. Now is a good time to start putting together some general information to smooth out the process:

- App name

- Description (up to 4,000 characters)

- Keywords

- Large app icon (1024×1024 for iOS and 512×512 for Android)

- Screenshots (at least one 3.5-inch and one 4-inch for iOS; any two screenshots for Android)

Publishing Your Binary to the Store

You can create binaries for store submission directly from Titanium Studio. A publishing wizard steps you through the process of locating the certificates you created earlier.

iOS App Store Submission Process

Follow the steps outlined in this section to publish your app to the iOS App Store.

Signing Up for an iOS Developer Account

This is simply an online checkout process where you add the iOS Developer Program to your cart and pay using a credit card. Go to `https://developer.apple.com/programs/ios/` and click Enroll Now.

When you have completed this process, you will receive notification for signing up for the Apple Developer Program and iTunesConnect. The iTunes Developer Program website is where you manage the development-related activities, whereas iTunesConnect is for managing store-related activities.

Signing Your iOS Application

This is split into three separate steps:

- Creating your application ID

- Creating a distribution certificate for the application

- Creating a distribution provisioning profile for your application

These steps are pretty well documented in the Appcelerator website and also on Apple's Developer Member Center; there are no Appcelerator-specific adjustments required in this process. See the respective sites for details.

Creating an iTunes Connect Record

The iTunesConnect record will hold all of the information required to publish your binary to the App Store. You create the record first so Appcelerator IDE can associate the application binary with the record for you.

These steps are pretty well documented in the Appcelerator website and also on Apple's Developer Member Center; there are no Appcelerator-specific adjustments required in this process. See the respective sites for details.

After you follow all of the steps, you know your process is completed when you see the "Waiting for Upload" message appear as the app status in iTunesConnect.

Publishing from Titanium Studio

Right-click your project and then choose Publish ➪ Distribute - Apple iTunes Store, as shown in Figure 13-1.

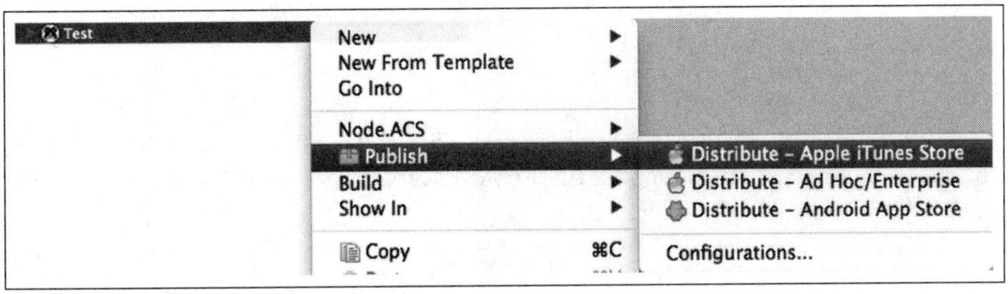

FIGURE 13-1: The Publish menu in Titanium Studio.

You'll see the screen in Figure 13-2. You must belong to the iOS Developer Program to proceed further.

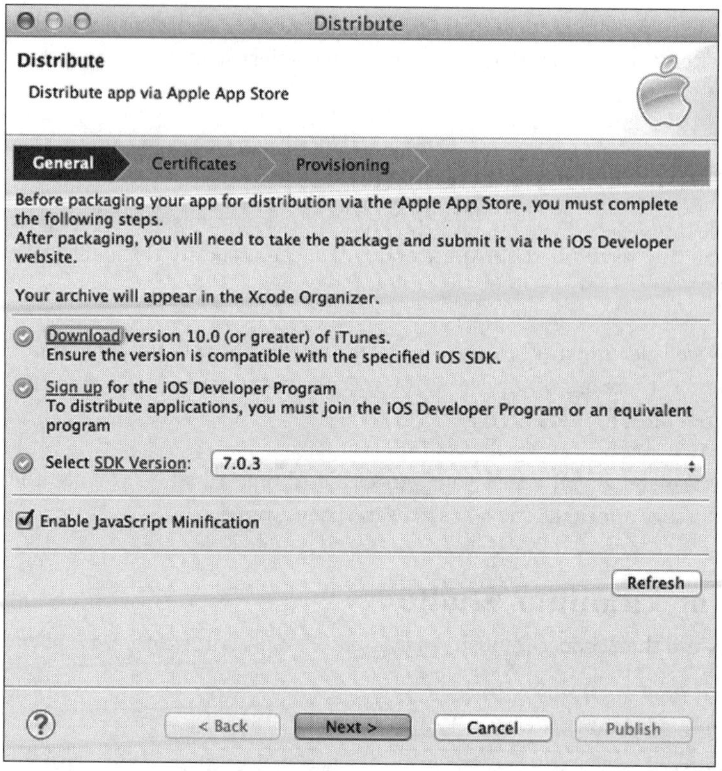

FIGURE 13-2: Distribute wizard: General.

Click Next to see screen Figure 13-3, which deals with certificates. For Select Distribution Certificate, choose the Distribution Certificate you created earlier in the Member Center. For Select Keychain, use the system defaults.

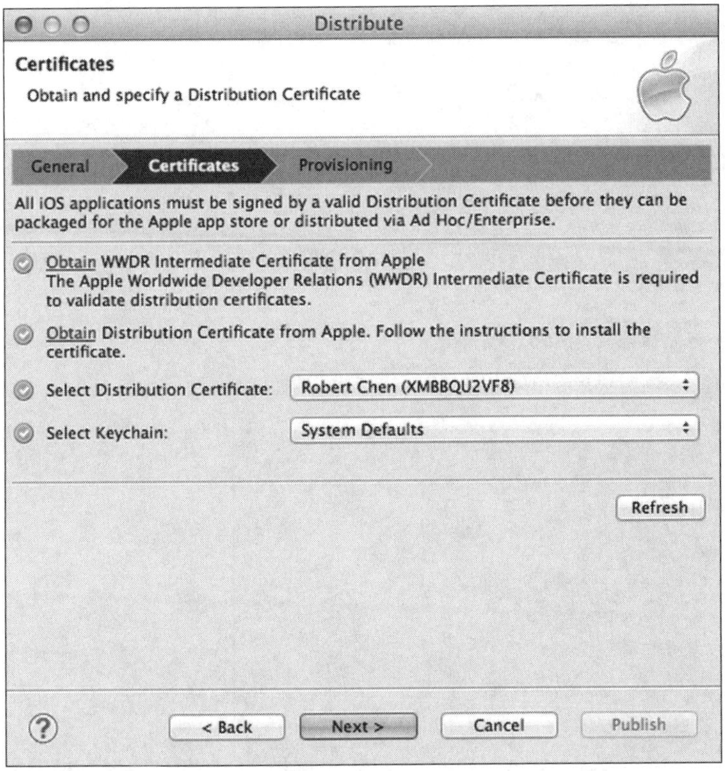

FIGURE 13-3: Distribute wizard: Certificates.

For Select Provisioning Profile, choose the distribution provisioning profile you created earlier in the Member Center. See Figure 13-4.

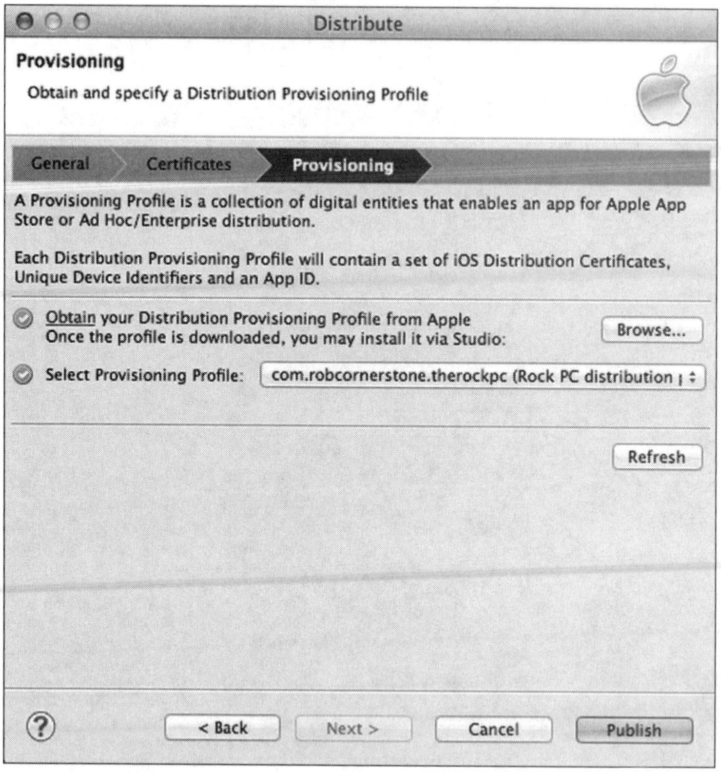

FIGURE 13-4: Distribute wizard: Provisioning.

When you're prompted to access the keychain, click Always Allow. See Figure 13-5.

FIGURE 13-5: Always allow keychain access.

You may see the System Preferences open. If so, click OK. See Figure 13-6.

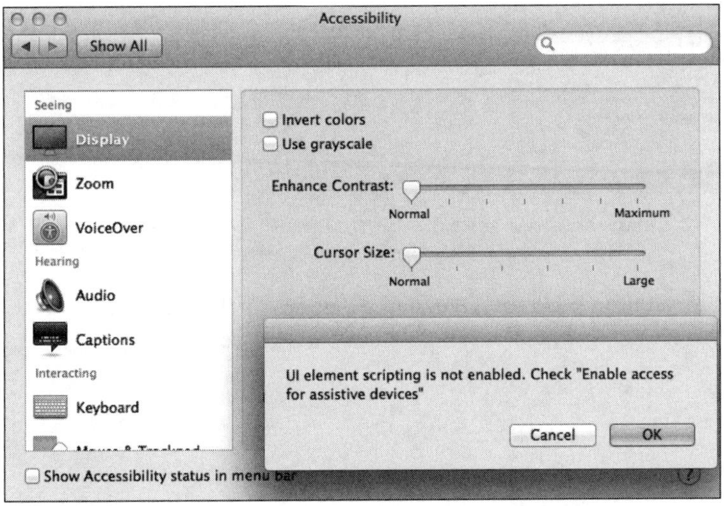

FIGURE 13-6: System Preferences Accessibility window.

You should see that the project was built successfully based on the output displayed on the console, as shown in Figure 13-7.

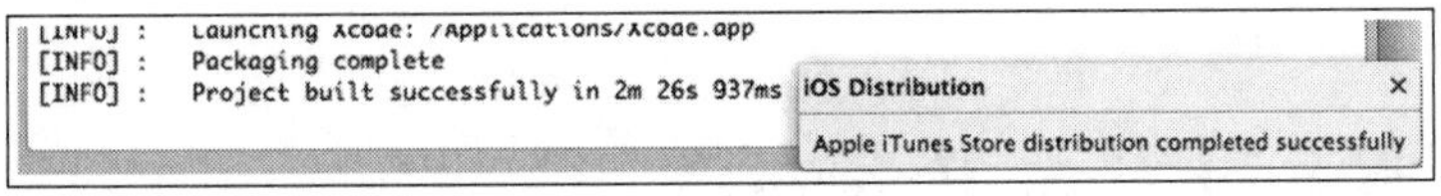

FIGURE 13-7: Success message from Titanium Studio.

Uploading Your Binary to the App Store

When the build is complete in Titanium Studio, you will see that Xcode has launched into the Organizer; see Figure 13-8.

Click the Archives tab, select the application you just built, and click Distribute. Follow the prompts to complete the validation of your application and submission to the App Store.

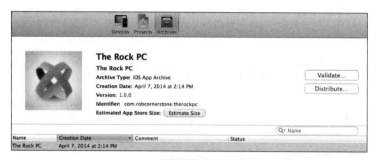

FIGURE 13-8: The Archives tab in the Xcode Organizer.

Over the next few days (exact timing will vary), keep an eye on status changes. Once you see "Ready for Sale," your app is live. Here are the various status changes you will see:

- Upload Received

- Waiting For Review

- In Review

- Processing for App Store

- Ready for Sale

For your first app version, you can control the exact launch date of your app by manipulating the availability date. Version updates give you the option of releasing manually.

Google Play Submission Process

Follow the steps outlined in this section to publish your app to the Google Play Store.

Signing Up for a Google Play Developer Account

Similar to the iOS Developer Program, this is a checkout process where you purchase a Developer Account. Visit the following link to get started: `https://play.google.com/apps/publish/signup/`.

Select the I Agree checkbox and click Continue to Payment. See Figure 13-9.

Next you will see a standard credit card form. Complete the form and click Buy.

After the purchase is complete, fill out a form with some basic personal information. Click on Complete Registration when you're finished. See Figure 13-10.

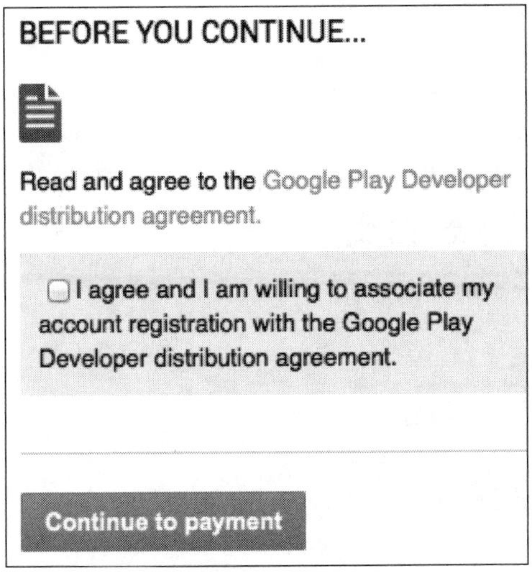

FIGURE 13-9: Accept the developer agreement.

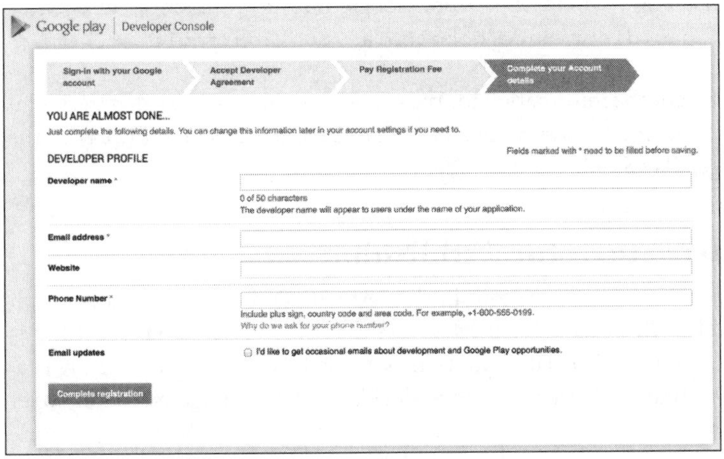

FIGURE 13-10: Complete the Account details.

Now you have access to the Developer's Console: `https://play.google.com/apps/publish`. Click on Publish an Android App on Google Play to create an app store listing. See Figure 13-11.

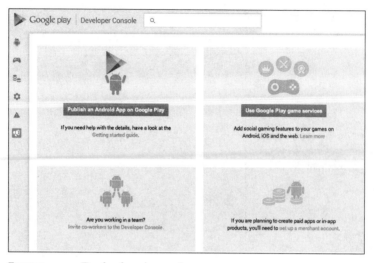

FIGURE 13-11: The developer's console.

Learn more about publishing Android apps from Google's documentation at `https://developer.android.com/distribute/googleplay/publish/register.html`.

Follow the prompts to fill out the information for the application. You will be using the metadata you captured earlier in the process and setting images for the icon and display of the application in the Google Play Store.

Generating a Keystore for Publishing

There are two ways to deploy an application: in debug mode and in release mode. Both involve signing your APK with a digital certificate. Note that the APK is not encrypted; it is only signed to identify the developer. Titanium transparently takes care of the signing process in debug mode. The tradeoff is that the target device must be configured to developer mode.

Release mode needs to be used for Google Play. The APK is signed with a digital certificate, to which you as the developer have sole access to the private key. This certificate cannot be forged, so users can rest assured that app updates originate from you. This also means that you lose the ability to update your app if you lose the private key.

See `http://developer.android.com/tools/publishing/app-signing.html` for more information.

A keystore is a local database containing private keys and public certificates. You'll need to create a keystore for your app named myApp:

```
cd ~/Documents
keytool -genkeypair -v -keystore myApp.keystore -alias myApp -
  keyalg RSA -sigalg SHA1withRSA -validity 10000
```

In this example, you are creating a file located at `~/Documents/myApp.keystore`. Titanium will need this location later.

The `-alias` used is myApp. Titanium will ask for the alias.

The `-validity 10000` is the length in days, which works out to 27 years (and exceeds the 25-year requirement).

Fill out the certificate information as follows:

```
What is your first and last name?
  [Unknown]:  John Doe
What is the name of your organizational unit?
  [Unknown]:  myCompanyName
What is the name of your organization?
  [Unknown]:  myCompanyName
What is the name of your City or Locality?
  [Unknown]:  Washington DC
What is the name of your State or Province?
  [Unknown]:  DC
What is the two-letter country code for this unit?
  [Unknown]:  US
```

You will be prompted for a password. This is your keystore password, as required by Titanium.

```
Enter key password for <myApp>
```

Save your keystore and password in a safe place.

Publishing to Google Play

Right-click your project and then choose Publish ➪ Distribute - Android App Store, as shown in Figure 13-12.

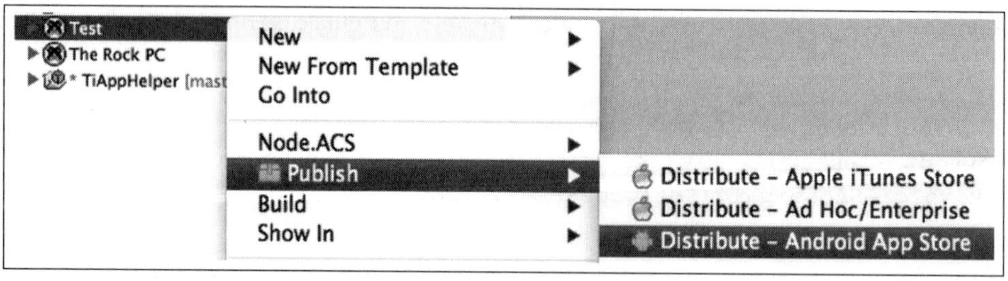

FIGURE 13-12: Publish menu in Titanium Studio.

For Distribution Location, browse to your desktop for easy access. For Keystore Location, point to the `myApp.keystore` file you created earlier in Documents. Enter the keystore password and key alias you used when you created the keystore. Finally, click Publish. You'll see something similar to Figure 13-13.

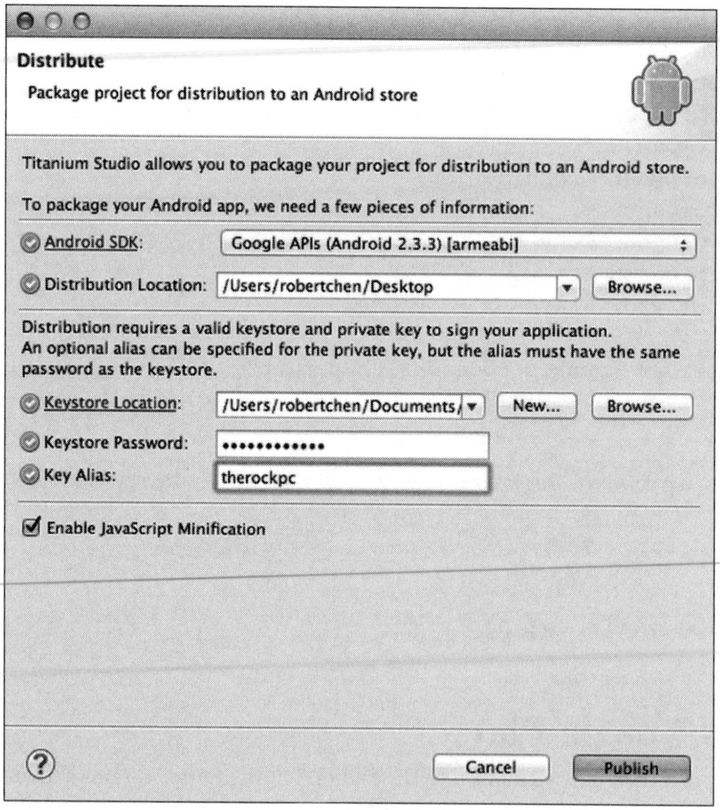

FIGURE 13-13: Entering keystore information into the Distribute wizard.

When the build process is complete, you will see output in the console of Titanium Studio, as shown in Figure 13-14.

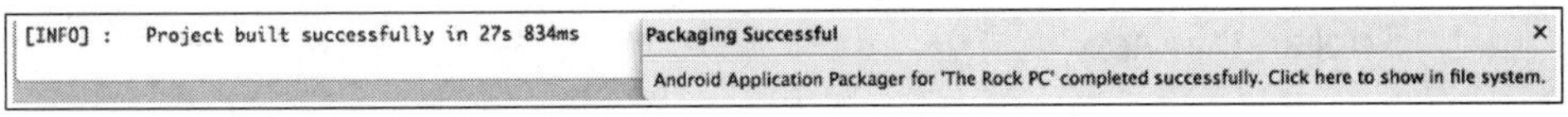
[INFO] : Project built successfully in 27s 834ms
Packaging Successful
Android Application Packager for 'The Rock PC' completed successfully. Click here to show in file system.

FIGURE 13-14: Success message from Titanium Studio.

Go back to the Developer Console window in your browser and select APK from the left navigation menu, as shown in Figure 13-15.

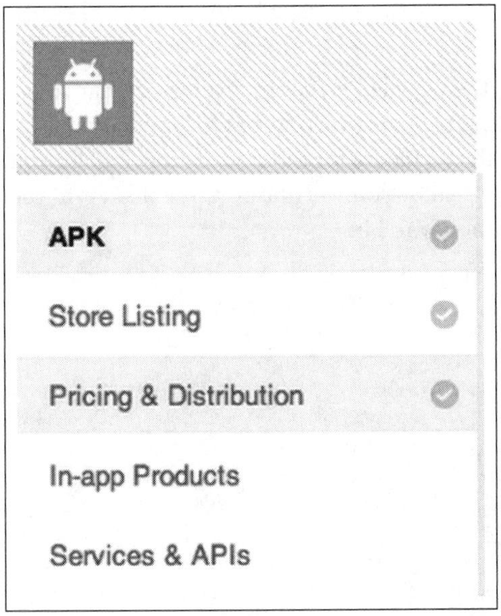
APK
Store Listing
Pricing & Distribution
In-app Products
Services & APIs

FIGURE 13-15: Google Play developer console menu.

Follow the directions provided to upload your APK to Google Play. Once the application is successfully uploaded, you should see a menu on the top right of your browser indicating the app is ready to publish. Select Publish This App to release your app on Google Play. It may take several hours (exact timing will vary) before your app becomes live in the store. See Figure 13-16.

FIGURE 13-16: The Ready to Publish option appears when the store listing is complete.

Summary

Publishing your app to the Apple App Store or the Google Play Store involves similar steps. You first register for a developer account and then create a certificate to sign your application. Next, you create an app record and fill out the metadata for the store listing. Finally, you create a distribution build in Titanium Studio signed by your certificate and upload it to the store. All that's left is to sit back and watch the money roll in!

Index